Blasphemy, Islam and the Stat

This book draws on the work of Rawls to explore the interaction between faith, law and the right to religious freedom in post-Soeharto Indonesia, the world's largest democracy after India and the United States. It argues that enforcement of Islamic principles by the state is inconsistent with religious diversity and the country's liberal constitution. The book thus contributes to understanding the role of religion in the development of democracy in the world's largest Muslim nation. A key objective is to test the argument that Rawls' thinking about public reason cannot apply to the case of Indonesia, and Muslim states more broadly. The book therefore contributes to emerging scholarship that considers Rawls in a Muslim context. In addition to examining public reason in detail and considering critiques of the concept, the work highlights the fact that the theory was created to deal with value pluralism and is therefore relevant in any religious setting, including an Islamic one. In doing so, it emphasises that Islam is multifaceted and demonstrates the difficulties, and negative consequences, of integrating faith and law in a liberal state.

Stewart Fenwick is an Honorary Professor of the Australian Catholic University at the Institute for Religion, Politics and Society, and an Associate of the Centre for Indonesian Law, Islam and Society, and the Asian Law Centre, University of Melbourne, Australia. He was awarded the Harold Luntz Graduate Research Thesis Prize for 2015 at the Melbourne Law School, and was awarded the Chancellor's Prize for Excellence in the PhD Thesis for 2016 at the University of Melbourne.

ICLARS Series on Law and Religion

Series Editors:

Silvio Ferrari
University of Milan, Italy

Russell Sandberg
Cardiff University, UK

Pieter Coertzen
University of Stellenbosch, South Africa

W. Cole Durham, Jr.
Brigham Young University, USA

and

Tahir Mahmood
Amity International University, India

The *ICLARS Series on Law and Religion* is a new series designed to provide a forum for the rapidly expanding field of research in law and religion. The series is published in association with the International Consortium for Law and Religion Studies, an international network of scholars and experts of law and religion founded in 2007 with the aim of providing a place where information, data and opinions can easily be exchanged among members and made available to the broader scientific community. The series aims to become a primary source for students and scholars while presenting authors with a valuable means to reach a wide and growing readership.

Other titles in this series:

Religion and Equality
Edited by W. Cole Durham, Jr. and Donlu Thayer, Brigham Young University, USA

Church and State in Scotland
Francis Lyall, University of Aberdeen, UK

Religion as Empowerment
Edited by Kyriaki Topidi and Lauren Fielder, both at University of Lucerne, Switzerland

Religions and Constitutional Transitions in the Muslim Mediterranean
Edited by Alessandro Ferrari and James Toronto

Blasphemy, Islam and the State

Pluralism and liberalism in Indonesia

Stewart Fenwick

Routledge
Taylor & Francis Group

LONDON AND NEW YORK

First published 2017 by Routledge

2 Park Square, Milton Park, Abingdon, Oxfordshire OX14 4RN

711 Third Avenue, New York, NY 10017

Routledge is an imprint of the Taylor & Francis Group, an informa business

First issued in paperback 2018

British Library Cataloguing in Publication Data
A catalogue record for this book is available from the British Library

Library of Congress Cataloging in Publication Data
Names: Fenwick, Stewart, author.
Title: Blasphemy, Islam and the state : pluralism and liberalism in Indonesia / Stewart Fenwick.
Description: Abingdon, Oxon ; New York, NY : Routledge, 2017. | Based on author's thesis (doctoral—University of Melbourne, Melbourne Law School, 2015) issued under title: Is Rawlsian liberalism compatible with Islam? : a case study of post-Soeharto Indonesia. | Includes bibliographical references and index.
Identifiers: LCCN 2016015763 (print) | LCCN 2016016187 (ebook) | ISBN 9781138694675 (hbk) | ISBN 9781315527697 (e-book) | ISBN 9781315527680 (Web PDF) | ISBN 9781315527673 (ePub) | ISBN 9781315527666 (Mobipocket)
Subjects: LCSH: Islam and state—Indonesia. | Blasphemy—Law and legislation—Indonesia. | Freedom of religion—Indonesia. | Religious pluralism—Islam. | Rawls, John, 1921–2002. | Liberalism.
Classification: LCC KNW2688 .F46 2017 (print) | LCC KNW2688 (ebook) | DDC 342.59808/5297—dc23
LC record available at https://lccn.loc.gov/2016015763

ISBN: 978-1-138-69467-5 (hbk)
ISBN: 978-1-138-36285-7 (pbk)

Typeset in Galliard
by Apex CoVantage, LLC

For my children

Contents

Preface

This book is based on my Doctoral thesis, completed in 2015. The research was conducted over a long period of time in a wide variety of settings. Some of my early study of John Rawls was undertaken in the very traditional setting of Duke Humfrey's Library, Oxford University. Here I was able to read a number of dissertations that addressed Rawls' work in detail; interest in Rawls only increased during the years I spent on this task.

While resident in Indonesia from 2004 to 2008 I learnt first-hand about the blasphemy regime from colleagues in the legal aid world. I accompanied them to court sessions in the trial of Lia Eden and her followers in the Central Jakarta District Court, and I visited the defendants in the cells behind the courthouse. Not the least of my 'field' experiences was my visit to Lawang, East Java, in early 2008, to meet with Yusman Roy, the main subject of this book. During this trip I was also kindly provided by legal aid staff with a set of DVDs containing recordings of his 2005 trial, which provided me with valuable insights into the dynamics of the time.

My research presents, largely, a description of events and of key legal and constitutional issues relating to blasphemy in Indonesia. It is, in the main, a statement of the 'who' and the 'what'; it is not, in any major sense, a statement of the 'why'. I provide details about the events leading up to the trial of Yusman Roy, and describe the posture of other key players but I have not attempted a detailed explanation of why things occurred in the way they did. This is because my research was not sociological, and I did not collect direct, personal input from the many actors involved. It was also important, in my view, for institutional voices to be heard, and I was fortunate to have access to sufficient documents to do this.

This book is fundamentally an inquiry into the nature of authority – legal, religious and political. As my primary discipline is law, this inquiry took me into new territory. Taking up a case study of blasphemy in an Islamic setting led me to explore Islamic religious doctrine and the nature of religious authority in Indonesia, and to interpret and apply Rawls' notion of public reason. I hope that I have done justice to these important elements of the study. These dimensions to the research should be understood for the way they assist in elaborating the different layers of the case study, which should itself be seen as providing insight into the evolution of law and constitutionalism in post-Soeharto Indonesia.

My wider interest has for some time been the study of Asian approaches to the rule of law. The research forming the basis of this book in fact first took the form of a study of the 'liberal' aspects of rule of law, before evolving quickly into a national case study. I am certainly not alone in considering Rawls, religion, and the state but my point of origin may be somewhat different to that of others. Specifically, I explore the legal and constitutional aspects of Rawls' later work, and the special role of independent courts in a constitutional democracy. I am highly conscious, also, of the difficulties arising in comparative legal study. Competence in one legal system is challenging enough, and so it has always seemed to me slightly foolhardy to claim any real ability in a different legal system. I have, however, relied on authoritative sources in my work, and Indonesian civil society has focused intently over many years on the same subjects considered here.

I am very thankful for the detailed and thoughtful feedback provided by my thesis examiners, and by independent reviewers on behalf of the publisher. I have taken this commentary into account, and also tried to have regard to work published since my research was completed. I chose to divide my treatment of Rawls into two parts. His later political philosophy and notion of public reason is discussed early in the book, and I turn to the question of applying Rawls in an Islamic setting at the end. This was done in order to provide adequate space for a review of his thinking and responses from some (but by no means all) of his critics. I have focused on those issues and criticisms that I think best highlight his relevance for this case study.

It is not just scholarship that has continued to evolve in recent times. Indonesian society, politics, law, and its Islamic institutions are, self-evidently, not static. The single prosecution examined here remains relevant, and both it and the decision of the Indonesian Constitutional Court (*Mahkamah Konstitusi*) on the Blasphemy Law, remain key legal milestones. The matter of defining 'blasphemous' behaviour in law is also still current, as a draft revision of the Criminal Code is before the Indonesian national legislature at the time of publication, and it includes provisions addressing conduct that offends against religion.

This book would not have been possible without the help of friends and colleagues in the Indonesian legal community. In particular I thank Uli Parulian Sihombing and Erna Rataningsih, especially for providing documents which were critical to producing a detailed case study. Saiful, of LBH Malang, generously hosted my meetings with Yusman Roy, and provided additional material which was greatly appreciated. Other valuable help was provided by Wahyu Widiana, Ramelan, Hasbi Hasan, and staff at the library of MUI. My thanks also go to Dina Afrianty who facilitated my participation in conferences, allowing me to present and test key elements of my work, and with whom I had productive discussions about my objectives.

I am extremely grateful to my primary supervisor, Tim Lindsey, for his guidance and friendship over many years. His support and faith in my capacity to undertake this work was a critical factor in its completion. Sadly I was not able to finalise my work before my parents left us, but I hope it acts as an inspiration to my children. Translations from Indonesian sources are my own, as are any errors more generally.

Stewart Fenwick

Abbreviations

DPR	*Dewan Perwakilan Rakyat* (People's Representative Council)
FPI	*Front Pembela Islam* (Islamic Defender's Front)
FUI	*Forum Umat Islam* (Islamic Community Forum)
HAM	*Hak Asasi Manusia* (Human Rights)
HTI	*Hizbut Tahrir Indonesia*
ICCPR	International Covenant on Civil and Political Rights
JIL	*Jaringan Islam Liberal* (Liberal Islam Network)
KomnasHAM	National Human Rights Commission
LBH	*Lembaga Bantuan Hukum* (Legal Aid Foundation)
MK	*Mahkamah Konstitusi* (Constitutional Court)
MMI	*Majelis Mujahidin Indonesia* (Indonesian *Mujahidin* Council)
MUI	*Majelis Ulama Indonesia* (Ulama Council of Indonesia)
NU	*Nahdlatul Ulama* (Awakening of the *Ulama*); Indonesia's largest mass Muslim organisation
PBB	*Partai Bulan Bintang* (Crescent Moon and Star Party)
Persis	*Persatuan Islam* (Islamic Union)
PPP	*Partai Persatuan Pembangunan* (United Development Party)
UDHR	Universal Declaration of Human Rights

Glossary

aqidah Islamic creed
bid'ah innovation (deviation from Islamic tradition)
Bupati Regent (District Head)
dasar negara basis of the state
fatawa plural form of *fatwa*
fatwa ruling or opinion by Islamic religious scholar
fiqh Islamic jurisprudence
hadith sayings of the Prophet Muhammad
hajj pilgrimage to Mecca
ibadah religious duties of worship and ritual
ibadat singular form of *ibadah*
Imam leader of congregation, or one competent to lead prayer
Jaksa Public Prosecutor
kepercayaan belief
Ketuhanan Yang Maha Esa Belief in Almighty God
madzhab school of jurisprudence in Sunni Islam
Mahkamah Agung Supreme Court
Mufti Islamic scholar qualified to produce *fatawa*
Muhammadiyah Indonesia's second largest mass Muslim organisation
negara hukum law state
Pancasila The Five Principles (forming Indonesia's state philosophy)
penodaan disgracing
Peraturan Regulation
pesantren Islamic boarding school
qanun Regional Regulation in Aceh
Rechstaat Law state
Reformasi Reformation
santri student at *pesantren*; also devout practicing Muslim
sesat deviant
sholat Islamic ritual prayer

sunna 'ways of the Prophet Muhammad'; his words and deeds as witnessed and transmitted by his companions

syariah Islamic law

ulama Islamic scholar

umat community of the faithful

undang-undang statute (passed by the DPR)

1 Islam and pluralism

Setting the scene – *sholat dwi bahasa*

In the early evening of Friday 6 May 2005, the leader of a small Islamic boarding school, or *pesantren*, in the East Java town of Lawang was arrested. Muhammad Yusman Roy was interrogated by police throughout the night of 6 May and into the early hours of Saturday 7 May on the basis of a report made to the police by members of the local branch of the *Majelis Ulama Indonesia* (MUI, the Ulama Council of Indonesia). The substance of the report was that Roy had, since 2003, taught the practice of performing *sholat*[1] in Arabic, as is customary, but accompanied by Indonesian translation. This was a teaching alleged to be a deviation from the rules for ritual prayer, as stated in three *fatawa* issued by different branches of MUI. Roy was to go on to spend 18 months in prison for his practice of dual-language prayer, described in Indonesian as *sholat dwi bahasa*, following prosecution under provisions of Indonesia's so-called 'blasphemy laws'.[2]

Roy was raised by his mother after she separated from his Muslim father, and she herself was a Catholic prior to the marriage.[3] Roy later lived with his father and converted to Islam. He pursued a career in boxing and was exposed to petty crime but, after finding a translation of the Qur'an in a book store, Roy was inspired to study Islam for many years with a teacher in Surabaya, the provincial capital of East Java. He went on to establish the *pesantren* and later went on the *hajj*, during which Roy felt that he received guidance from God. Shortly afterwards, Roy began to practice dual-language prayer in private and gradually began to promote it to his students, and the local community.

---

1 Islamic ritual prayer – *salat* – in Indonesian.
2 The legal regime is considered at length in Chapter 2. An Amnesty International (2014) report examines the subject at length. See also the report by Human Rights Watch (2013) into the treatment of religious minorities in Indonesia, Margiyono (et al. 2011), and Marshall and Shea (2011) for a global study of blasphemy (including in Indonesia).
3 Biographical information drawn from LBH Surabaya (2005). See also Hosen (2012) for his detailed portrait of Roy and the circumstances of his prosecution, which I take up in Chapter 5.

Roy's *pesantren*, titled the *Pondok Itikaf Jamaah Ngaji Lelaku,*[4] was quite modest in size, and situated at the edge of a small river just off the main road running through Lawang, which is a town approximately 20–30 minutes' drive from the regional centre of Malang. It consisted of a small compound comprising a house, stables, and a small open-sided meeting place of around 8 x 3 metres, in which Qur'anic study sessions were held. The name of the *pesantren* provides some indication of Roy's religious mission. While difficult to translate precisely, it indicates that the *pesantren* was a place for a group of faithful to gather (*Jamaah*) to undertake current or lawful (*lelaku*) study of the Qur'an (*Ngaji* – a colloquial form of *mengaji* – from *kaji*, to review/assess). The word *itikaf* carries two meanings: derived from Arabic, it can mean praying in the mosque for some length of time, and it also is used to refer to a period of retreat in the Roman Catholic church.[5] The letterhead of the *pesantren* carries the slogan *Memahami Terjemahan Ayat–Ayat Suci Al-Qur'an – Hadist* which can be translated as 'Understanding Translations of the holy verses of the Qur'an and [of] Hadith'. Thus, particularly through the slogan on the letterhead, Roy clearly promoted the distinguishing feature of his teaching.

Roy received support from the well-known Indonesian legal aid institution *Lembaga Bantuan Hukum* (LBH – 'Legal Aid Foundation'), from its offices in Surabaya and Malang, in defending the criminal charges raised against him. In a publication released prior to his trial (LBH Surabaya 2005), the legal aid organisation describes prosecutions based on religious grounds as amounting to the 'criminalisation of religious freedom'. LBH Surabaya thereby labelled the case as fundamentally being about discrimination against minority groups, indeed minorities within the same religion. The publication called on the state and its various institutions to submit to the supremacy of the national Constitution of 1945, which guarantees protection for religious freedom and its divergent expressions. Religious groups also must acknowledge Constitutional rule, the publication stated, without reserve, and MUI should not monopolise the interpretation of religious texts, nor seek to eliminate other interpretations.

There are two other interesting characteristics about Roy's case. The *pesantren* was governed by a foundation with a board consisting of Roy and his wife, and a further twelve individuals filling roles including deputy director, treasurer and ordinary members. In short, Roy was not acting alone. He was clearly the leader of the *pesantren*, and the guiding hand behind the concept of *sholat dwi bahasa*, but he conducted his affairs transparently, and in the company of a number of supporters. The other fact is the efforts to which Roy went in order to obtain official sanction for his teachings. LBH Surabaya (2005) identified over twenty separate communications between Roy and various agencies and institutions between 2003–2005 including the Department of Religion, the National Police, MUI, the National Human Rights Commission and the President. These will

---

4 *Pondok* – in this context, a dormitory (Solahudin 2008: 6) but also cottage, or retreat.
5 'itikaf' (Stevens et al. 2004: 397). See also Solahudin (2008: 17).

be considered later, in Chapter 5, but clearly the state, in the broadest sense, was fully on notice as to Roy's activities, his motivations and objectives for a long period of time. Despite this, the question of the status of Roy's teaching was only resolved through the application of the criminal law.

Ritual prayer – a Pillar of Islam

In order to understand the reason criminal charges might be laid in response to the format of prayer in an independent *pesantren*, it is necessary to appreciate the significance of ritual prayer in Islam. The experience of Islamic faith is framed by the Five Pillars of Islam: 1) the proclamation of faith; 2) performance of ritual prayer; 3) payment of purification tax (*zakat*); 4) fasting during *ramadan*; and 5) the pilgrimage to Mecca.[6] Through the proclamation of faith a person joins the *umma* – or the community of the faithful,[7] and the act of ritual prayer – the focus of the case study at the heart of the research – itself has a strongly communal nature. It is considered best to pray in congregation whenever possible, and Friday congregational prayer for men is considered mandatory by some. Prayer 'permeates' the life of a Muslim through the requirement for five daily prayers and, according to Hooker (2003: 90), features in Indonesian *fatawa* because prayer is a subject of 'intense interest' to the Muslim community.[8]

Despite its critical role, Islamic ritual prayer 'is nowhere described or exactly regulated' in the Qur'an (Gibb & Kramers 1974), and is considered – compared to ritual in other major faiths – to be 'the most intractable to anthropological analysis' (Bowen 1989: 600). The procedure for conducting *sholat* is, however, largely consistent across the Muslim world,[9] and comprises a series of movements and recitations known as a *raka'at* (a 'unit' of prayer), their number varying according to which of the five daily prayers is being performed. Each unit of prayer comprises the recitation of the *Fatihah*, the first *Surat* (Indonesian – *Surah*; verses)[10] of the Qur'an, usually recited only by the *Imam* in congregation, followed by the recitation of other Qur'anic verses and then by ritual prostration, conducted twice and accompanied by a set of utterances for each phase of the prostration, and concluding once more with the *Fatihah* and short Qur'anic

---

6 See Alavi (2007) and Cornell (2007).

7 In Indonesian also *ummat* and *umat*.

8 *Fatawa* is the plural form of *fatwa*, an opinion on a point of Islamic law by a Muslim religious scholar. The nature of *fatawa* in Indonesia is discussed in Chapter 4. All matters connected with ritual law – *ibadat* – fall within the domain of the *fatwa* (Masud et al. 1996: 19). *Ibadat* is the plural form of *ibadah* and refers to the religious duties of worship including the pillars of Islam, striving to live in the path of God, the condition of purity required for worship and Qur'anic recitation; '*Ibadah*', *Oxford Dictionary of Islam* (2003) (ODI). Available in Oxford Reference Online. www.oxfordreference.com.

9 This discussion draws on Alavi (2007: 11–17), Bowen (1989: 600–601), Muhaimin (1995: 91–104) and '*Salat*', in Gibb & Kramers (1974) (henceforth SEI).

10 According to Saeed (2006: 19) most Muslims around the world would be able to recite the *Fatihah* in Arabic due to the frequency with which it is used.

verses. Despite the lack of prescription contained in the Qur'an, conducting *sholat* according to correct procedure is critical. This is because 'an invalid prayer is tantamount to no prayer at all and thus constitutes, if no compensatory measures are taken, a sin of omission' (Weiss 1996: 66).[11] In the case of Indonesia, Bowen (1989: 601) observes that there has been a 'particular urgency' about local discussion of *sholat* driven by confrontations between reform-minded Muslims and defenders of older procedures, a subject which will be taken up in Chapter 4.

The heart of the doctrinal issue in the case study is the bond between ritual prayer, recitation of the Qur'an, and the fact that in Islam the Qur'an is considered the literal word of God revealed in Arabic to Muhammad. The Qur'an acknowledges the variety of languages spoken by humankind, but Arabic 'has always enjoyed special importance in both the Islamic religion and the Islamic civilization' (Mir 2007: 47). The text itself also stresses the divine nature of the revelation and the absence of any human element in its production; the revelation came directly from God 'to protect it from any human-induced errors or inaccuracies' (Saeed 2006: 16). Hence, according to the mainstream view, 'the *language* of revelation is an essential aspect of its divine content' (Saeed 2006: 17). For this reason, a translation of the Qur'an is not the Qur'an, and 'only the Arabic Qur'an may be recited in formal prayers' (Mir 2007: 50).

The importance of ritual prayer in Islam and its required form, including the role of Arabic in Qur'anic recitation, is clear from the foregoing discussion. However, the events of the Roy case, and the debate concerning the validity of his specific teaching, show that, in reality, practice may vary from what is prescribed. Indonesia is the world's largest Muslim nation, but was also 'the least Arabized of the major Islamic countries' and 'Malay' can be considered the language of Southeast Asian Islam (Madjid 1994: 59, 62). More particularly, the question arises as to whether Roy should be seen as a radical, a reformer, or merely isolated and on the very fringe of Islamic practice. The following section takes up this question.

Diversity, divergence and authority in Islam

The important communal nature of Islam was identified above, and so the faith involves 'more than just a personal relationship with God'; it contains a set of social obligations which 'entails a relationship with a community of believers and a society' (Cornell 2007: xix). Glenn (2000: 165) also observes that the general absence of institutional structures, including in the sense understood in other legal systems, means that 'Islamic law is simply sustained by the Islamic community'. There is a particular dynamic between members of the community of believers, and also with the society in which that community lives: 'throughout

---

11 Mahmood (2005: 123) provides an account of ritual prayer in Cairo that broadens the components of its execution beyond these core elements, including in particular its internal or emotional dimensions. Debates about different dimensions of ritual worship have also been part of Indonesian Islam, as will be seen in Chapter 4.

Islamic history, the traditions of the majority of believers always had to be served, even by those who chose to reject them' (Cornell 2007: xix). Hooker (2002: 214) – writing in the context of Islam in Southeast Asia – explains 'the whole syariah discussion' assumes a static *umma* 'in which social, linguistic and cultural differences could be subsumed in submission to God', but goes on to observe that this ideal was never a practical reality. More importantly, 'variation and variety are the defining characteristics of Islamic law in Southeast Asia' (Hooker: 2013: 185). Bowen's (1989) detailed study of several debates in Indonesia over the performance of ritual worship demonstrates how prevalent diverse practices have been. Bowen (1989: 601) argues that such cases can be 'motivated by larger debates about the nature of community and society', and by movements in Islamic reform more widely.[12]

The notion of who, or what, is the Islamic community is infused with issues of sectarianism, orthodoxy and heterodoxy, and this is no less the case in Indonesia than in any other part of the Muslim world.[13] The history of sectarianism in Islam is indeed 'long and complex' (Hooker 2003: 66), and at its extremes, sectarianism touches on the field of heresy (questions of variation, innovation and heresy are dealt with in Chapter 4). The Prophet Muhammad is said to have proclaimed that Islam would divide into seventy-three sects,[14] and that the followers of all but one would go to hell. Sunni Muslims have declared themselves the chosen sect, entitled the *Najiyah* (although the other sects also claim to be the saved ones), but the four schools within Sunni Islam (see below) are not themselves properly considered sects, although they are characterised by varying interpretations of the faith and differences in ritual practice. Taylor (1967: 199) argues that the tradition which provided for seventy-three sects shows 'the insistence upon drawing up lines of definition of the *umma*'. He also proposes that the concept of 'sectarian' lies in the ground between 'ecumenical' and 'heretical' and that there is a natural relationship of tension between what is considered orthodox, and what heterodox, in Islamic movements and doctrine (Taylor 1967: 197). In the contemporary world, this tension is now also 'between transcendent norms with their claims to divine sanction and ideas of the rule of law' (Salvatore and Eickelman 2004: xiv).[15]

Syariah is comprised of both divine sources (the commands and prohibitions found in the Qur'an and *sunna*) and human sources, or *fiqh*, being specific rulings based on understandings and interpretation of syariah using other sources

---

12 The particular cases he raises will be taken up in Chapter 4, but in general they concern situations where a social group 'has emphasised certain features of the salat in its efforts to define or maintain a particular social form' (Bowen 1989: 609).

13 See for example Fathurrahman (2011) who considers the 'discourse of controversy' between orthodox and heterodox views of Islam expressed in Islamic manuscripts in Indonesia since the sixteenth century.

14 'Sects of Islam', *A Dictionary of Islam* (Hughes c.1885).

15 Salvatore and Eickelman (2004: xiv) suggest that the *umma* will never agree on 'error'.

(Saeed 2006: 44). Syariah is therefore concerned with the fulfilment of prescribed duties (Saeed 2006: 43) and has been described as 'theology in legal form' (Hooker 2002: 213).[16] Much of the substance of Islamic law can be found in *fiqh* covering both matters of ritual (*ibadat*) and human relations (*muamalat*) (Glenn 2000: 160). *Fiqh* developed within Sunni Islam in four directions, expressed within the four schools of Islamic law (or *madhhab*), each of which prevails in different parts of the Islamic world: the Hanafi; Shafi'i (prevailing in Indonesia); Maliki; and Hanbali.[17] Islam does not, as may commonly be assumed, adopt a binary system of approved and forbidden conduct (echoing the familiar distinction between food that is considered *halal* or *haram*). Rather, five classes exist to classify conduct: compulsory (*wadjib*); rewarded (or recommended – *mandub*); indifferent (*mubah*); disapproved (or reprehensible – *makruh*); or, forbidden (*haram*).[18] There is flexibility both within the categories and in the determination of their boundaries (Glenn 2000: 185–186).

A *fatwa* is a ruling on a question submitted about a point of Islamic law produced by a person with the authority to do so.[19] Traditionally the *fatwa* is understood as being personal, in that it is non-binding and intended to provide guidance to the person seeking to have their question answered, who may decide not to follow it and seek another opinion. *Fatawa* have however routinely been collected and used as references because they are a valuable guide to how to respond to real situations. In some Muslim states *fatawa* may be used as a source of guidance in Islamic courts by the judge (*qadi*). The work performed in the *fatwa* (at the 'meeting point between law and fact') is the 'juristic labour' that 'marks the relation of *sharia* . . . to the concrete world of human affairs' (Masud et al. 1996: 3).[20] The nature of *fatawa* in Indonesia and their use by MUI will be considered in Chapter 4, however it has been noted that the *fatwa* has a variety of characteristics including a political dimension, with *fatawa* appearing at 'key historical junctures' as an expression of a religious perspective on political events (Masud et al. 1996: 28). Religious and doctrinal disputes comprise an 'entire branch' of *fatwa* activity, but social issues and social relations also feature in some collections (Masud et al. 1996: 28–29). The relative importance of 'old-style fatawa categories' is shifting and whilst the coverage is now broader in its 'social address', at the same time there is a more specialised interest in 'religious' issues (Masud et al. 1996: 29).[21]

16 It cannot be overlooked, when making a comparison with legal systems, that syariah is 'a complex ethico-legal tradition' (Hefner 2013: 3).
17 Glenn (2000: 179) notes that there may originally have been hundreds of schools of Islamic law.
18 See '*Sharia*', in SEI.
19 This discussion draws on Glenn (2000: 165–166), Hooker (2003: 1–2, 229, 257), Hooker and Lindsey (2002), Masud (et al. 1996), and SEI. Masud (et al. 1996) provide a detailed explanation of the development of *fatawa* out of the original process of direct consultation with the Prophet Muhammad.
20 The world of the *fatwa* is a world of 'competing opinions' (Masud et al. 1996: 19).
21 For example, more than half of some Middle Eastern collections now fall into religious categories of ritual law, creed (*aqidah*) and Qur'anic interpretation (Masud et al. 1996: 29).

Islam, the constitution and the state

The discussion in the previous section provides a brief introduction to Islam as a normative domain, in order to appreciate how and why Roy's 'deviant' approach came to be criticised by MUI. The doctrinal issues form an important part of the case study, but the objective of this book is to understand the implications of the experience of individuals like Yusman Roy for the nature of contemporary Indonesian constitutionalism. As seen above in the observations of his legal defence team, prosecuting Indonesian citizens for their religious beliefs and practices is arguably a question of discrimination, and contrary to the human rights protections enshrined in the Constitution. This section considers the history of engagement between proponents if Islam and the normative order of state law.

The case study raises important questions about the public role of Islamic organisations such as MUI, and in particular, the place of religion in public life. There are two aspects to this religious dimension. One is the place of religion in relation to the state and national law. The other is the nature of authority within Indonesian Islam itself, and the special status afforded to MUI. The nature of the Blasphemy Law in Indonesia, its application in Roy's case, and the susceptibility of conduct such as his to charges of blasphemy will be examined in detail. Briefly, however, it is understood that 'expressing religious opinions at variance with standard Islamic views could easily be looked on as blasphemous' (Hassan 2006: 136). It is therefore critical to understand how Islamic orthodoxy is expressed in Indonesia, and how it interleaves with state power in the application of criminal law. Together, these issues go directly to the basis of legitimate law and authority in democratic Indonesia which are key matters addressed in Rawls' work.

The question of the basis of state authority and the nature of constitutional power is dealt with at length by Nasution (1992). Nasution's (1992: 403) starting point is the observation that at the time of Indonesian independence from colonial rule in 1945 'it was clear that this [independent] state was intended to be a constitutional state in which the freedom of the Indonesian people to govern themselves was firmly secured'. Establishing a constitutional state was part of the broader project of independence and 'it was within this institutional framework that a democratic society could be developed' (Nasution 1992). Under Soeharto, however, Indonesia 'deviated fundamentally from the modern ideal of constitutional government' (Nasution 1992: 404). This deviation was built on the framework provided by the 1945 Constitution, which enabled the emergence of two dictatorships (under both Soeharto, and Indonesia's first President, Soekarno) (Lindsey 2008: 23).[22] Central to the authoritarian model of governance was the idea of the 'Integralist State' developed from the thinking of the Indonesian legal scholar Raden Soepomo (Bourchier 1999; Lindsey 2008: 29).

22 See Indrayana (2008: 106–123) for a discussion of the authoritarian features of both presidencies.

The Integralist State was not openly promoted as an authoritarian model[23] but rather on the basis of an organic state or 'family' principle in which ruler and society were united (Butt & Lindsey 2012: 8–9). A consequence of the adoption of this model was that the Constitution lacked fundamental mechanisms to challenge state power (Lindsey 2008: 29; Butt & Lindsey 2012: 8).[24] This model was accepted at least in part because it was argued that it reflected a traditional Indonesian approach to harmony and consensus (Bourchier 1999: 186) and it has also been identified with an ancient Javanese concept of the unity of all things, microcosm and macrocosm (Butt & Lindsey 2012: 8–9; Nasution 1992: 421–422). Despite this, Bourchier (1999: 186) details critical ways in which the notion of integralism was also sustained by traditions of political philosophy inherited from Dutch legal thought. Indonesian constitutionalism, according to Bourchier (1999: 186–190), has reflected elements of both Positivism and Romanticism, but there is a particular congruence between integralism and European legal Romanticism.[25] He argues in particular that Indonesian Dutch-educated lawyers sympathised with a 'communalistic and anti-liberal' stream of thinking that emerged in Europe following the French revolution and industrialisation (Bourchier 1999: 190).

Nasution (1992: 408–410) adopts the phrase 'the problem of power' to explain evolving attitudes to the place of the individual in relation to the state at different points in Indonesia's constitutional journey. The Integralist State completely negated the problem of power as it could not be envisaged that the ruler would *not* exercise power in the peoples' interest, or that it might lead to repression (Nasution 1992: 422). Conversely, during the debates on constitutional amendment by the Constituent Assembly during the 1950's, the majority of that body 'recognised that state power should be limited by human rights and the rule of law, and that government should be accountable for its use of power' (Nasution 1992: 408).[26] Integralism is, however, only one of several competing ideologies which have played a part in the development of Indonesia's constitution. Butt and Lindsey (2012: 7) argue that three 'strains of opinion' have regularly surfaced in debates about Indonesia's Constitution: integralist/authoritarian,

---

23 Although both Nazi Germany and Imperial Japan were referred to by Soepomo in the course of explaining why the model was suitable to Indonesia (Butt & Lindsey 2012: 8).

24 Indrayana (2008: 123–140) provides a comprehensive assessment of the shortcomings of the 1945 Constitution including, in addition to the lack of checks and balances, being 'executive heavy' and containing unclear provisions, too many delegations to statute, and legal vacuums.

25 Bourchier (1999: 186–187) describes Positivism as the 'tradition of legal philosophy that sees law as emanating from state authority' and Romanticism as the tradition 'which holds that law is legitimate only if it arises organically from the history and culture of particular civilisations'.

26 Key stages of constitutional development including the work of the democratically elected Constituent Assembly are dealt with in Chapter 3. This body was established to consider constitutional reforms (Butt & Lindsey 2012: 4).

liberal-democratic and Islamic. Indeed, Linnan (2007: 274) observes that public law in Indonesia has 'been the subject of repeated disputation from multiple sides', and that this is part of an established pattern reflecting 'a lack of consensus at the level of state purpose'.

The fall of Soeharto in 1998 was followed by a period of transition during which four sets of constitutional amendments effectively 'dismantled' integralism (Butt & Lindsey 2012: 19–25). This constitutional reform process, at the heart of large scale political and social transformation known as *Reformasi*,[27] was completed 'against expectations' (Lindsey 2008: 23). This was because of the significance that the amendments held for the very nature of the Indonesian state (Lindsey 2008). Notwithstanding the passage of the four sets of amendments,[28] Lindsey (2008) argues the process of constitutional amendment was not necessarily satisfactory, nor is it complete. Linnan's observation (above) regarding the lack of consensus about state purpose is borne out by the different, and arguably conflicting, philosophical bases evident in the Constitution: the state philosophy of *Pancasila*;[29] a socialist oriented provision (art 33) providing for national ownership of resources; the pressures of Islamisation; and, a human rights framework demonstrating commitment to a wide range of individual rights (Linnan 2007: 271–274). Despite this, the reformed Constitution is an 'incomparably better document' than it was before amendment (Lindsey 2008: 45). It must be noted that Islam is not mentioned in the Constitution, but the question of whether, or how, to find a place for Islam in the Constitution is taken up below.

One of the key reasons for this successful transition from authoritarianism to a liberal democratic system is that throughout the Soeharto era there was a 'persistent assertion of rule of law and universal values', albeit on the 'margins' of public life (Lindsey 2004: 296–297). After Soeharto, integralism quickly vanished from public life, to be replaced with the language of human rights (Lindsey 2004: 297). Nasution (1992: 407) also argues strongly that the validity of human rights had been clearly acclaimed in the workings of the Constituent Assembly, which saw them as 'inherent in human nature and existing in every human civilisation'. However, the existence of competing strains of opinion, as noted above, means that there has in fact been a 'flip-flop between whether the

27 *Reformasi* (Reformation) was unleashed by the departure of Soeharto in May 1998 (Lindsey 2012a: 3).

28 The First amendment included provisions reversing elements of executive power; the Second included a raft of new human rights provisions and expanded regional autonomy; the Third introduced direct Presidential election, reshaped legislative powers and instituted judicial review in a Constitutional Court; and, as part of the Fourth amendment, the notion that Islamic law be entrenched in the Constitution was rejected (Butt & Lindsey 2012: 20–23).

29 Five principles appearing as part of the Preamble to the Constitution and accepted as expressing the core state philosophy (Butt & Lindsey 2012: 13). *Pancasila* is addressed in Chapter 3. The inclusion of a commitment to belief in God in the *Pancasila* is a significant issue in the context of the issues explored in the research.

citizen exists for the state's benefit or vice versa', which effectively describes the differences between proponents of integralism and human rights between 1945–1998 (Linnan 2007: 277).

Another critical concern regarding the nature of Indonesian citizenship is the way in which the coexistence of plural legal systems – particularly elements of Islamic law – sits with ideas about equality before the law embodied in the national legal system (Linnan 2007: 272). Indeed, there has been concern that Islamic groups would seek to qualify human rights through a filter of radical intolerance (Lindsey 2004: 313). Indonesia is not an Islamic state and was founded as a pluralist entity, but there has been a 'strong demand for imposing Sharia voiced by radical conservative groups' in the post-Soeharto era (Anwar 2007: 186), when restrictions on their ability to express their views publicly that prevailed under Soeharto were lifted (Lindsey 2012a: 42–45). These groups identify Islam with syariah, and consider the concept of pluralism itself as offensive to Islam (Anwar 2007: 203–205). A counter view was proposed by Madjid (1994: 76), who argued that Indonesia could offer itself as a 'laboratory for developing modern religious tolerance and pluralism'. This pluralism has not been confined to interfaith pluralism, but has been identified clearly as involving a pluralism of views within Indonesian Islam (Hefner 1995: 41). The present challenge, however, is more complex ('daunting indeed'), and is a result of the fact that 'Muslim publics seem to be drawn to both shari'a and democracy' (Hefner 2011b: 4). Indonesia presents a special case of the tension that is 'pervasive' in most Muslim-majority lands – that between the desire for both democratically accountable government, and to give Islamic values greater public prominence (Hefner 2011a: 283).

Liberal voices have long been heard in Indonesian Islam and perhaps foremost among these was Madjid, who dealt directly with the questions of liberalisation of Islamic thought and the concept of secularisation in the early 1970s (Bourchier & Hadiz 2003: 82–92). Contemporary Indonesia has therefore seen the rise of a more progressive and liberal approach to the interpretation of Islam, which has the objective of promoting a 'more moderate form of Islam' (Anwar 2007: 216–227). Anwar (2007: 243) explains, however, that political Islam in post-Soeharto Indonesia has been 'coloured by the contest' between these progressive voices and radical-conservative voices. Bruinessen (2013: 3–6) summarises the evolution of contemporary Islamic thought as reflecting a 'conservative turn' in which not only progressive liberal thought but other moderate voices in mainstream Islamic organisations have been disempowered.[30] Indeed, while the membership of MUI was expanded in 2005 to include conservative Islamist representatives (Ichwan 2013: 64), no liberal or minority Muslim groups were

---

30 This evolution may well reflect a broader trend in the Muslim world. According to Salvatore and Eickelman (2004: xx) there are signs that debates about 'what constitutes "good" or authentic Islam' are becoming more competitive and expansive and it is 'one of the paradoxes of modern Muslim publics is that despite this . . . in many Muslim-majority states and communities, the public good is increasingly defined within the parameters of Islam'.

admitted (Bruinessen 2013: 6). Mohamad (2007: 165) also notes that the theology of some liberal Muslims in Indonesia involves an approach that in the past has been condemned as apostasy.[31] The rise of 'uncivil' elements of Muslim society will be considered further in Chapter 4, but the Indonesian case shows how 'proponents of authoritarian variants of Islamic law' can gain an influence disproportionate to their numbers in society (Hefner 2011a: 309).

This issue is, however, one of long-standing and reflects an entrenched and deep conflict between politically active Muslims who have 'looked with suspicion on the state' leading to 'mutual suspicion between Islam and the state' (Effendy 2003: 2). Indeed, Effendy (2003: 224) echoes the observation of Linnan (above) about the lack of consensus as to state purpose, concluding that Indonesia has been unable to conduct an uninterrupted dialogue about the 'proper role and position of religion in the state' and that it is time the political and religious elites reached 'an appropriate settlement'.[32] A significant player among the religious elites is MUI itself which has exploited its 'semi official religious authority' to advance a 'puritanical' version of Islam based on Sunni orthodoxy (Ichwan 2013: 61).[33] It has thus been able to influence public debate on Islamic public policy, and to establish itself as a de facto 'official national mufti' (Lindsey 2012a: 124).[34] This influence was reflected in the statements of the immediate past President of Indonesia, Susilo Bambang Yudohyono, who not only called on MUI to help form state policy on Islam but appeared to suggest that its rulings in *fatawa* would guide the state (Lindsey 2012a: 128–129).[35] Given that it was once considered that many Muslim leaders had renounced an 'aspiration for monopolistic unity' in Indonesian Islam (Hefner 1995: 41), the rise of MUI and the institutionalising of Islam is a particularly important development for the purposes of the research.

Hosen (2007: 226) frames the question succinctly: 'can a state be at once truly democratic and in some sense Islamic in character?' It is important to note

31 Mohamad refers specifically to the 'hermeneutics' approach to Islam adopted by Ulil Abshar Abdalla, who is a leading figure in liberal Islam in Indonesia and played a role in the case study. Debates concerning orthodoxy and deviation are by no means confined to modern Indonesia. Disagreements as to doctrine have led in centuries past to attempts to marginalise opposing views, revealing a 'dark side to the social history of religion' in Indonesia; a tendency that continues to the present day (Fathurrahman 2011: 471).

32 Hefner (2013: 24) proposes that 'serious disagreements' among Indonesia's elites about how to balance religious freedom and social cohesion influence the interpretation and application of the law relating to religious freedom. These legal and constitutional issues will be considered in detail in the subsequent chapters.

33 'Puritanical' here is defined as Islamic thought and practices imbued with teachings that emphasise the purity of the faith from polytheistic and associated beliefs including blasphemy, heresy, heterodoxy, liberalism, secularism and pluralism (Ichwan 2013: 91 n5).

34 A *mufti* was traditionally a scholar independent of the state and qualified to provide religious rulings or *fatwa* (Hooker 2003: 1). MUI's position as self-appointed leader of Indonesian Islam is addressed in Chapter 4.

35 MUI does in fact play an official role in areas such as the management of Islamic banking and finance (Lindsey 2012a: 154), see further Chapter 3.

that Islamic political parties have acknowledged that 'sovereignty belongs to the people' and that these same parties were active participants in the decision to reject the formal acknowledgement of syariah in the most recent round of constitutional amendments (Hosen 2007: 228–229). Despite this, there remains an Islamic agenda within the Indonesian legislature (the *Dewan Perwakilan Rakyat* (DPR) or People's Representative Council) by which supporters of syariah seek to 'ensure that no law should contradict Islamic teachings' (Hosen 2007: 231). In a similar vein, the failure to secure constitutional recognition of Islam also led to a drive to enact Islamic principles in regional regulations (Bush 2008; Salim 2008: 175). This rising influence of Islam on the national legal system since the 1990s, however, falls short of 'real' or 'complete' syariah. It is not entirely syariah, as it is enacted in man-made law (Salim 2008: 177), and it is the result of mediation by the state between proponents and opponents of Islamisation (Lindsey 2012a: 3).

While the Indonesian state does respond to pressure for greater recognition of syariah, Islamic law remains within the 'formal legal and administrative institutional framework of the state' (Lindsey 2012a: 3). Thus, the state 'stands in the middle', both regulating Islam and mediating the outcome of challenges through legal mechanisms, including the courts (Lindsey 2012a: 4). Nonetheless, as seen above, there are divergent approaches to interpreting and applying syariah. This means that in circumstances such as those arising in the case study, it remains necessary to resolve the issue of which Islam, or who's Islam, should apply. The book also considers how the boundaries of these previous mediations between the state and Islam are tested, or extended, by the Blasphemy Laws.

Contribution of the research – why Rawls?

The preceding introduction to key issues that have arisen in Indonesian constitutional studies is included not as a literature review, but to provide context, as these issues will be discussed in the coming chapters. They are also included as they demonstrate the challenges that have arisen, and continue to arise, in establishing democracy in the world's largest Muslim nation. According to Hefner (2011b: 1), questions such as the nature of syariah in modern Moslem democracies, the concept of pluralist citizenship, and the place of those professing a 'non-conforming variety of the faith' are among the most decisive for 'assessing the future of the modern Muslim world'. I have chosen to deal with these issues by applying the work of John Rawls to the case of Indonesia. The next chapter provides an introduction to Rawls' political liberalism and the concept of public reason, and I also review some, but not all, criticisms of Rawls. As I observed in the Preface, I am reading Rawls primarily from a rule of law perspective, and this is not the work of a political scientist, but a lawyer and student of Asian law. I come back in the final chapter to the application of Rawls' thinking to Muslim states, and Indonesia in particular. I will explain briefly the challenges associated with this project, but fuller attention is paid to the contrasting approaches to the use of Rawls in non-Western settings in that final chapter.

The discussion in the preceding section demonstrates that while Indonesia has transformed into a liberal democracy, to date there has been limited attention paid to how this reflects any more comprehensive political theory, and to what extent.[36] It was seen that Western political theory has been – at the least – latent in previous constitutional orders. It is also accepted that different strains of thought have driven constitutional debate, and it is acknowledged that the current Constitution reflects divergent influences. A small number of scholars have sought to apply John Rawls' concept of public reason to political and legal affairs in Indonesia (An-Na'im 2008; Bowen 2003, 2005; Elson 2010), with differing results. There is also a body of scholarship considering Rawls in the context of Muslim states and Islamic thought (An-Na'im 2008; Bahlul 2003; Bilgin 2011; Fadel 2007–2008, 2008), and other work exploring Rawls in the context of Muslim minorities in established democracies (March 2009). Rawls and key concepts forming part of his thinking have also been applied in work exploring Islam, democracy and secularism more generally (Asad 2003: 2–8; Dalacoura 2003: 19–20; Hashemi 2009: 25–27).

The reason that Rawls appears to demand consideration is because of his focus on precisely the issues evident in the case of Indonesia. Rawls is concerned fundamentally with the survival of constitutional democracy and how religious and secular doctrines can 'get on together and cooperate in running a reasonably just and effective government' (Bilgin 2011: 4). Scholars have also noted the particular relevance of Rawls to questions of religion. It may be that this dimension of Rawls' work has been neglected or, indeed, that his own treatment of religion has been misunderstood (Dombrowski 2001: ix; Maffettone 2015: 8). Dombrowski (2001: x) argues that in fact an interest in religion can be seen throughout Rawls' career. According to An-Na'im (2015: 277–78), there is an increasing need to consider Rawls' thinking, given the facts of deeper religious diversity and the realities of an increasingly interdependent world.

One question underlying this body of work is whether Rawls' thinking should in some way be disqualified from application outside a Western social or political setting. Arguments have been raised in the literature as to the relevance of a political philosophy derived from a particular historical experience, although what is considered a value of the 'West' or the 'East' is a subject of debate (Lindsey 2004: 286–287).[37] As will be discussed further in the following chapter, there are strong arguments raised about any claim that political liberalism is derived from a 'Western' political tradition, and that the political values ascribed to the liberal tradition are somehow embedded in a Western tradition. The idea of respect,

---

36 Hefner (2013: 19) states that studies of religion in post-Independence Indonesia were not usually directly concerned with 'liberal and/or human rights based measures of religious freedom'.

37 Asad (2003: 13) observes that 'although the West contains many faces at home it presents a single face abroad'.

states Nussbaum (2015: 64), 'is not especially Western'. Further, as noted above, Western philosophical thought has already been applied to Indonesia: European legal and philosophical influences were manifest in the post-Independence Constitution, and it has arguably been very influential for later political regimes, such as Socialism under Soekarno.

Indonesian scholars have also accepted that the point of origin of different theories does not present an insurmountable barrier to their application to Indonesia. For example, Mohamad (2007: 164) argues that most Muslim states embrace secularism. Azra and Hudson (2008: 1) have also dealt directly with the argument that 'Western political concepts are difficult to apply to Islamic societies', asserting that there is much scholarship which accepts that 'concepts from Western political theory are compatible – to a lesser or greater degree, depending on individual interpretations – with a rational interpretation of Islamic universalism'. This is a view shared by scholars writing outside the Indonesian context. Salvatore and Eickelman (2004: xx) note that 'Islamic ideas of the common good shift in content and elaboration over time', but they 'may often converge with Western understandings of such major issues as democracy and tolerance for religious diversity'. Ultimately, the study of Indonesian Islam inevitably involves confronting the issue of understanding the impact of multiple external influences, including those most directly associated with a faith rooted in the Arab Middle East. Hooker (2013: 236–237) has invoked the notion of 'Arab intellectual imperialism' in discussing the idea of local adaptations of Islam. Moreover, Indonesian scholars deal regularly with, in particular, the influence of Arabic in the development of language and the study of Islam (Madjid: 1994; Umam: 2013).

A recurring preoccupation of Rawls' was to understand how a just, well-ordered society could be maintained (Freeman 2007: 460). He therefore developed the 'ideal of a democratic society . . . in terms of the political autonomy of free and equal citizens who agree for a number of different reasons to a liberal conception of justice' (Freeman 2007: 461). Both Bilgin (2011) and Fadel (2008) accept virtually without qualification that Rawls' political liberalism can make a positive contribution to analysis of Muslim democracies. Bilgin (2011) does not, however, explore any national case studies, nor does he address Indonesia in any detail. Fadel (2008) has a different focus, and primarily identifies elements of Islamic thought that are compatible with Rawls. An-Na'im (2008: 1) adapts Rawls' notion of public reason in pursuit of his own project which is fundamentally concerned with the experience of Islamic faith in Muslim states, and he considers Indonesia as one of his case studies of the relationship between Islam and the state. Bowen (2003, 2005) considers Rawls briefly, and argues that his work is not compatible with conditions in Indonesia, due to the significant role Islam plays in public discourse.

For Bilgin (2011: 45) political liberalism

> should be rather agreeable to most citizens of faith in Muslim societies . . . the citizen of faith is reassured by the inclusive outlook of political

liberalism in achieving and maintaining the political consensus. Political liberal expression of liberal democracy aims to be inclusive and just.

The notion of state neutrality is central to liberal thought and political liberalism in particular, but, while charged by critics with a 'secular bias', it does not seek to be 'non-religious' (Bilgin 2011: 41). Its neutrality 'expresses a moral commitment to reaching terms of political association on which all citizens can reasonably agree' (Bilgin 2011: 42). The reason that neutrality and a search for consensus might be valuable is articulated by Fadel (2008: 7): pluralism and specifically intra-Muslim pluralism has become 'an indelible feature of Muslim moral and political life'. Fadel goes on:

> Given Rawls' status among liberals, his analysis represents a plausible starting point for a systematic analysis of the relationship of fundamental Islamic theological, ethical and legal concepts to those of modern liberalism.

There is therefore a dual aspect to the application of Rawls to a state such as Indonesia. First, it is valuable to assess the current state of Indonesian constitutionalism with a model of liberalism. The history of debate over the place of Islam in the state was sketched above and, as Bush (2009: 8) observes, these have been 'some of the fiercest debates waged in the country's history'. The Roy case study, a prosecution under blasphemy laws, demonstrates an important contemporary dimension to the ongoing debate about the recognition of aspects of Islamic law and the nature of the Indonesian state.

Second, the defining characteristic of the case study is that it shows that members of the majority faith are not immune from allegations of blasphemy. This is entirely consistent with the experience throughout Indonesian history, which demonstrates that, albeit perhaps counter-intuitively, 'most of the conflicts involving Islam' have been intrafaith rather than interfaith – 'conflicts among Muslims themselves' (Bush 2009: 8–9).[38] In modern Indonesia, this conflict included debate over what Madjid considered the liberating potential for the *umat* of secularisation, leading to his call for a reform movement that was both non-traditionalist and non-sectarian (Bourchier & Hadiz 2003: 89–91).[39] Put simply, the sheer diversity of religious opinion confronting Muslims 'on every conceivable issue' militates against arguments that Rawls should not be considered in a Muslim context (An-Na'im 2015: 263).

---

38 A finding implicit from the discussion about the diverse contours of Islam outlined in this chapter, but also supported by Hirji (2010). Hirji (2010: 7–8) takes up the subjects of 'intra-communal difference and religious plurality' among Muslims and also observes: 'Muslims who mark their identity in strictly religious terms are not all the same and do not have identical interpretations of their foundational texts'.

39 For a detailed examination of the concept of secularisation and its application in the Indonesian context see Hefner (1995).

The particular objective of this book is, in short, to conduct a more comprehensive analysis of the applicability of Rawls' political liberalism to the case of Indonesia than has been done to date. In particular, in looking at a case study of religious freedom, the research explores the prospects for what Hefner (2013: 24) describes as the 'civic-pluralist understanding of religious freedom', which, in his view, faces 'severe obstacles'. These obstacles include different views of what is legitimate religion; non-secularist views of the state; divergent views of 'what is required for human flourishing'; and, a lack of willingness to enforce existing laws and constitutional provisions on religious freedom (Hefner 2013). With respect to the contribution of political liberalism, the research revisits and extends the analysis of Bowen, and re-evaluates the way in which An-Na'im adapts Rawls. It does so, in particular, by considering key criticisms of Rawls and considering whether those criticisms withstand scrutiny within the context of the Roy prosecution and the blasphemy regime. The aim of this exercise is, fundamentally, to view Indonesia's Constitution, and constitutional thinking about human rights, through the lens of a model of liberal political philosophy.

Chapter outline

The book deals, in turn, with each of the main subjects set out above. Separate consideration is given to Rawls' political philosophy; the Indonesian constitutional, legal and human rights framework so far as it relates to religious freedom; the nature of Islam outside the state legal framework, including the place of MUI; and, the Roy prosecution (in two chapters).

In Chapter 2, 'Rawls and the challenge of faith', I deal at length with Rawls' political liberalism, which is the wider political theory within which his idea of public reason sits. Political liberalism is, for Rawls, a 'limited' form of liberalism and does not require that liberal values prevail as against other comprehensive moral or ethical belief systems. Rather, Rawls argues, it provides a means to ensure that in cases of 'constitutional fundamentals' state institutions and decision makers, including judges, are not motivated by arguments founded in any particular value system, where there is likely to be conflict as to the accepted outcome. I consider some criticisms of this framework, including the 'communitarian critique', which claims that Rawls' concepts remain rooted in liberal individualism; arguments that the need for an 'overlapping consensus' is impractical and that a pragmatic '*modus vivendi*' among competing comprehensive value systems is more feasible; and objections to the restrictions some claim Rawls places upon religion in public life and political interchange. I argue, in response, that Rawls' critics agree on the underlying fact of pluralism, and there is consensus that fundamental rights such as freedom of religion should be respected in all circumstances.

In Chapter 3, 'Faith and freedom in Indonesian law', I highlight how Indonesian law both promotes and protects religion. The Constitution and specific laws remain neutral as to faith, and religious freedom has been protected since independence. Nonetheless a framework of criminal offences and administrative measures provides the basis for managing a range of different conduct, from acts of religious deviancy through to acts affecting public order, such as forms of vilification. I propose that this amounts to a de facto blasphemy regime because offences against God as such are not regulated, but the interpretation and application of the law favours the protection of religious orthodoxy. This results in large part from the preambular *Pancasila* declaration in the Constitution which has been interpreted by the Constitutional Court, and is widely accepted in broader scholarship, as effectively requiring a high degree of religiosity in Indonesia. I identify key contributions from the Constitutional Court: inviting religious scholars to play a role through framing religious standards; reading down individual rights in the Constitution; and advancing a conservative and literalist interpretation of permitted exceptions in the Constitution's human rights provisions. The long-standing debate about the *dasar negara*, or basis of the state, has been cast in terms of secular versus religious governance, but appears to have reached a new stage in its development. Islam is still not a state religion but now has a more prominent, and secure, place in law and policy than ever before.

In Chapter 4, 'MUI – The institutionalising of Indonesian Islam', I address in detail the policy and stance of the Ulama Council of Indonesia. First, I place the issue of innovation in the context of long-standing debates within Islam (also seen in Indonesia) over claims of deviancy and, more critically, apostasy. Piety acts as a social marker, and the relative stance of individual Muslims and/or parent organisations on matters of doctrine has been used as a basis for classifying approaches to Islam in Indonesia. MUI, a non-government religious organisation, is active in law and policy formulation and in its efforts to control the spread of doctrinal innovation. In contrast to the traditional status of religious rulings, the *fatawa* of the MUI are presented as authoritative and binding rulings, and are increasingly being given status in the law-making process. MUI has actively embraced more radical and conservative elements and seeks to marginalise liberal voices. Despite its unofficial, non-government status, the organisation plays a critical role in establishing public standards in matters of Islamic faith.

Chapters 5 and 6 relate at some length the events of the case study and draw extensively on Indonesian language documents obtained during field work. In Chapter 5, 'Case Study Part 1 – The language of devotion', I relate the facts of the case and the circumstances leading up to the prosecution of Yusman Roy. The chapter traces the interaction at the local level of several protagonists: Roy himself as the leader of the *pesantren*; MUI at the sub-national level; other local *ulama* (Islamic scholars); and law enforcement and other government agencies. The case evolved against a background of both national and international tensions post the 9/11 attack on the Twin Towers, and I argue that the prosecution of Roy parallels the rise in conservative Islamic action generally in 2005 in Indonesia. I document also the close relations between MUI representatives and government agencies and officials, and highlights the role of *fatawa* and Islamic reasoning in the legal process. I argue the case study can be seen as a microcosm of the wider conflict between liberal and conservative Muslims.

In the second part of the case study, Chapter 6, 'Case Study Part 2 – Innovation on trial', I look at the court process, principally at the District Court level. The trial itself in large part focused on the issue of whether Roy's promotion of dual-language prayer was indeed deviant according to Islamic thought. I outline prosecution and defence arguments, as well as the evidence of a wide range of expert witnesses. The District Court ultimately did not uphold a charge that Roy's behaviour 'disgraced' Islam, but it did not remove itself from this religious issue explicitly on the basis of lack of competence holding, rather, that a difference of opinion among expert witnesses prevented it making such a finding. Instead, it upheld charges that the promotion of Roy's unorthodox Islamic practices included the expression of hostility, hatred or contempt (under vilification offences) against Sunni Muslims. To this extent, the trial rests, at least indirectly, on judgments about doctrine and acceptable religious practices. I argue that the trial can be considered a continuation by formal legal means of the debate between representatives of different approaches to Indonesian Islam identified in Chapter 5. It is characterised, however, by a lack of rigorous legal analysis of the elements of the offences, and a willingness to entertain religious argumentation.

In Chapter 7, 'Islam, public reason, and the State', I address the central objectives of the book. Based on the consideration given in Chapter 2 to Rawls' political liberalism as a model for a well-governed constitutional democracy, I revisit the scholarship which has dealt with Rawls and Muslim states, including Indonesia. Bowen (2003, 2005) argues that Rawls cannot apply in Indonesia without modification and that reasoning there is 'public and also Islamic'. An-Na'im (2008) argues that Rawls' framework is compromised (largely on political rather than philosophical grounds), but advances a concept he describes as 'civic reason'. Bilgin (2011) raises little objection to the use of Rawls in Muslim settings. Such concerns about the application of Rawls to the case of Indonesia reflect the critiques discussed in Chapter 2, and I maintain that there remains no fundamental reason why a theory designed to establish a mechanism for debate among value systems in constitutional democracies cannot be adopted for Indonesia. The case study reinforces that value pluralism can exist within belief systems as well as among them (the case study reflecting an intra-Islamic dispute), and the 'Western' origins of this framework do not disqualify it from consideration. In the case of Indonesia, the existence of religious argumentation in public institutions, the promotion of religiosity more generally, and the protection of Islamic orthodoxy by MUI serve to qualify the liberal principles embedded in the prevailing constitutional order. Rawls' model is deliberately ideal, and utopian, but I argue that his thinking is applicable to a case of intra-Islamic pluralism in a modern, Asian democracy.

2 Rawls and the challenge of faith

Political liberalism is a theory that seeks to provide a framework for dealing with value pluralism. While a descendant of previous forms of liberal political thought, Rawls uses it to distinguish between decisions made through political actions and processes in a constitutional democracy, and those derived from other, comprehensive, value systems. He acknowledges, for example, that liberalism itself and his earlier work on justice as fairness are themselves comprehensive value systems. What I think is especially interesting about his approach is that Rawls goes to some lengths to explain how political liberalism responds to the Western historical experience of entrenched religiously based conflict. Indeed, his notion of public reason is a key concept that seeks to reconcile religion and politics (Maffettone 2015: 9). It is for this reason, and his focus on constitutional democracy at work, that his thinking appeals to me for its potential, valuable, contribution to understanding legal and political development in Indonesia.

I also highlight the special role played by the judiciary in public reason. In this book we will see both trial and superior courts at work. Rawls himself focuses particular attention on the role of superior courts in contributing to stability in a democratic state. I think it is valuable to see how lower courts also face issues of constitutional fundamentals, and are therefore also potentially charged with a duty to operate in a manner consistent with the principles of public reason. Rawls proposes a theoretical model, and provides relatively few examples in support of his concepts. This book provides a more detailed, worked example of how his thinking can apply to a quintessential issue of religious freedom – the application of Indonesia's Blasphemy Law. Fundamentally, I argue here that both Rawls and his critics share an aversion to political regimes that fail to protect fundamental rights relating to religious freedom and expression.

Political liberalism

Liberalism is not easy to describe or to define,[1] but Arblaster (1984: 15, 55) proposes that the concept of individualism is at its core, and that freedom is a fundamental liberal value.[2] It has been described as the intellectual strand that binds together modern Western political, social and economic life (Hayek 1982: 119–120; Voegelin 1974), and it informs systems of government, individual consent being a fundamental principle of liberal political theory (Kahn 1999: 58; Loughlin 2003: 13). It is a doctrine closely associated with the rule of law (Steiner and Alston 1996: 190) and with fixing 'moral limits to the powers of government' (Larmore 1990: 339).

Rawls' work on political liberalism developed out of his earlier and foundational writing on justice as fairness (Rawls 1971).[3] There have been other expressions of political liberalism, but O'Neill (1997: 411) argues that, on its adoption by Rawls, the phrase gained 'a new meaning'.[4] Prior to developing his ideas on political liberalism, Rawls proposed a 'baseline' of social and economic primary goods, and equal access of all people to these primary goods (Rawls 2002: 41).

1 See, for example, Cumming (1969: 2) and Tamanaha (2004: 32). 'Like any tradition of thought, liberalism is marked by disputes among its adherents as well as by disagreements with its adversaries' (Larmore 1990: 339).
2 Larmore (1990: 343) observes that the thinking of Kant and Mill on individualism (which Larmore argues can be further reduced to ideals of autonomy and individuality) stand out as the most widely known versions. According to Larmore (1990) 'individualism' amounts to a demand that we should always maintain only a 'contingent and never a constitutive allegiance to any substantial view of the good life, that is, to any concrete way of life involving a specific structure of purposes, significances, and activities (e.g., the life devoted to art, or to a career, or to a particular religion)'. Mill (in *On Liberty*) remarked on the importance of exercising key human faculties (perception, judgment, mental activity, moral preference) through making a choice – 'He who does anything because it is the custom makes no choice . . .' (Larmore 1990: 343).
3 John Rawls' *A Theory of Justice* precedes by twenty years his work on political liberalism and public reason. *A Theory of Justice* can be said to be his primary work, and in it Rawls aimed to provide an alternative account to utilitarianism, based on the social contract tradition (Campbell 2001: 92; Freeman 2003: 1; Rawls 1993: xiv–xv). (The social contract being an idea of society 'as a fair system of cooperation between citizens regarded as free and equal', and utilitarianism being an idea of society as a social system 'organised so as to produce the most good summed over all its members' (Rawls 2001: 95–96)). Justice as fairness is at the centre of this earlier work and it is presented 'as a universal moral ideal to be aspired to by all societies', but shares with his later work the objective of working out a 'realistic utopia' – a realistic ideal of justice (Freeman 2003: 2). Rawls also applies his later concepts to the field of international relations in *The Law of Peoples* (2002). I will not deal here with this dimension of his work but see, for example, Tasioulas (2002).
4 Ackerman (1994: 364) writes of 'political liberalism' – 'a distinct approach to the problem of political power' – but again without identifying a source for the term. Larmore (1990) published on the subject prior to the release of Rawls' fully fledged account in 1993 (*Political Liberalism*). Cf. Halliday and Karpik (1997), who deploy the phrase in their work on the legal profession and the rule of law without reference to any source.

Any departure from this baseline requires agreement among citizens that such departure would be to the benefit of all, particularly the least advantaged (Rawls 2002). This process rests upon Rawls' idea of the 'original position'. This is a hypothetical agreement that he describes as a 'model of representation for liberal societies' (Rawls 2002: 30), which in turn rests on the idea of the 'veil of ignorance' (Rawls 1993: 304–305).[5]

Rawls (1993: 38) re-worked his theory of justice realising that his initial concepts represented a comprehensive moral framework in its own right, and may not be acceptable to those supporting rival conceptions of justice:

> Since there is no reasonable religious, philosophical, or moral doctrine affirmed by all citizens, the conception of justice affirmed in a well-ordered democratic society must be a conception limited to what I shall call 'the domain of the political' and its values.

Rawls' political liberalism departs from justice as fairness in that there is no longer congruence of 'the Right with a shared intrinsic Good' but rather a congruence between a 'publicly justifiable conception of justice with different and competing comprehensive ethical views' (Freeman 1994: 641).[6]

The idea of justice remains, however, fundamental to Rawls' approach to liberalism and is reflected in his placing priority on the 'right over the good' (Rawls 1993: 173–211).[7] The inherent link between Rawls' political theory and law and justice gives rise, for example, to the claim that Rawls can been seen as the 'perfect philosopher of the rule of law' (Kahn 1999: 20), and O'Neill (2015: 84) remarks on the importance for Rawls' thinking of 'both order and the rule of law'. It could, therefore, be said that placing precedence in basic justice over civil peace is a benchmark of his political liberalism (Larmore 2003: 385). Rawls himself acknowledges that purporting to establish an idea of justice that is independent of any particular conception of the good appears problematic

---

5 Individuals come to agree to the principle of justice as fairness because their social status and their particular allocation of goods is obscured by this 'veil' and, being deprived of this particular knowledge, individuals arrive at principles of justice which carry only those restrictions which might arise as though they were designing a system in which their places in life were assigned at random (Rawls 1993: 304–305; Nagel 1999: 38).
6 Habermas (2010: 450) characterises this shift in thinking as the result of two decades of reflection on the question of whether common practical reason had 'enough substance to rival a *moral* theory intrinsically linked to religion'. Political liberalism is not remote from his earlier work, and Rawls (1993: 43) links together a series of 'abstract conceptions' in his exposition of political liberalism including the notion of the original position. See also Nussbaum (2015: 29) who argues much of that written about 'alleged differences' between the two major works is misleading.
7 Sandel (1994: 1766–1776) deals with this philosophical question at length, and I will return to his critique below. See also Campbell (2001: 103) on the rule of law question. The importance of public reason for the role of courts is taken up further below.

(Rawls 1993: 174). Rawls (1993) explains (in reply to his own questioning on this point) that giving priority to 'right' means that the 'principles of political justice impose limits on permissible ways of life; and hence claims citizens make to pursue ends that transgress those limits have no weight'.[8]

The problem that Rawls seeks to address is the difficulty that arises from the existence of competing viewpoints within a democratic society: 'How is it possible that there may exist over time a stable and just society of free and equal citizens profoundly divided by reasonable though incompatible religious, philosophical, and moral doctrines?' (Rawls 1993: xviii). This, itself, is an attempt to deal with 'the big problem of justification' – that is, how or why would people put aside their deepest convictions in favour of 'narrower political values'? (Nagel 2003: 76–77). This question is, in fact, shared by much of contemporary political philosophy in which liberal theorists are

> all concerned with the question of whether and how the ideal of public justification, variously understood, could be realised under the circumstances prevailing in modern societies, chief among which is the persistence of an irreconcilable plurality of world-views among citizens.[9]

For Rawls (1993: xxiv), political liberalism originates in the Reformation, with its 'long controversies' over religious toleration.[10] Division of faith led to the emergence, within the same societies, of rival forms of authority because individuals were in no doubt as to either the nature of the 'highest good' or of the basis of moral obligation, which was divine law ('moral theology gave them complete guidance') (Rawls 1993: xxii, xxiv). The problem thrown up under these circumstances was, therefore, how could society even be possible when it involves different faiths (Rawls 1993: xxiv, 303).

---

8 A distinction can be made between two conceptions of justice: 'those that allow for a plurality of reasonable though opposing comprehensive doctrines each with its own conception of the good, and those that hold that there is but one such conception' (Rawls 1993: 134). Nagel (2003: 74) expresses this a little differently and, relating back to liberal political philosophy, refers to the 'typical liberal demands of tolerance and individual liberty'. 'It is the value of mutual respect which limits the grounds on which we may call on the collective power of the state to force those who do not share our convictions to submit to the will of the majority' (Nagel 2003: 75).

9 See Hayfa (2008: 3), who deals in detail with Rawls, Jurgen Habermas and Richard Rorty, but also identifies Charles Larmore, Bruce Ackerman and others. See Habermas (2006) for a discussion of similarities and differences in his and Rawls' responses to the underlying issue of pluralism and tolerance.

10 Franck (1997: 609) sets out at length the emergence of the notion of toleration, and its establishment through legislation in Britain, noting that it was 'not a sentiment familiar anywhere in Europe before the sixteenth century'. According to Rawls (1993: xxii), Medieval Christianity was marked by a tendency toward an authoritarian, institutional form of religion and in which doctrine and adherence to creed was seen as a way to salvation.

Rawls (1993: 11) acknowledges that this political conception is, at the same time, also a moral conception – meaning 'its content is given by certain ideals, principles and standards; and that these norms articulate certain values, in this case political values'.[11] He asserts, however, that the values underpinning political liberalism are 'so to speak, political not metaphysical' (Rawls 1993: 10).[12] Rawls (2002: 166) declares that this is not 'an individualist political conception' as it aims to protect 'the various interests in liberty, both associational and individual'. He also distinguishes clearly the 'full autonomy of political life' from 'ethical values of autonomy and individuality, which may be applied to the whole of life' – the 'weight of ethical autonomy' is left to be decided by citizens in the light of their comprehensive doctrines (Rawls 1993: 78).

Rawls (1993: 135) also deals specifically with the nature and workings of liberal democracy,[13] noting that 'no comprehensive doctrine is appropriate as a political conception for a constitutional regime'. He stresses that political power in a constitutional regime is 'ultimately the power of the public, that is the power of free and equal citizens as a collective body' (Rawls 1993: 136). Rawls (1993: 137) reinforces this notion with the 'liberal principle of legitimacy':

> our exercise of political power is fully proper only when it is exercised in accordance with a constitution the essentials of which all citizens as free and equal may reasonably be expected to endorse in the light of principles and ideas acceptable to their common human reason.

The political culture of modern democratic society, Rawls (1993: 36–39) argues, is characterised by diversity of reasonable comprehensive doctrines as 'permanent feature of the public culture of democracy', and difference is so fundamental a feature of society that even the shared understanding of a single comprehensive religious, philosophical, or moral doctrine 'can be maintained only by the oppressive use of state power'.

---

11 The distinction with a moral conception being that it covers a wider range – seeking to cover 'all recognised values and virtues within one rather precisely articulated system' (Rawls 1993: 13). Elsewhere, Rawls (2002: 143) states that 'political values are not moral doctrines' although he does acknowledge that liberal political principles and values are 'intrinsically moral', and claims they 'fall under the category of the political', whereas moral doctrines are considered to be on a par with religion and philosophy. Larmore (1990: 346) similarly observes that that there is a 'minimal' moral basis to liberalism, but 'it cannot be trivial . . . nor is the form of the political association it secures of small importance'.

12 'Political liberalism is not comprehensive liberalism' (Rawls 1993: xxvii). Challenges raised against this notion are discussed below. As Ackerman (1994: 373) observes: 'The entire point of the project is to avoid rendering liberal theory hostage to any particular metaphysical view'.

13 In the words of Freeman (1994: 633), Rawls sets out the 'public ethics of the political domain of a democracy'.

Overlapping consensus

The importance of equality among citizens gives rise to a 'crucial assumption' that citizens will have fundamentally different conceptions of the good that are 'incommensurable and irreconcilable' (Rawls 1993: 303). In this way, citizens are no longer bound by a single conception of the good, such as a religious faith or philosophical doctrine, 'but on a shared public conception of justice appropriate to the conception of citizens in a democratic state as free and equal persons' (Rawls 1993: 304). The objective is not to replace the various different comprehensive views (Rawls 1993: xviii), rather citizens are expected to share a 'focal political conception' as well as their own 'reasonable doctrines' (Rawls 1993: xix). The outcome of this process is an 'overlapping consensus' of 'reasonable comprehensive doctrines' which, while deeply opposed, live together through affirming the 'political conception of a constitutional regime' (Rawls 1993: xviii). Rawls (1993) therefore also distinguishes between 'public' and 'non-public' bases of justification – the first is generally acceptable to citizens on fundamental political questions; the latter belongs to the many comprehensive doctrines, and is 'acceptable only to those who affirm them'. This 'dualism' is a feature of the 'special nature of democratic political culture' (Rawls 1993, xxi).

Comprehensive doctrines belong to what Rawls (1993: 14) describes as the 'background culture' of civil society and contain the values that apply to personal, family and associational realms. Public culture for Rawls (1993: 13–14) consists of the 'political institutions of a constitutional regime and the public traditions of their interpretation (including the judiciary)'. The background culture is 'the culture of the social, not the political', the culture of daily life (Rawls 1993: 14). Individuals affirm the political conception from within their own comprehensive doctrines of which it becomes a 'constituent part' (Rawls 1993: 147) – to maintain hopes of the hegemony of their own value system is inconsistent with the 'idea of equal basic liberties for all free and equal citizens' (Rawls 2002: 137). Rawls (1993: 146–147) proposes the positive engagement with the political values he propounds is required in order that social consensus is more than a mere *modus vivendi*.[14] He argues that in the conflict between Catholics and Protestants during the sixteenth century 'the principle of toleration was honoured only as a modus vivendi' and should either side gain its way, it would impose its 'own religious doctrine as the sole admissible faith' (Rawls 2002: 149).

14 He uses the example of a treaty between two states which is adopted merely because it seems prudent to adopt an equilibrium point, with both states standing ready to pursue their independent objectives should circumstances change (Rawls 1993: 147). In the context of social relations, Rawls (1993: 147) explains that a *modus vivendi* arises when consensus is based on self or group interests and political bargaining – in such a situation 'social unity is only apparent, as its stability is contingent on circumstances remaining such as not to upset the fortunate convergence of interests'.

Further, a comprehensive doctrine can be considered 'reasonable' when it affirms the political conception of justice and the 'corresponding political institutions: equal basic rights and liberties for all citizens, including liberty of conscience and the freedom of religion'; a comprehensive doctrine that cannot support such a democratic society is 'unreasonable' (Rawls 2002: 173).[15] The existence of 'unreasonable' doctrines is not a failure of public reason, but 'rather it indicates that there are limits to what public reason can accomplish' (Rawls 2002: 178).

Rawls (2002: 149) also addresses, albeit indirectly, the position of Islam with respect to his theoretical framework. In his review of the question of how people of faith can maintain both their comprehensive doctrine and a reasonable political conception that supports a reasonable constitutional democratic regime, Rawls quotes An-Na'im. In a lengthy footnote, Rawls (2002: 151 n46) refers specifically to An-Na'im's explanation that syariah can be interpreted so as to support constitutional democracy. Rawls argues (2002) that this description of Qur'anic support for the notion of non-discrimination in gender and religion is a 'perfect example of overlapping consensus'. Freeman (2007: 383–384), speaking in the context of a society based on Islamic principles (in his example Saudi Arabia), points out that simply identifying shared values in a society is not the same as identifying that public reason exists; public debate based on shared religious values only indicates that the same comprehensive value system prevails.

Public reason

Public reason is defined by Rawls (1993: 10) as 'citizen's reasoning in the public forum about constitutional essentials and basic questions of justice'.[16] It 'belongs to a conception of a well-ordered liberal democracy' (Rawls 2002: 131) and it specifies 'the basic moral and political values that are to determine a constitutional democratic government's relation to its citizens and their relation to one another' (Rawls 2002: 132). The concept is rejected by those who also reject constitutional democracy, as the nature of the political relations among people is critical (Rawls 2002). 'The zeal to embody the whole truth in politics is incompatible with an idea of public reason that belongs with democratic citizenship' (Rawls 2002: 132–133).[17]

15 'As examples, consider the many fundamentalist religious doctrines, the doctrine of the divine right of monarchs and the various forms of aristocracy, and not to be overlooked, the many instances of autocracy and dictatorship' (Rawls 2002: 173). Rawls (2002: 178) also believes every society will normally contain unreasonable doctrines that are not compatible with democratic society, although they are a 'threat to democratic institutions since it is impossible for them to abide by a constitutional regime except as a modus vivendi'.

16 Rawls (1993: 213) does not offer a view on the derivation of the phrase 'public reason' but says the idea is 'often discussed and has a long history'. Cf. Finnis (2007), below.

17 'Political liberalism will live or die in an effort to construct a constitutive form of public reason – one that allows very different sorts of people to reason together on fundamental questions of social justice' (Ackerman 1994: 368).

Public reason is 'public' in three ways: it is the reason of free and equal citizens ('the public'); it concerns the public good, being 'questions of fundamental political justice' ('constitutional essentials and matters of basic justice'); and, 'its nature and content are public', that is, it is expressed through public reasoning among a family of 'reasonable conceptions of political justice' (Rawls 2002: 133). Citizens must offer each other 'fair terms of cooperation' according to what they consider 'the most reasonable conception of political justice' and the proposer must consider it reasonable for others to accept them – this being 'the criterion of reciprocity' (Rawls 2002: 138).[18] This ensures 'stability for the right reasons, that is secured by a firm allegiance to a democratic society's political (moral) ideals and values', as democracy 'necessarily requires that, as one equal citizen among others, each of us accept the obligations of legitimate law' (Rawls 2002: 150).[19] Public reason is an appeal to the use of state power: it is advanced by citizens in 'making their political justifications to one another when they support laws and policies that invoke the coercive powers of government concerning fundamental political questions' (Rawls 2002: 165–166).[20]

There are three specific public forums in which public reason is seen. These are: 'the discourse of judges in their decisions, and especially of the judges of a supreme court';[21] the discourse of government officials especially chief executives and legislators; and, the discourse of candidates for public office (Rawls 2002: 133). Public reason is framed in terms of the political conception of justice which 'is broadly liberal in character' (Rawls 1993: 223). Rawls (1993) explains that this means:

1   it specifies certain basic rights, liberties, and opportunities (of the kind familiar from constitutional democratic regimes);
2   it assigns special priority to these rights, liberties, and opportunities; and
3   it affirms measures assuring all citizens adequate all-purpose means to make effective use of their basic liberties and opportunities.

Public reason must be justifiable to all under the principle of political legitimacy and, in making justifications, it is permissible only to appeal to 'presently

---

18 'In this case we reason from what we believe, or conjecture, may be other people's basic doctrines . . . and seek to show them that, despite what they might think, they can still endorse a reasonable political conception of justice' (Rawls 2002: 152).
19 In an echo of the argument about *modus vivendi*, Rawls (2002: 150) adds that public reason should not serve simply to 'quiet divisiveness and encourage social stability'.
20 Rawls again draws on a historical example of religious persecution. He observes that 'a persecuting zeal has been the great curse of the Christian religion', and that Christianity has historically sought to punish heresy and stamp out by persecution and religious wars what it regarded as false doctrine and to do this 'required the coercive powers of the state' (Rawls 2002: 166 n75).
21 Indeed, for Rawls (2002: 134) public reason applies 'more strictly to judges than to others'.

accepted general beliefs and forms of reasoning found in common sense, and the methods and conclusions of science when these are not controversial' (Rawls 1993: 224). Rawls (1993: 227) elaborates on what constitutes a constitutional essential; they are of two kinds:

a   fundamental principles that specify the general structure of government and the political process: the powers of the legislature, executive and the judiciary; the scope of majority rule; and

b   equal basic rights and liberties of citizenship that legislative majorities are to respect: such as the right to vote and to participate in politics, liberty of conscience, freedom of thought and of association, as well as the protections of the rule of law.

Whereas comprehensive doctrines form part of the background culture, Rawls admits scope for reliance on arguments founded in reasonable comprehensive doctrines in public reason. He does this by introducing the notion of a 'wide view of public political culture' (Rawls 2002: 152). In what Rawls (2002: 144, 152) describes as 'the proviso' he accepts the introduction into debate 'at any time' of comprehensive religious or nonreligious doctrine, provided that, subsequently, 'properly public reasons' (or 'proper political reasons'), are given to support the principle being argued for.[22] Rawls (2002: 143) specifically distinguishes public reason from secular reason and secular values because secular reason is itself an example of a 'comprehensive nonreligious' doctrine.

Rawls (2002: 166) notes also, however, that there is a wide acceptance of religion in American life.[23] Rawls (2002: 166–168) therefore considers whether public reason either unreasonably limits the range of topics available for discussion, or whether it may lead to a 'stand-off' by failing to bring about decisions

22   This is consistent with Rawls' (2002: 127) observation that 'political liberalism does not dismiss spiritual questions as unimportant', rather it establishes a 'division of labour between political and social institutions'. Larmore (2003: 386–387) does not find this evolution of public reason convincing and considers its provisions vague, preferring the original formulation which permitted departures from the rules applying to the content of public reason. Habermas (2006: 8–9) argues that it is unreasonable to expect individuals to justify their public political statements independently of their 'religious convictions or world views'; this is a restriction that should apply only to public officials or candidates for office. In its earlier formulation, Rawls (1993: 251) argues that 'the appropriate limits of public reason vary depending on historical and social conditions'; an 'exclusive' view of public reason might hold that comprehensive doctrines should never be used in public reason, while an 'inclusive' view sees citizens presenting 'what they regard as the basis of political values rooted in their comprehensive doctrine, provided they do this in ways that strengthen the ideal of public reason itself' (Rawls 1993: 247).

23   Tocqueville, according to Rawls (2002: 167), viewed the separation of church and state in America as one the of the main causes of the strength of its democracy. 'Political liberalism accepts Tocqueville's view and sees it as explaining, so far as possible, the basis of peace among comprehensive doctrines both religious and secular' (Rawls 2002: 167 n76).

on matters in dispute. Referring to examples of debate touching on religious themes in American public life (prayer in school and abortion), Rawls (2002: 166) remarks on the benefits of the separation of Church and state, which 'protects religion from the state and the state from religion' and 'citizens from their Churches' as well as from one another.[24] Here Rawls (2002: 168) returns to the role of public officials, proposing that a 'political rule of action' must be laid down and all must 'reasonably endorse the process by which a decision is reached':

> Thus, when there seems to be a stand-off, that is, when legal arguments seem to be evenly balanced on both sides, judges cannot resolve the case simply by appealing to their own political views. To do that for judges is to violate their duty.[25]

Public reason – if pursued properly and sincerely – does not result in an outcome that is necessarily 'true or correct' but rather one that 'is reasonable and legitimate law' (Rawls 2002: 169). As regards the position of Roman Catholics, for example, Rawls (2002: 170) suggests that they may mount arguments in public reason and should these fail to win support, they are not obliged to exercise the right to abortion. Forceful resistance to legitimate law is 'unreasonable', but it is consistent with public reason for Catholics to continue to argue against the right to abortion and for the Church to require its members to follow its doctrine (Rawls 2002: 170).[26]

The role of courts

As seen above, Rawls places particular emphasis on the role of courts as a forum in which public reason is deployed. Public reason applies to citizen and public officials equally, and according to Rawls (1993: 216) 'it applies in a special way

---

24 'And it is also a grave error to think that the separation of church and state is primarily for the protection of secular culture; of course it does protect that culture; but no more so than it protects all religions' (Rawls 2002: 166). Here, again, Rawls (2002: 166 n74) refers specifically to the Christian institution of the church, and asserts that freedom to change one's faith is protected, as heresy and apostasy are not crimes.

25 Rousseau (quoted in Freeman (2007: 403)) expressed a similar view in relation to the work of the magistrate: 'His own reason ought to be suspect to him, and the only reason he should follow is the public reason'.

26 Rawls (1993: 249–250) also provides an example of the use of religiously inspired argument in the public sphere using Dr Martin Luther King as his example. The American civil rights movement demonstrated the deployment of non-public reason supported by the conclusions of public reason – in the case of King, appealing to the political values expressed in the Constitution (Rawls 1993: 250). 'Religious doctrines clearly underlie King's views and are important in his appeals. Yet they are expressed in general terms: and they fully support constitutional values and accord with public reason' (Rawls 1993: 250 n39).

to the judiciary and above all to a supreme court in a constitutional democracy with judicial review'. This special role makes courts 'the exemplar of public reason' (Rawls 1993: 216) and it 'applies more strictly to judges than to others' (Rawls 2002: 134–135).[27] Rawls (1993: 235) argues that 'public reason is the sole reason the court exercises' as judges are required to make the grounds of their decisions

> consistent and fit them into a coherent constitutional view over the whole range of their decisions. The role of the justices is to do precisely that and in doing it they have no other reason and no other values than the political.

When justice or constitutional essentials are at stake, the outcome is considered legitimate law if the government official pursues the principles of public reason (Rawls 2002: 137). A number of arguments are made to substantiate this position (Rawls 1993: 231–240). In brief, they amount in large part to a defence of the judiciary as a central part of a rule of law system, balancing the authority of other branches of government. More specifically, they include the argument that the judiciary is the only public institution that applies public reason alone: judges 'must appeal to the political values they think belong to the most reasonable understanding of the public conception and its political values of justice, and public reason' (Rawls 1993: 236).

In expressing opinions on matters of constitutional interpretation, judicial reasoning must fit the relevant body of constitutional materials and be justified 'in terms of the public conception of justice or a reasonable variant thereof' (Rawls 1993: 236):

> In doing this it is expected that the justices may and do appeal to the political values of the public conception whenever the constitution itself expressly or implicitly invokes those values, as it does, for example, in a bill of rights guaranteeing the free exercise of religion, or the equal protection of the laws.

27 Rawls (1993: 231–232) discusses five principles of constitutionalism in support of the role of courts, and a supreme court in particular: the distinction between constituent power of the people and the framework regulating ordinary power; the distinction between higher and ordinary law; a democratic constitution as a principled expression in a higher law of the political ideal of the people; that constitutional essentials are fixed in a democratically ratified constitution; and, that in a constitutional government ultimate power cannot be left to any one branch of government. He explains that constitutional democracies are therefore 'dualist': the constituent power and higher law of the people coexists with ordinary power and the ordinary law of the legislature (Rawls 1993: 233). 'A supreme court fits into this idea of dualist constitutional democracy as one of the institutional devices to protect the higher law' (Rawls 1993: 233).

Justices cannot involve personal morality, 'nor the ideals and virtues of morality generally . . . Equally, they cannot involve their or other people's religious or philosophical views' (Rawls 1993: 236). They must appeal 'to the most reasonable understanding of the public conception and its political values of justice and public reason . . . that they believe in good faith . . . that all citizens as reasonable and rational might reasonably be expected to endorse' (Rawls 1993). The court's work in resolving fundamental political questions gives public reason 'vividness and vitality in the public forum' (Rawls 1993: 237).

Commentary and critique

Rawls' political liberalism has been the subject of extensive commentary, and several key dimensions are addressed in this section. I do not attempt to deal with the full range of literature addressing Rawls, nor to provide a comprehensive analysis of his critics. Some commentary reflects opinion based in competing approaches to political philosophy, some of which is strident. Other critique argues, with less vigour, that there are weaknesses in Rawls' framework, or parts of it. What I hope to achieve is to identify some of the key issues that I see as critical for the broader issues dealt with in this book. As a result I draw in particular on some sources at the expense of others. Four issues will be dealt with here: arguments that Rawls' whole scheme is flawed, particularly in its apparent claim to universality; opposition to the notion of an overlapping consensus, and – correspondingly – the promotion of *modus vivendi* as a rival concept; claims that public reason is prejudicial and indeed antithetical to religion; and, the role of courts.

Political but still liberal

Rawls' efforts to develop a liberalism based on a 'limited' moral conception have been criticized in the so-called 'liberal–communitarian debate' (Sandel 1994: 1766), characterised by Larmore (1990: 349) as a 'dispute between individualism and tradition'.[28] This debate was advanced by those seeking to challenge

---

28 A label described by Sandel (1994: 1766) himself as 'somewhat misleading'. See, for example, Nagel (1999: 40) where he describes the 'communitarian objection' and Campbell (2001: 111) who refers to the 'communitarian critique of Rawls'; see also the extensive list of references in Sandel (1994: 1767 n13). According to Sandel (1994: 1767) the description of the debate is misleading because those mounting the critique were not arguing that rights should rest on values and preferences prevailing 'in any given community in any given time' but instead 'whether rights can be identified and justified in a way that does not presuppose any particular conception of the good'. What is at issue is not the 'relative weight of individual and communal claims' but the relation between the right and the good (Sandel 1994). See also Taylor (1995) who explains that a stark division between liberals and communitarians is not feasible

aspects of 'contemporary rights-oriented liberalism' (Sandel 1994: 1766) and, in particular, the priority of the right over the good (Sandel 1994: 1768):[29]

> As a philosophical matter, our reflections about justice cannot reasonably be detached from our reflections about the nature of the good life and the highest human ends. As a political matter, our deliberations about justice and rights cannot proceed without reference to the conceptions of the good that find expression in many cultures and traditions within which those deliberations take place.[30]

Put another way – political liberalism is a project in which 'all really important decisions about human rights and the common good would banish concern for truth' (Finnis 2011: 18). Notwithstanding his criticism (dismissing Rawls liberalism as a 'ramshackle project'), Finnis (2011: 4) accepts the reality of the underlying challenge of diversity: 'the standing possibility that political community and its underlying civil society will be torn apart by civil strife between adherents of different religions or religious creeds'.[31]

An important dimension to this debate is the 'competing conceptions of the person' entailed in the opposing views of liberalism, and opposition to Rawls is an expression of resistance to the notion that 'we can make sense of our moral and political obligations in wholly voluntarist or contractual terms' (Sandel 1994: 1768).[32] It could be argued that the underlying roots of Rawls' thinking, such as his 'original position', reflects an 'extreme methodological individualism' (Campbell 2001: 111), although Larmore (1990: 350) counters that while there is 'a certain individualism' inherent in citizens operating in the political realm, this does not imply 'a broader individualism'.[33]

---

29 According to Sandel (1994: 1766) there are two dimensions to this: first, 'the right is prior to the good in the sense that certain individual rights "trump", or outweigh, considerations of the common good'; second, 'in that the principles of justice that specify our rights do not depend for their justification on any particular conception of the good life'.

30 Larmore (1990: 350) appears to agree, proposing that while political liberalism does require that citizens rank the norms of 'rational dialogue and equal respect above their other commitments', this does not undermine their commitment to a substantial idea of the good life. Cf. Campbell (2001: 111) who describes Rawls as adopting an approach which produces a 'model for society which is lacking in the specific ties of culture and particularity which give our lives meaning and content'.

31 Diversity of views is 'readily explicable, "predictable"', because under ideal conditions everyone would concur in a 'true' judgment, but actual epistemic conditions are far from ideal and therefore almost all religious beliefs must contain a measure of falsity because of the fact they conflict (Finnis 2011: 3).

32 See also Sandel (1984: 5), where he observes that privileging individual freedom threatens alternative conceptions of society. Recall that Rawls' earlier work was based in the social contract tradition.

33 Rawls (1993: 27) holds that even the key concept of the original position does not presuppose a particular metaphysical conception of the person. Campbell's (2001: 92–123)

A further extension of this debate is whether political liberalism is an inherently Western phenomenon (Gray 2000a: 163; 2000b: 23; Larmore 1990: 351–352, 356–357).[34] Larmore (1990: 351) declares that the particular conception of the person underlying political liberalism is largely confined to modern Western societies. He considers liberal theory is a 'latecomer' that follows from the development of a minimal set of criteria that should suffice to provide the conditions for its adoption – 'geography, a common language, and a common historical experience (including the memory of past controversy, even civil war)' (Larmore 1990: 352). Gray (2000a: 163) concludes, with greater force, that Rawls promotes a 'Eurocentric philosophy of history' and that his claims of not privileging a morality of 'autonomy and individuality' do not stand up: Rawls distils the 'individualist' form of life in contemporary Western culture, most importantly that of the United States.[35] Gray (2000a: 164), though (like Finnis), does not dispute the existence of pluralism, and agrees that the task of liberal political philosophy is 'finding reasonable terms of coexistence among different communities and ways of life'.

This criticism has, in turn, been rejected by Inoue (1999: 48) who considers Gray's 'post-liberalism' as incorporating a 'condescending deference to the Asian values discourse' and indulging in the 'Orientalist identity script'.[36] Similarly, Ivison (2002: 43) quotes from Chakrabarty who, although emphasising that liberalism has 'played a part in assimilating "all other possibilities of human solidarity"', also suggests that European historicism can be critiqued without abandoning

---

review of Rawls addresses almost exclusively his earlier work, and deals only quite briefly with political liberalism.

34 Gray (2000b: 23) states that a claim for the universal relevance of political liberalism reflects a positivist philosophy which affirms that as societies become more modern they are bound to become more alike: 'the belief that modern societies will everywhere converge on the same values does not result from historical inquiry. It is a confession of faith'. Modernisation and autonomy do not necessarily go hand-in-hand, and autonomy may not be a prerequisite for flourishing in all, or even most, modern cultures (Gray 2000a: 162). Cf. Inoue (1999: 44), who considers that the diversity among many Asian societies requires the development of liberal democracy, to counter conflict and tension.

35 According to Gray (2000a: 164), invoking this conception of the person ('a human being disembodied from any constitutive communal attachment and emptied of any distinctive cultural and historical identity') is a celebration of an 'anaemic pluralism of life-plans'; this conception has 'no authority, and little interest, for anyone else'.

36 The phrase 'Asian values' describes what was, essentially, a political movement including prominent Southeast Asian national leaders (Lee Kuan Yew, Singapore, Dr Mahathir Mohamad, Malaysia, and Soeharto of Indonesia), founded in an argument that 'Asians shared distinct values that were incompatible with values shared by Westerners and that therefore the West should not rely on its construction of human rights to intervene in affairs of Asian states' (Lindsey 2004: 286). See also Inoue (1999) and, in the context of Indonesia, Nasution (1992: 404). 'Asian values', argues Lindsey (2008: 286–287) 'seemed central to the anti-democratic Indonesian polity', but the notion was effectively erased from Indonesian public life with the arrival of post-Soeharto reforms after May 1998.

European thought altogether: 'by analogy it means criticising liberalism without abandoning a commitment to justice, freedom or human well-being'. Nussbaum (2001: 889) argues that it did not require the 'so-called modern era or the European Enlightenment' to forge principles such as the respect for difference. Gray (2000b: 3–4), too, observes that recognition of pluralism pre-dates the modern era. Equally, Franck (1997: 598) argues that the Western provenance (in a narrow chronological sense) of ideas such as toleration and disestablishment (separation of Church and State) did not prevent them appealing, centuries after their emergence, to leaders such as Nehru and Mandela. Further, he notes that 'modern "Western" liberal values, with their emphasis on individual personal autonomy and human rights, are no emanation of some deep cultural tradition of the societies of Europe and North America', providing examples of the painful and long history to religious toleration in these regions (Franck 1997: 615).

A variant of the communitarian critique is the observation that democratic citizenship is a fundamental assumption in Rawls' work (O'Neill 1997: 416–421). The process of 'sharing principles and standards for the fundamental arrangements of life' is 'more or less what it is to be a citizen of a democratic society' (O'Neill 1997: 421). Since the individuals whom Rawls brings together already share a political identity, they 'therefore have powerful motives for seeking agreement on basic principles and institutions' (O'Neill 1997: 422).[37] Extending these thoughts further, Ackerman (1994: 364) highlights the fact that Rawls' exposition of political liberalism 'conceals an alarming tendency to glorify the nation-state'.[38]

Larmore (1990: 343) suggests that the source of the objections to Rawls lies in the 'powerful critique of individualist ideals' that is a central strand of the Romantic movement.[39] Romantic thinkers have 'stressed the values of belonging and custom' (Larmore 1990: 343),[40] whereas political liberalism relies on abandoning 'the cult of wholeness', embracing differentiation between citizenship and other roles in which the good life is pursued (freeing individuals from 'status

---

37　Campbell (2001: 219) argues that a 'barrage of criticism' led Rawls 'to retreat into a more secure but less daring position from which he holds himself out as doing no more than providing a path to a pragmatic political consensus in certain types of liberal society'. Cf. Rawls (1999: 439): 'the virtues of political cooperation that make a constitutional regime possible are, then, *very great* virtues'.

38　This is a 'vision of the self that finds expression in the ideal of the state as a neutral framework' (Sandel 1984: 5). Correspondingly, O'Neill (1997: 18) observes that the 'power of Rawls's conception of public reason is drawn from its connection to his account of *citizens*': 'being a citizen with a sense of political identity . . . is constitutive of reasonableness'.

39　Larmore (1990: 344) accepts that this approach is not definitive of the Romantic movement but asserts that German, French and English Romantics were concerned with 'a new respect for tradition and belonging, along with a rejection of the supposedly shallow and dangerous individualism of the eighteenth century'.

40　Some ways of life are not based on allegiance as a matter of decision but are instead '*constitutive* of what we hold to be valuable' (Larmore 1990: 351)

and ascription') (Larmore 1990: 351).[41] It is not belonging itself which holds the main value in this school of thought, but the possibility that the ideals of autonomy and individuality 'effectively blind us to the real merits of many ways of life' (Larmore 1900: 344).[42]

In summary, Sandel (1994: 1793–1794) argues there are moral and political costs associated with Rawls' political liberalism. The moral cost arises from the potential that 'a political conception of justice sanctions toleration of a grave moral wrong' (Sandel 1994: 1793). The political cost is the fact that democratic politics 'cannot long abide a public life as abstract and decorous, as detached from moral purpose as Supreme Court opinions are supposed to be' (Sandel 1994: 1793–1794). This form of politics merely 'generates its own disenchantment', and creates a moral void that opens the way for the 'intolerant and the trivial' (Sandel 1994: 1794).

Modus vivendi preferable

The preceding objections about the fundamental premises of political liberalism are accompanied by other criticisms of political liberalism in practice. While approaches differ, a number of objections have been raised with the concept of an overlapping consensus. Finnis (2011: 52) mounts a substantial criticism of political liberalism, claiming it is 'crippled by its ambiguity and unprincipled exception making'. If decision making can only proceed on the basis of those reasons that are part of an overlapping consensus (where all reasonable people could reasonably be expected to affirm them), then this is a proposition that under ideal epistemic conditions 'excludes precisely nothing', and under prevailing conditions also excludes little or nothing simply because, as Rawls accepts, 'reasonable people can and do hold some unreasonable views' (Finnis 2011: 52). Finnis (2011: 52) goes on to note that 'it follows that for all practical purposes there is no interestingly substantive view that *all* reasonable people agree to'.

It is also argued that the separation of political and personal identities, together with all questions of cultural, morality and tradition 'brackets' comprehensive doctrines (O'Neill 1997: 413; Sandel 1994: 1777–1782). If 'bracketing our moral and religious convictions is necessary if we are to secure social cooperation on the basis of mutual respect', how can it be guaranteed that there is no competing interest within a comprehensive view that is more important

---

41 See, for example, Gray (2000b: 11–12), who argues that value pluralism arises not from the plurality of divergent ideals of individuals but rather 'rival claims of ways of life'. Cf. Inoue (1999: 46), who argues that the multiculturalist critique of liberal rights promotes the group over the individual and therefore is incompatible with liberal tolerance, 'insofar as it denies an individual member the right to criticise and attempt to revise the dominant beliefs and practices of her own cultural community and to move out of it if she loses faith in it'.

42 Larmore (1990: 344) adds that 'some fairly horrible ways of life can become customary'.

(Sandel 1994: 1777)? Many conflicts are 'deep conflicts' that challenge the 'basic framework of moral assumptions and political procedures' that are assumed by Rawls (Bohmann 1995: 254).[43] These conflicts (arising from ethnic, cultural and religious diversity) are so serious as to pose 'intergroup dilemmas' and therefore challenge the process of adjudication of such conflicts (Bohmann 1995: 254–257).

This argument is taken up by Gray (2000b: 1), who offers an alternative view of liberalism, proposing that the task is to 'refashion' liberal toleration 'so that it can guide the pursuit of *modus vivendi* in a more plural world'. He argues that overlapping consensus is far from evident in most 'later-modern societies' and, where a liberal rights-based discourse exists, its 'hegemony' is only skin deep (Gray 2000b: 13).[44] He declares that a 'strictly political liberalism . . . is an impossibility' because central elements of liberalism (such as rights and justice) only have content 'insofar as they express a view of the good' (Gray 2000b: 19).[45]

Liberalism, according to Gray (2000b: 1), must give up 'the search for a rational consensus on the best way of life'. Gray (2000b: 2) distinguishes two strands of liberalism by their approach to toleration: Rawls' thinking exemplifies 'the liberal project of a universal regime';[46] the second strand expresses 'the liberalism of peaceful coexistence'. Gray (2000a: 164) identifies Hobbes as a key source for the latter approach, stating that this form of liberalism 'extends to private belief the radical tolerance of indifference'.[47] One solution proposed is the Ottoman

---

43 Cf. Nussbaum (2001: 886–887), who argues that it is precisely because disagreements persist 'at a very deep level' that 'respect for our fellow citizens seems to demand that we acknowledge this fact, refraining from building our basic political principles around any one of the contested comprehensive doctrines'.

44 Ethical life is 'inescapably hybrid' and the pursuit of individual autonomy often conflicts with 'allegiance to an established community' (Gray 2000b: 13). Cf. Sen (2006), who addresses the issue of multiple identities at length but comes to a different conclusion as to the implication for rights.

45 'If we differ about the good life, we are bound to differ about justice and rights' (Gray 2000b: 19).

46 He describes this as a 'recent orthodoxy', in which the liberal state is not just one among a number of possible forms of regime but 'is the only mode of political organisation that can ever be fully legitimate' (Gray 2000b: 14). Gray (2000b: 31) ties universalism to Berlin, who he states held a conviction that there is a 'basic knowable human nature', whereas Mill affirmed that human good is found in divergent ways of life. Cf. Berlin (1984), where he, in fact, describes the need to balance between individual aims and other value claims, and states explicitly that there are many (incompatible) absolute claims.

47 See also Larmore (1990: 346). Freeman (2003: 278) explains that Hobbes was, along with Rawls, a social contractarian and that concern for social stability is a common feature of such theories. Hobbes believed that near absolute sovereignty was essential for stability, but later theorists see that among rational actors 'indifferent to one another and motivated only by their particular interests' there may be little need for coercive force: 'stability is achieved as the result of practical compromise among essentially conflicting interests' (Freeman 2003: 278). Not surprisingly, Nussbaum (2015: 23) describes Rawls' *Political Liberalism* as 'an extended rejoinder' to Hobbes' *Leviathan*.

millet system which enabled the practitioners of diverse religions to live as communities within the Ottoman Empire but under the jurisdiction of their own religions (Gray 2000b: 109). This approach is also taken by Kymlicka (1992: 35) who also refers to the millet system in considering the possibility of toleration among groups, and questions the claim that 'we must tolerate dissent within a religious (or ethnic) community'.[48]

In contrast, Inoue (1999: 45), argues the millet system is 'not a full-fledged moral alternative' to liberal tolerance but a preliminary step toward it. Importantly, he highlights that the experience of reform in the millet system forms part of the history of Turkey's constitutional democratic politics and helps break down the 'contemporary Orientalist stereotype of "Islam as the fanatic fundamentalism"' allowing us to appreciate 'the Islamic potential for liberal tolerance' (Inoue 1999: 46). An-Na'im (2011), too, considers the nature and history of communal religious affiliation in Islam and declares them 'now obviously totally untenable' (2011: 327). This is, at least in part, because of their incapacity to tolerate dissent and debate (An-Na'im 2011: 333).

Gray (2000b: 20) acknowledges that there are at least some limits to *modus vivendi*, and therefore considers it is 'impossible in a regime in which the varieties of the good are seen as symptoms of error or heresy'.[49] As with other forms of liberalism, it resists totalitarianism and fundamentalism (Gray 2000b: 20). Larmore (1990: 346) goes further, stating that *modus vivendi* contains defects which arise from the fact that this approach to toleration relies solely on 'strategic considerations' and is driven by 'purely prudential motives'. These defects are: 1) instability – because bargaining power is relative and changeable, potentially undermining the motivation to uphold any agreement; and, 2) lack of efficacy – prudence itself has never succeeded as an organising principle as it involves 'maximisation of individual preference-satisfaction' (Larmore 1990).

The religious objection

Political liberalism has been considered as 'an attack on religion', notwithstanding that, according to Scanlon (2003: 166 n14), Rawls does not claim that religious views 'need to be reformed and become tolerant'. Spinner-Halev (2008: 553–556), for example, claims that Rawls conceives of religion as simply a matter of belief, whereas many religious people want not only freedom to believe but freedom to practice in the social space. Rawls, he claims, 'blithely dismisses the importance of traditional religions in the modern world' and that 'justice must guide society's

---

48 Kymlicka (1992: 54) does not reject comprehensive liberalism, but argues it is important to 'recognise that there are limits to our ability to implement and impose liberal principles on groups that have not endorsed those principles'.

49 According to Gray (2000b: 20), however, liberals and pluralists part company when one regime is set up as a standard for all.

institutions *and* people's beliefs' (Spinner-Halev 2008: 558). Finnis (2011: 2–3) asserts a close relationship between faith and reason: 'religion is fundamentally an operation of reason. . . . And since it is a matter of reason, religion shares in reason's radically public character'. Adapting the language of Rawls, Finnis (2011: 3) proposes that reason does not 'run out, or become non-public' when based on matters divine.[50] It follows that 'since reason is in all these respects inherently public, there is no real need for the phrase "public reason"' (Finnis 2011: 4).

Reinforcing his attack on public reason, Finnis (2007: 2) attributes the entry of the phrase into English discourse to Satan in Milton's *Paradise Lost*.[51] He then corrects this attribution, identifying an earlier source – Hobbes' *Leviathan* (Finnis 2007: 2). Hobbes discusses the miracle of transubstantiation (specifically, whether it may be taught that miracles occur) and states that, while an individual may have their own private views of miracles, 'when it comes to confession of that faith, the private reason must submit to the public' (Finnis 2007).[52] Finnis (2011: 8) asserts that Rawls 'excludes' all comprehensive doctrines from public deliberation concerning constitutional fundamentals, and draws on Thomas Aquinas in proposing that 'one should be willing to argue out all questions of moral (and therefore political and legal) conduct and decision with all the intellectual resources one can get'.

The application of religious values in practice can be seen in the example of the attitude of the Catholic Church to abortion (Rawls 1993: 243; Sandel 1994: 1778). Rawls (1993: 243), as seen above, uses it to illustrate his argument that in specific cases 'which doctrine is affirmed is a matter of conscience for the individual citizen', but affirms that comprehensive doctrines 'run afoul' of public reason when they 'cannot support a reasonable balance of political values'. He argues that there are at least three important political values engaged by abortion: due respect for human life; the ordered reproduction of society over time; and,

---

50 Finnis (2011: 3) also here refers to Thomas Aquinas' notion of 'natural reason' in which Aquinas links reason and 'public divine revelation'.

51

> . . . yet public reason just –
> Honour and empire with revenge enlarge'd
> By conquering this new world – compels me now
> To do what else, though damn'd, I should abhor'.
> So spake the Fiend, and with necessity,
> The tyrant's plea, excus'd his devilish deeds.

52 Finnis (2007: 2 n2) quotes Hobbes: 'we are not every one to make our own private reason or conscience, but the public reason, that is the reason of God's supreme lieutenant, judge; and indeed we have made him judge already, if we have given him a sovereign power to do all that is necessary for our peace and defence. A private man has always the liberty, because thought is free, to believe or not believe in his heart those acts that have been given out for miracles. . . . But when it comes to confession of that faith, the private reason must submit to the public; that is to say, to God's lieutenant'.

the equality of women as equal citizens (Rawls 1993: 243 n32). Rawls (1993) concludes that a reasonable balance among these principles gives a woman the right to end her pregnancy in the first trimester as 'the political value of the equality of women is overriding, and this right is required to give it substance and force'.

Sandel (1994: 1778) responds with the argument that if the Catholic Church were in fact 'right about the moral status of the fetus' then there is no clear reason why political values of toleration and equality should prevail in the case of abortion. Returning again to the underlying philosophical proposition of the priority of the right over the good, Sandel (1994: 1778) argues that the case for abortion rights 'cannot be neutral with respect to moral and religious controversy' because in this case respecting a woman's rights depends on showing that there is a relevant moral difference between aborting a young foetus and killing a child.

Finnis (2011: 35), too, focuses on the importance of morality, arguing there is a moral duty in individuals to 'seek the truth about reality's most fundamental shape' a duty only fulfilled if authentically pursued, and not 'prejudiced, corrupted, and even nullified by coercion and psychological pressure'.[53] That is, the political community has a public duty to respect and leave uncoerced all 'conscientious religious beliefs and acts . . . even beliefs that include much that is false and acts that are accordingly ill justified' (Finnis 2011: 35).[54] Gray (2000b: 1077), too, holds that any regime that seeks to do systematic injury to the individual pursuit of interests 'that make any kind of life worthwhile' is illegitimate.

Finnis (2011: 101) explores the potential limits on arrangements by which the state may 'recognise and favour religion' (referencing the Vatican Council) or, as he calls it, the 'peak question': 'what if anything may be stipulated constitutionally and legally about the true religion'. He nominates the following: measures to manage or in some way restrict faiths whose beliefs present a threat to public order;[55] an obligation not to hold out any one religion as the 'true religion'; a duty not to make subscription to any one religion a prerequisite for

---

53 An argument contained in the Second Vatican Council Declaration on Religious Liberty (Finnis 2011: 35 n48).
54 Finnis' views are heavily influenced by Christian thinking. He argues, for example, that if a basis for the defence of religious freedom can be found in political liberalism, it can be found nowhere better than in 'the developed Christian teaching' (Finnis 2011: 53).
55 In relation to public order see Gray's (2000b: 112) reference to Spinoza in support of the view that 'the rights of religion and the outward observance of piety should be in accordance with public peace and wellbeing, and should therefore be determined by the sovereign power'. Finnis (2011: 94) also affirms there is a human right 'to be immune from coercion by individuals, groups, governments, or laws, in one's religious or religiously motivated acts, provided they are in line with public order'. He includes among those things worthy of protection by the state adherence to, and proclaiming, 'a religion which one believes to be true but is in fact false' (Finnis 2011: 94).

public office; a duty not to seek to direct the true religion by claiming power to make appointments to its representatives or give or withhold ratification of doctrinal pronouncements; acceptance that individuals 'can rightly and should take into account the firm moral teachings of a religion if it is the true religion, so far as its teachings are relevant to issues of law and government'; and, finally, that 'in establishing their constitutional arrangements a people might without injustice or political impropriety record their solemn belief about the identity and name of the true religious faith and community' (Finnis 2011: 100–102).

A note on courts

It was seen above that political liberalism applies to what O'Neill (1997: 422) describes as a 'closed yet democratic society', one in which citizens are likely to already agree on 'general principles and standards' and reasoning among these people with a shared political identity is supported by powerful motive for seeking agreement – public reason is by definition an insider's reasoning. A similar argument is raised in relation to the operation of courts as a key institution in Rawls' framework. Bohmann (1995: 261) notes that the way in which courts operate may in fact work to reduce participation, and to exclude through their practices and cultures. Bohmann (1995: 262–264) argues instead for 'plural public reason' because a singular standpoint is inadequate to deal with the diversity of standpoints in modern democracies.[56] Rawls appears to argue that conflict should be avoided, whereas the civil rights and feminist movements have shown how it can be necessary to deem issues public, and to drive development of public consciousness where 'the meaning and scope of public values' is contentious (Bohmann 1995: 264).[57]

Gray (2000b: 16) also sees flaws in Rawls' account of the role of courts and argues that placing judicial review in such a central position removes all fundamental issues from political deliberation, thus rendering Rawls doctrine 'a species of anti-political legalism'.[58] Cohen (2003: 118), too, deals with the important questions raised by Rawls' reliance upon courts: 'It is hard to see

---

56 A point echoed by Ivison (2002: 48), who adds that the real complexity of multicultural societies today may demand 'more complex and multilayered forms of political identification and association'.

57 See O'Neill's (1997: 420) commentary on Rawls' view of society (a 'closed' political society) and who constitutes 'the public': 'in real life persons are often unsure about their sense(s) of political identity. . . . A central objective of politics may be the reconstrual of political identities'. Hayfa (2004: 246) refers to this as the 'constituency problem' – any account of public reason must specify some criterion to whom it applies, and this criterion itself represents a 'prior framework condition for the process of justification'. Cf. Ivison (2002: ix), who suggests that indigenous peoples may in fact have been able to adapt and co-opt liberal democratic thought to their own ends.

58 'Contemporary liberal orthodoxy is a species of legalism, in which virtually every important issue of public policy is treated as a question of fundamental rights' (Gray 2000b: 116).

how any serious theory of justice' could result in an 'institutional conclusion' of this kind without considerable additional argument. He observes that it is a matter of the particular political traditions of any country as to the 'division of deliberative labor' and the role of a supreme court (Cohen 2003: 119).

Agreement and divergence

There are, broadly, two dimensions to the critiques of Rawls' political liberalism. Some commentary, such as that of Sandel, Gray and Finnis, amounts to a rejection of the entire framework. This approach is grounded in an objection to Rawls' 'limited' liberalism. Other commentary, including that of O'Neill, deals more with the mechanisms Rawls develops for the application of his theory (although her work also contains a challenge to the liberal notions underpinning Rawls). This commentary tends to take issue with the logic or the practicality of the theory in practice. In the case of the religious objection, this is expressed in terms of both dimensions, and commentary displays a deep concern with the absence in political liberalism of any identifiable moral foundation to political decision making. It is also evident in the commentary on the limitations of public reason as a justificatory mechanism.

The first challenge (the so-called communitarian critique) at its heart rests on rejecting the priority of the right over the good (as Rawls expresses it). This is seen clearly in the work of Sandel, but also in Finnis, particularly in his references to the role of the 'true faith'. It is not clear how a fundamental philosophical difference such as this can be easily resolved, if at all. Arguments in support of this critique point to the role in Rawls' work of a particular conception of the individual. Rawls' earlier, foundational, work on justice as fairness clearly rests on certain assumptions about the place of individuals in society. It presents key elements (the veil of ignorance and original position) which, while highly theoretical, assume certain capacities or competencies of individuals. These are not explicit elements of political liberalism, but are clearly related. There is evidently a baseline of individual capacity assumed in political liberalism, but this is entirely consistent with Rawls' stated objective of exploring the workings of a democratic system, including the relationship between individuals, and between individuals and the state. Critics agree with Rawls on the importance of fundamental freedoms, including the freedom of religion (see further below). This acknowledgment of the importance of certain fundamental rights itself involves the recognition of individual capacity – the capacity to exercise choice in matters of faith, which dilutes the impact of this critique.

According to Larmore, the communitarian critique reflects another Western philosophical tradition, Romanticism. As noted in the Chapter 1, Bourchier (1999) explores the role of Romanticism in the development of Indonesian constitutionalism. He confirms Larmore's observations on the inclination of Romantic thought, stating that it is 'typically hostile to the rationalism and universalism of the Enlightenment' and indeed was characterised, at least in part, by its rejection of social contract theory (Bourchier 1999: 187). The idea of a social contract, it was seen above[59], forms a fundamental pillar of Rawls' thinking. More relevantly for the study of Rawls, given his emphasis on democratic procedure and the development of legitimate law, Bourchier (1999) adds that the tradition of Romanticism 'holds that law is legitimate only if it arises organically from the history and culture of particular civilisations'. Presumably, Indonesia's democratic transition with its comprehensive re-working of the Constitution must be taken to form part of its history and cultural development.

As observed in Chapter 1, 'Western' intellectual traditions have already been identified as having influence upon the development and interpretation of constitutional principles and the nature of state authority in Indonesia. A further counter argument raised against the presumption that Western values cannot apply elsewhere is that the core notion of equality is not necessarily a Western value, and that Western history itself does not demonstrate a consistent pattern of liberal tolerance. Furthermore, Inoue argues firmly against the assumption that liberal democratic traditions cannot be adopted in Asian states, particularly given Western influence began to be significant in Asia since as early as the sixteenth century. It is critical to observe also that Rawls is dealing with theory and there is no overarching claim made that the United States, or other Western democracy, establishes a standard. It has in fact been claimed that 'no nation on earth has achieved the kind of social justice to which political liberalism aspires' (Ackerman 1994: 377).[60]

Different visions of the state appear to influence the observations of commentators, particularly Gray and Finnis. They both recognise the importance of state authority and, in particular, the need for public order which is raised, for example, in relation to the rights of religious minorities. In response to this question – which is an issue at the heart of the book – it is worth restating Rawls' objective. The big question for Rawls is what the 'extent and the admissible grounds' are for the exercise of state power (Nagel 2003: 74). Rawls (2002: 138) is concerned with the 'fundamental political relation of citizenship':

> how, when constitutional essentials and matters of basic justice are at stake, citizens so related can be bound to honour the structure of their constitutional democratic regime and abide by the statutes and laws enacted under it. The fact of reasonable pluralism raises this question all the more sharply, since it means that the differences between citizens arising from their comprehensive doctrines, religious and nonreligious, may be irreconcilable. By

---

59 p20, n3.
60 See also Freeman (1994: 652), who claims that the United States only 'faintly approximates' the ideal of public reason; and Nussbaum (2001: 900), who reflects on the limitations of public deliberative culture in American politics and (2015: 61) goes further to criticise Rawls' claim that political liberalism owes its origins merely to Western constitutional democracies. Cf. Schaefer (2007: x-xi), who is a critic of Rawls and argues that the United States emulates a variant liberal model and that Rawls' claims are not consistent with the constitutional traditions of that nation.

what ideals and principles, are citizens who share equally in ultimate political power to exercise that power so that each can reasonably justify his or her political decision to everyone?

Rawls' focus on constitutional democracy has been criticised, first, as evidence of a retreat from a more comprehensive philosophical doctrine, and, second, for addressing (merely) a political reality. In short, the claim is made that his whole edifice arguably conceals rather modest foundations. Rawls himself counters that the behaviours required of his scheme are founded on 'very great virtues' and his scheme is designed to address a critical issue, which is the experience of fundamental freedoms. His framework is explicitly directed at the logic and processes of developing legitimate law, and proper bounds on the exercise of state authority. Rawls identifies his subject quite transparently; its wider relevance is a matter for further exploration in particular contexts. Constitutional democracy is not a purely Western phenomenon and therefore the potential scope of application is as broad as the experience of democracy.

Overlapping consensus is the subject of criticism with both a philosophical and pragmatic basis. Overlapping consensus is required by political liberalism because of the fact of pluralism. To a large extent the concerns about this concept are an extension of the fundamental philosophical challenge; competing views of the good life mean that conflicts of values are so deep that there is no hope of consensus. Nonetheless, there is a suspicion that Rawls' approach involves a kind of 'liberal camouflage for much more partisan arguments' and the proposed 'ecumenical appeal' of his liberalism is, in fact, hollow (Nagel 2003: 77). This response arises despite the fact that – in the words of Habermas (2010: 450) – the 'liberal conception of justice acquires flesh and blood in a political community only when it finds support in religious and metaphysical contexts'.[61]

Modus vivendi is offered as a preferred mechanism because it is seen as a better solution to the fact of pluralism. One reason for this alternative is based on a fundamental philosophical difference about the nature of justice. Another reason (advanced by Finnis) is that overlapping consensus is a solution to a problem that does not exist, and is a deeply flawed or simply impractical notion. Rawls advances overlapping consensus because it reflects the logic of his fundamental proposition (no single value system may prevail), and because it adds an element of positive affirmation by citizens in a democracy. There are difficulties associated with testing the existence in practice of a theoretical proposition or concept, such as overlapping consensus, although Gray (2000b: 139) suggests it is seen in some 'late modern societies'. Perhaps more importantly, Gray (2000b: 20) proposes an important limit to *modus vivendi*: it is 'impossible in

---

61 Citizens find a 'reasonable' concept of justice convincing only when affirming this from within their own comprehensive doctrine: 'this idea forms the kernel of *Political Liberalism*' (Habermas 2010: 451).

a regime in which the varieties of the good are seen as symptoms of error or heresy', the sign, he says, of an illiberal regime.

Public reason is criticised by those who prefer to see a substantive role for comprehensive value systems in public discourse. Rawls at no point dismisses the importance of the values of the 'background culture'. Equally, he explicitly rejects the possibility that political liberalism promotes a role for secularism, or any other non-religious value system. Furthermore, while attracting some criticism, his 'wide view' of public reason specifically permits reference to comprehensive doctrines. Therefore, on the basis of Rawls' own thinking, there is at first glance little to be made of a number of the criticisms mounted against public reason.

Rawls (1993: 136) deploys the concept of public reason – a process of public justification – in connection with the question of the 'legitimacy of the general structure of authority'. Public reason provides stability 'for the right reasons' and in this way, is closely aligned to the notion of consensus discussed above. As Ackerman (1994: 386) puts it: the 'civic discourse' of public reason is part of a 'common effort to control the basic structures of society that would otherwise evolve by mere force or accident'. This view stands in contrast to Gray's (2000b: 19) sobering alternative: 'peaceful coexistence is not an *a priori* value'. If no comprehensive doctrine may prevail (on questions of constitutional fundamentals) then, logically, argumentation cannot proceed on the basis of seeking to trump another's point of view – political liberalism simply rules out the objective, or potential, of hegemony.

Commentary regarding the special role afforded courts in political liberalism is consistent with other writing about the cultural nature of law. Kahn (1999: 39) proposes that the 'rule of law is a social practice' that leads to a set of beliefs about the self and community, leading to the conclusion that law is socially constructed, and so, contingent.[62] Rawls writes predominantly about the political construction of legitimate law, not about the operation of law as such. However, it is important to acknowledge concerns about the role of courts given the well-established critique of law as a social and cultural construct. I deal directly with the contribution of judges at different levels by reviewing in detail a case of religious freedom. This case study deals with issues of the criminal procedure and judicial review and therefore the role of such a key state institution is of central importance and debates about the feasibility of public reason applying to judges highly relevant.

The religious objection combines philosophical challenges to the world view that critics claim is imposed by Rawls' thinking, and complaints about the restrictions placed by the requirements of public reason on the content of public discourse. Habermas (2010: 442–443) holds that Rawls has unique standing

---

62 Kamenka and Tay (1980: 3) observed some time ago that we now 'insist' that 'law stands neither above nor outside society, but within it, and that it does not make its own history'.

due to the 'systematic attention' he pays to religious and metaphysical pluralism, indeed being the 'first major political philosopher' to take the issue seriously.[63] Rawls seeks to provide a scheme for 'determining the legitimacy of the exercise of power by a state over all its citizens' (Nagel 2003, 78) but, despite this, political liberalism has 'fed subliminal resentment within religious circles concerning the justification of constitutional principles' (Habermas 2010: 451). A liberal constitution is, however, designed to guarantee equal scope to all citizens for religious freedom and shield public bodies from religious influence – 'the secularisation of the state does not entail the secularisation of society' (Habermas 2010: 451). This point, moreover, appears to be acknowledged even by Finnis (2011: 5) who argues that the resolution to the issue of pluralism is 'the secular and religious realms exist in parallel, within the hearts and mind of the believer and in public forms – church and state – each free from the supervisory management of the other'.[64]

Despite building political liberalism as a solution to historical experience with religious conflict, Rawls does not deal with many practical examples in developing political liberalism. It has in fact been alleged that Rawls' work lacks a sound empirical base (Schaefer 2007: 13). In his defence, Nussbaum (2001: 900) points out that Rawls 'is not doing sociology, he is doing normative (indeed ideal) theory'. This book is in part directed at exploring a particularly relevant case study – freedom of religion – which engages directly both with the foundation question of pluralism, the issue of fundamental constitutional rights, and the mechanism of public reason. While not raised directly by the commentaries discussed above, a further dimension to the religious objection could be to ask how or why religious conflict in sixteenth-century Europe might provide in any way a relevant model? The history of European, religiously based conflict, is an example of intra-religious conflict; two rival branches of Christianity in competition. This setting is arguably relevant for Indonesia, a Muslim majority nation, which is experiencing both intra-faith tension and a debate about the role of the majority faith in law and state governance.

Conclusion

Rawls and key critics are in agreement about the fact of pluralism, the need for toleration in response to this fact, and the need to uphold respect for basic

---

63 Moreover, drawing on a study of Rawls' early academic work, Habermas (2010: 448–449) observes that 'the history of John Rawls' work exhibits a philosophical reshaping of religious ideas' and remarks that Rawls' earlier strongly religious convictions were shaken after service in World War II. See Loobuyck & Rummens (2011) for an account of the similarities and differences between Habermas and Rawls concerning the place of religious argument in the public sphere.

64 It is not clear how this perspective links with Finnis' desire to see constitutional recognition of faith – indeed of the 'true faith'.

rights including, in particular, religious freedom. The key point of contention is the philosophical basis for the concepts or mechanisms deployed in response. There is fundamental disagreement with Rawls about the priority of the 'right' over the 'good', which, at its most basic level, involves a difference about the value afforded to individual equality. Rawls, however, confines his efforts to working through the logic of, and necessary procedures at work in, the modern constitutional state. He does not seek to describe or explain the nature or interplay of values across society as a whole. His scheme in fact acknowledges the breadth of all domains of thought, belief and association.

Whether practical or not, and whether pursued imperfectly or not, Rawls' framework arguably provides a more consistent and internally coherent response to the reality of value pluralism than alternative approaches. Critiques that it is based on 'foreign' philosophical concepts are rejected and, in any event, may not apply in the Indonesian setting, given the framework of the Indonesian state is the product of colonial influence and, subsequently, independent domestic reforms (a subject taken up in the following chapter). Some critics are vulnerable to claims of inconsistency as they provide a largely similar response as Rawls to the fundamental question of the rights of the individual with respect to pursuit of religion, and freedom from arbitrary state interference. While political liberalism evolved from and incorporates elements of Rawls' own particular notion of justice, it is specifically confined to political relations in a constitutional democracy. His thinking is, moreover, grounded in the historical experience of religiously-based conflict in Western European history. Rawls' particular response to the inherent potential for divisions based on conflict among value systems including interpretations of faith is a theoretical model for developing and maintaining a well-ordered democratic society.

3 Faith and freedom in Indonesian law

In this chapter I consider the way Indonesian law both promotes religion and protects religious freedom. These different, but not necessarily mutually exclusive, objectives sit within a constitutional framework that provides a special place for religion, without establishing a state religion, and that promotes human rights, including freedom of religion. Islam itself does not receive special constitutional recognition or protection, but consideration will be given to the way the history of constitutional development and reform, as well as contemporary jurisprudence, helps to provide special status for faith and, in particular, the majority religion, Islam. Scholarship and judicial decisions, particularly those of the Constitutional Court (*Mahkamah Konstitusi* or MK), reveal that the nature of the Indonesian state remains a matter of open debate. Indonesia has traditionally been described as neither secular nor religious, and I consider the extent to which this view of the state remains appropriate. The objective is to consider the essential qualities of Indonesia's modern democratic state, with particular attention paid to the questions raised in the previous chapter about the fact of liberal pluralism as a social reality.

At key points in contemporary Indonesian history it has been agreed that the Constitution should remain neutral as to religion, notwithstanding the Islamic affiliation of the majority of the population. This chapter will look at the debate around the basis of the state – or *dasar negara* – and what this demonstrates about thinking on the subject of pluralism. While religion has been, and continues to be, seen as a cornerstone of Indonesian constitutionalism (and accordingly is non-negotiable) the Constitution provides for a pluralist perspective. It recognises religious freedom, and does not identify a special role for Islamic law, despite repeated attempts to make this so. It may be possible to argue that Islam is a constitutional orphan, but it is not forgotten and remains a subject of much attention. It is strongly held to be a valid source of Indonesian law, albeit within certain limits.

One of the most important questions for the purposes of the case study is to understand the origins, nature and operation of the elements of the Criminal Code that were brought to bear in the prosecution of Yusman Roy. I introduce some interesting commentary on the nature and origins of the relevant laws, but there is more research left to be done to identify sources of, or inspiration for, specific provisions. Subsequent to the events of the case study (detailed in Chapters 5 and 6) this legal framework was challenged in the MK, and the decision that followed is discussed at some length in this chapter. This decision is one of several that have dealt with matters of faith, and the manner in which aspects of Islamic law form part of the legal landscape. I consider these decisions briefly to provide further context for the case study and application of a liberal political analytical framework. Specific questions that arise include how to understand prosecutions such as this within the higher-level debate over the role of Islam in state and law, and the way the right to religious freedom is interpreted by the MK.

The promotion and protection of religion

The foundation of state engagement with faith is found in the words of the Constitution's preamble, which includes the well-known five principles or *Pancasila*, opening with the declaration that Indonesia is a state based on Belief in Almighty God.[1] The Constitution does not recognise a state religion, but this notionally secular foundation has been repeatedly debated in post-Independence Indonesia, and remains contested. Moreover, human rights, and the protection of religious freedom in particular, are counterbalanced by other laws protecting religion (often described as blasphemy laws, a description that will be considered in more detail below). There are also a number of areas of accommodation in both law and administration that mean that there are, in fact, numerous points of contact between state and Islam.

Religious freedom

The overarching principle in the preamble, that Indonesia is a state sustained by faith, is partnered with a clear recognition of the right to freedom of religion. Freedom of religion is, in fact, mentioned twice in the Constitution, first in art 29 (in terms echoing the preambular statement):

1) The State shall be based upon the Belief in Almighty God.
2) The State guarantees all persons the freedom of worship, and each according to his/her own religion or belief.[2]

---

1 The Indonesian wording is *Ketuhanan Yang Maha Esa*, and can also be translated as Belief in the One and Only God, or Belief in the One Almighty God. The origins and interpretation of the phrase are considered further below. The other principles are [2] just and civilised humanity, [3] the unity of Indonesia, [4] a democratic life led by the wisdom of thoughts in deliberation amongst representatives of the people, and [5] achieving social justice for all the people of Indonesia. The name of the doctrine is derived from Sanskrit (*panca* – five, *sila* – principles) and was developed during negotiations over the first post-Independence Constitution – see further below. It became in particular a key plank of New Order ideology and continues to drive public debate about the nature of the Indonesian state, see Salim (2007) and Ichwan (2006: 93–99).

2 There is an important distinction in Indonesia between 'religion' and 'beliefs'. Traditional belief systems (*kepercayaan*) are not illegal per se but have not been afforded the same status

Following the end of the Soeharto era (1966–1998), significant amendments were introduced including an expanded range of human rights.[3] Interestingly, art 29 was retained and freedom of religion was repeated, in a modified form, in art 28E:[4]

1) Every person shall be free to choose and to practice the religion of his/her own choice . . .[5]
2) Every person shall have the right of the freedom to believe his/her faith, and to express his/her views and thoughts, in accordance with his/her conscience.
3) Every person shall have the right of the freedom to associate, to assemble and to express opinions.

Article 28I of the Constitution appears to further strengthen the position of religious freedom, declaring it to be one of several 'non-derogable' rights (rights that 'cannot be limited under any circumstances'). This key provision is followed with art 28J (2) which states that rights may be restricted by law including in order to satisfy 'just demands' based on morality, religious values, security and public order.

Religious freedom is also protected under the Human Rights Law (Law 39/1999) adopted under the Habibie Presidency, prior to the constitutional amendments.[6] Article 22 provides that:

1) Everyone has the right to freedom to choose his religion and to worship according to the teachings of his religion and beliefs.
2) The state guarantees everyone the freedom to choose and practice his religion and to worship according to his religion and beliefs.[7]

---

as 'religions', and have been managed under a separate legal and administrative regime. See Alfitri (2008: 15–17) and Butt & Lindsey (2012: 240–243).

3 See Lindsey (2009) for a summary of the human rights amendments, which will be considered further below. Lindsey (2009: 274–277) notes that Indonesia has seen a parallel movement to both 'Islamise' laws and to institutionalise international human rights.

4 The provisions appear in different chapters of the Constitution.

5 This provision also refers to other rights including the right to work, and freedom of movement.

6 In addition to providing a legislative mandate for the National Commission on Human Rights, previously empowered only by Presidential Decree, this law provides for a wide range of human rights and freedoms.

7 There are variations in the different formulations of the right to religious freedom, perhaps the most obvious being the explicit protection for freedom to worship found in the human rights legislation. This formulation of the right, however, is different in another critical way as it requires individuals to pursue their faith according to the teachings of that religion. The place of accepted teachings and the role of religious authorities in determining what is or is not consistent with Islam is a central issue in the book.

Law 39/1999 also establishes a direct link between international human rights standards and domestic law in art 7 (2): 'provisions set forth in international law concerning human rights ratified by the Republic of Indonesia, are recognised under this Act as legally binding in Indonesia'. Indonesia ratified the International Covenant on Civil and Political Rights (ICCPR) in 2005 (Colbran 2010: 680). Article 18 of this Convention provides:

1) Everyone shall have the right to freedom of thought, conscience and religion. This right shall include freedom to have or to adopt a religion or belief of his choice, and freedom, either individually or in community with others and in public or private, to manifest his religion or belief in worship, observance, practice and teaching.
2) No one shall be subject to coercion which would impair his freedom to have or to adopt a religion or belief of his choice.
3) Freedom to manifest one's religion or beliefs may be subject only to such limitations as are prescribed by law and are necessary to protect public safety, order, health, or morals or the fundamental rights and freedoms of others.
4) The States Parties to the present Covenant undertake to have respect for the liberty of parents and, when applicable, legal guardians to ensure the religious and moral education of their children in conformity with their own convictions.[8]

Religious freedom is therefore arguably the most strongly promoted right in Indonesia's human rights framework: it appears twice in the Constitution; in human rights legislation; and, indirectly through the recognition afforded to international law.

Laws protecting religion

A range of offences exist in Indonesian law, directed at different forms of conduct, and intended to provide protection for religion. They are not based explicitly in Islamic law and they existed in pre-Independence laws, some being a product of the colonial administration, with key provisions appearing in the chapter of the Criminal Code addressing 'public order'.[9] Together they aim to

---

8 The way in which the right to freedom of religion is expressed in international law is quite different to that found in the Constitution and legislation in Indonesia. Freedom from coercion, found in the ICCPR, is absent from the Indonesian provisions, and art 18 (1) of the ICCPR provides a much more expansive definition of the right; it also appears to acknowledge that the right may be an individual or a group experience.
9 Both the Indonesian Criminal and Civil Codes are products of the colonial period and the original versions of each are written in Dutch. See for example Hamzah (2010) and Bell

protect religion and its public expression and prefigure by many years the contemporary international debate concerning 'defamation of religion'.[10]

Presidential Decree 1/1965 Concerning Prevention of Abuse and/or Disgrace of Religion (*Pencegahan Penyalagunaan dan/atau Penodaan Agama*)
(1/PNPS/1965) was elevated to the status of statute (or 'law' [*undang-
undang*]) of the DPR in 1969,[11] thereafter being known as Law 1/PNPS/1965.
It is informally known as the 'Blasphemy Law' and, together with the Criminal
Code, provides the framework for the management of offences against religion
in Indonesia. The Law establishes administrative procedures for the control
of certain activities for implementation jointly by the Minister for Religion,
Attorney General (*Jaksa Agung*) and Minister for the Interior and the President. The joint Ministerial team[12] has the authority to warn individuals or
organisations considered to be conducting deviant activities, with failure to
heed a warning leading to criminal sanction, and a recommendation to the
President to disband any organisation involved. The relevant prohibition is
described as follows:

> It is prohibited for anyone to deliberately and in public to communicate,
> encourage, or to seek general support for the interpretation of a religion
> adopted in Indonesia or conduct religious activities that resemble such
> religious activities, such interpretations and activities being ones that deviate
> from the central teachings of that religion.

Should the activities continue, the Law provides for a jail term of five years
but establishes no procedure for the enforcement of this punishment. The
Law also inserted a new provision into the Criminal Code, art 156a,
providing:

(2008). According to Adji (1984: 74), some of the relevant criminal provisions were 'created for the interests and "convenience" of the "colonial administration"'.

10 See Blitt (2010) and Fenwick (2011b) on the protracted debate on defamation of religion
particularly in United Nations forums.

11 Law No 5 of 1969 Declaring Several Decisions and Regulations of the President to be
Laws (Lindsey 2012a: 402).

12 Known as *bakorpakem* (*Badan Koordinasi Pengawasan Kepercayaan Masyrakat* – the
Coordinating Body for the Monitoring of Mystical Beliefs in Society), the national team is
complemented by regional teams and is led by the intelligence division of the Attorney-
General's Office, pursuant to Decision of the Attorney General 108/JA/5/1984 On the
Establishment of the Coordinating Body for the Monitoring of Mystical Beliefs in Society.
It coordinates with other agencies to monitor belief systems to ensure that the principle of
Ketuhanan Yang Maha Esa is maintained, and that they do not endanger society (Crouch
2012: 6–9; Lindsey 2012a: 423). The Attorney-General's service (public prosecutor) has a
legislative mandate to monitor belief systems and prevent the misuse or insult to religion
under art 30 of Law 16/2004 on the Public Prosecutor.

Whosoever intentionally publicly expresses sentiments or commits an act:

a   that fundamentally and by its nature is hostile, abuses or disgraces a religion practised in Indonesia

b   with the intention that persons should not practise any religion at all that is based on Belief in Almighty God

is subject to a jail sentence of 5 years.

The elucidation attached to the original Decree states that its measures are not intended to restrict the practice of religion. The elucidation reinforces state guidance on religion by referring to the six most common religions – Islam, Christianity (meaning Protestantism), Catholicism, Hinduism, Buddhism and Confucianism. It goes on to add that other religions such as Judaism, Zoroastrianism, Shintoism and Taoism are not prohibited in Indonesia, and receive constitutional protection, so long as they do not breach the provisions contained in the Decree. The Decree was established at the urging of the then Minister for Religion with a view to ensuring national security, where abuse of religion could be seen as a threat to this goal, and to prevent the growth of sects and beliefs seen as contrary to doctrine (Colbran 2010: 681). Menchik (2014: 607) explains that the Decree formed part of then President Soekarno's efforts to 'mobilise support as the self-proclaimed leader of the Muslim world'. Six weeks after the Decree was signed by the President it was announced in joint statements by the major Muslim organisations[13] – Nahdlatul Ulama (NU), Muhammadiyah and Sarekat Islam – who declared (in turn) their support for Soekarno's policy of NASAKOM (an inclusive term for Soekarno's political ideology, which he claimed embraced nationalism, religion and communism) (Menchik 2014: 608).[14]

Two other provisions of the Criminal Code establish relevant offences. Article 156 provides:

Whosoever publicly expresses feelings of hostility, hatred or contempt toward one or more groups in Indonesian society, is liable to a jail sentence of no longer than five years or a fine. . . . The word group in this and the subsequent article means each part of Indonesian society which is different with one or several other parts because of race, country of origin, religion, place, origin, decent, nationality or status according to constitutional law.

13 NU and Muhammadiyah are described in Chapter 4.
14 Soekarno was later awarded the title 'Champion of Islam and Freedom in Asia and Africa' by the 1965 Islamic Asia-Pacific Conference, a successor event to the 1955 Bandung Asia-Africa Conference (Drakeley 2014: 202; Menchik 2014: 608). This period late in Soekarno's reign is more often associated with rising engagement with Communist China, see for example Ricklefs (2001: 336–337). Cf. Sukma (2003: 32–36), who does not remark on this dimension to Soekarno's international engagement in his study of Islam in Indonesian foreign policy, and indeed describes Islam as entirely absent from Soekarno's foreign policy.

The following provision, art 157, provides:

> Whosoever broadcasts, exhibits, or affixes writing or drawings in public, the contents of which contain statements of hostility, hatred or contempt between or towards groups in Indonesian society, with the intention that their contents be known or better known by the public, is liable to a jail sentence no longer than two and a half years or a fine.

Articles 156a and 157 are important for the case study, as they were the charges applied to Yusman Roy. I explore them in Chapter 6 and also in this chapter, below.[15] Briefly, art 156 could be said to be directed at hate speech or vilification, given its explicit focus on the act of expressing negative views about religion, and art 156a extends the form of the offence against religion by introducing the quite specific offence of *penodaan* which can mean, variously, 'staining', 'disgracing' and – possibly – 'desecrating'. Article 157 encompasses different forms of transmission or dissemination of offensive expressions through electronic media or public display.

Neither the administrative procedures nor the provisions of the Criminal Code above specifically seek to protect Islam. In contrast, the high-water mark of implementation of syariah remains the province of Aceh which possesses special authority to develop Islamic-inspired regulations.[16] These regulations, known as *Qanun*, apply only in the Province of Aceh and seek to implement syariah. They institute limited forms of corporal punishment as a sanction for certain offences.[17] In particular these regulations seek to control social conduct such as drinking, gambling and fraternisation among unmarried men and women. *Qanun* 11/2002[18] goes further and regulates the observance of Islamic faith in Aceh by addressing 'creed' (*aqidah*) and ritual observance (*Ibadah*) (Ichwan 2006: 248). In doing so it defines all schools of thought other than Sunni as deviant, and bans propagation of such beliefs (Ichwan 2006: 248). In this area of regulation, a special role is afforded the Acehnese Ulama council to determine, through *fatawa*, the particular forms of deviant belief giving rise to an offence (the role of MUI at national and local levels elsewhere in Indonesia is taken up in the following chapter). The regulation also establishes leaving the Islamic faith (*keluar dari aqidah*) as a criminal offence; that is, it

---

15 Articles 176 and 177 of the Criminal Code also protect religion through prohibiting disruption of religious gatherings and ridiculing of officials and ceremonies (Lindsey 2012a: 402–403).

16 For a detailed description of the regime applying in Aceh see Lindsey (2012a: 307–323) and Salim (2008: 143–167). The source of the Province's authority to adopt syariah is Law 18/2001 on Special Autonomy for the Province of Nanggroe Aceh Darussalam.

17 The first public caning took place in August 2005 (International Crisis Group 2006).

18 *Qanun* No 11 of 2002 on the Implementation of Islamic *Syariat* in the Fields of *Aqidah*, *Ibadah* and *Syi'ar* Islam.

enshrines the principle of apostasy. Aceh's capacity with respect to passage of local regulations is a result of the devolution of authority, under regional autonomy law, to local governments (Lindsey 2012a: 15–18). The primary distinction is that the devolution to Aceh specifically includes power with respect to matters of religion (but only Islam). The absence of specific authority to regulate matters of religion in other parts of Indonesia has not prevented local governments passing regulations touching on faith and morality (Bush 2008; Lindsey 2012a).

The law in action

Several accounts are given of the deployment of the Blasphemy Law providing very detailed analyses of the law in action, statistics, and descriptions of numerous case studies (Crouch 2012; Lindsey 2012a; Sihombing et al. 2012). Crouch (2012: 1, 14) has identified more than 47 prosecutions undertaken between 1998–2011, against over 120 individuals, in which there were only two acquittals. Margiyono (et al. 2011: 6) state that more than 150 individuals were subject to criminal process in the five years 2003–2008 alone. In contrast, the New Order period of Soeharto's rule as President (1966–1998) appears to have seen only ten prosecutions (Crouch 2012: 12). Among the contemporary cases many – perhaps the majority – of individuals appear to be Christian (40 individuals were all prosecuted in a single case), but the majority of trials in recent years have been prosecutions of Muslims (Crouch 2012: 13).

The New Order era prosecutions include the 1968 action against magazine editor H.B. Jassin who was charged over the publication of a short story that included comments deemed insulting to Islam, and which prompted an attack on the magazine's office (Lindsey 2012a: 403). In 1990, a tabloid editor was prosecuted for publishing the results of a reader survey that ranked the Prophet Muhammad at number 11 in a list of popular figures (Lindsey 2012a: 403–404). Two other cases, in 1995 and 1996, also involved public statements deemed offensive to Islam but the religious element in the first may have been secondary to other, controversial, political statements. The second case, which also involved acts of serious violence, has been described as 'engineered' – possibly as part of political manoeuvres relating to the rising public profile of the reformist Muslim leader Abdurrahman Wahid (Lindsey 2012a: 404–406). More characteristic of the Soeharto era was the deployment of the administrative processes of the executive agencies responsible for banning deviant sects. During the years of the New Order, dozens if not hundreds of sects were banned (Crouch 2012: 9; Lindsey 2012a: 419).

The use of the administrative procedures continued after the fall of Soeharto and over fifty bans are thought to have been issued across Indonesia at the local level (Crouch 2012: 10). The most prominent examples of the banning of groups deemed to be in breach of the provisions of the Law related to the Ahmadiyah faith, which was the subject of deadly protest action by hard-line Muslims (*garis keras*) and a controversial ban at the national level in 2008

(Crouch 2012; Lindsey 2012a: 421; Platzdasch 2011).[19] The 2008 ban was controversial due to the fact that it took place in highly charged circumstances. It followed on from the serious violence perpetrated against members of the faith; public interventions by MUI including the development of guidelines determining what amounted to deviancy;[20] and, the unprecedented 'Monas Tragedy' of June 2008 in which hardline Muslims led by the Islamic Defender's Front (FPI) disrupted a large peaceful protest in support of religious tolerance. The arrival of the ban was attended by contradictory statements by officials about its issuance (Lindsey 2012a: 419–428). Moreover, Ahmadiyah was subject to a number of other bans declared at the local level, some in pursuance of the national level Decree (Crouch 2012: 10; Lindsey 2012a: 427).

Notwithstanding the fact that Ahmadiyah has attracted such a high degree of opposition from Islamic groups, and ultimately legally sanctioned interference by the state, none of the organisation's members have to date been subject to prosecution under the criminal law (Lindsey 2012a: 419–420). This may be due to the fact that it is part of a larger international movement and is legally established in Indonesia (Lindsey 2012a: 420). Instead, Lindsey (2012a: 419) explains that the criminal law has 'typically been directed at small, often informal, local groups and their leaders' and, as noted above, it is likely the majority of cases are brought against Muslims. In addition to the case of Yusman Roy, other cases include the 2005 prosecution (in East Java) of the founder of a faith healing foundation (*Yayasan Kanker dan Narkoba Cahaya Alam* – the Natural Light Cancer and Narcotic Foundation) and the 2006 prosecution (in Sulawesi) of the founder of a sect which promoted a form of whistling prayer (Lindsey 2012a: 413–416). Both of these cases involved the promotion of variants of Islamic teaching, attracting the opposition of local branches of MUI and resulting in *fatawa* rejecting the teaching as deviant.

It has been argued that there is both a pattern to many prosecutions and, possibly, a discernible change in the volume of cases in Indonesia post-Soeharto. Case statistics that have been collected differ and do not show a consistent raise over time, but rather highs and lows (a low of one per year and a high of up to seven in another year) across the period 2003–2012 (Crouch 2012: 12; Sihombing et al. 2012: 72). What is apparent from the research is that there were few prosecutions prior to 2003 (Crouch 2012; Lindsey 2012a: 406; Sihombing et al. 2012). More significantly, the pattern observed in numerous cases reflects elements of what Olle (2006) describes as a 'campaign against heresy', in which MUI has played a key role. That is, small localised groups are subject to protest and sometimes violent action and their activities are formally

---

19 The religious movement, founded by Mirza Ghulam Ahmad in Pakistan in the late nineteenth century, is considered a variant of Islam and declared deviant due to the belief that its founder was successor to Muhammad (see Lindsey 2012a: 63).

20 I consider deviancy and related concepts in more detail in Chapter 4.

denounced in *fatawa* by MUI: key personnel are subsequently arrested and prosecuted (Fenwick 2011b; Lindsey 2012a: 418–419: Olle 2006 and 2009).[21]

State, law and religion

Analysis of the relationship between state, law and religion in Indonesia most commonly comprises identifying where Indonesia might be said to rest on a spectrum running from 'secular' to 'religious'.[22] The 'degree' of secularism in Indonesia has given rise to a range of formulations: Indonesia is 'not fully secular' (Otto 2010: 456); it is 'quasi-secular' or even 'pseudo-secularist' (Elson 2010: 329); and 'semi-secular' (Butt 2010: 299). The Department of Religion effectively opts out of the secular state. In its description of government policy (or 'wisdom' – *kebijaksanaan*) it states that Indonesia is neither secular nor religious (Department of Religion 2007: 12). An alternative approach considers the issue starting, as it were, from the other end of the spectrum, considering the degree to which Indonesia has been 'confessionalised'. Ichwan (2006: 15) proposes that, by force of the various mechanisms by which the state has engaged with faith (and Islam in particular), Indonesia has experienced a process of 'deconfessionalisation'.[23] It has been argued, in fact, that the state has successfully incorporated and subjugated Islam, making it a 'subsidiary part of national law and governance' (Otto 2010: 480), and in modern Indonesia doctrinal Islam and 'official' Islam have formed separate normative regimes (Hooker 2003: 245). Even so, tensions remain. These are seen in the post-*Reformasi* intellectual struggle between conservative and liberal Islamic voices in Indonesia (Anwar 2007: 236–243). Analysis of the history of the *dasar negara* question and jurisprudence reveals traces of the tension between social adherence to Islam and the constitutional and legal framework, which Effendy (2003: 14) ascribes

21 A study of 37 cases (Sihombing et al. 2012: 9–57) of prosecutions or other instances of alleged blasphemy bears out this conclusion (in 5 cases the study does not record criminal action). At least 17 of the 37 cases involved Islamic sects (including the Yusman Roy case). The study identifies MUI involvement in 9 instances, of which 4 include the issue of *fatawa*. There were 10 cases in which other Islamic organisations made objections to conduct or religious practices, or brought the matter to the attention of police, or were otherwise implicated in protest action (including the Department of Religion, the FPI, and the Indonesian *Mujahidin* Council (MMI – *Majelis Mujahidin Indonesia*)). Protest action, raids on premises of other violent mob activity occurred in 15 of the 37 cases reported and in 10 of these there was both a form of protest action and the involvement in some form of an Islamic organisation.

22 For commentary on the concept of the secular state and the distinction between secularism and secularity, which I do not pursue here, see Scharffs (2011).

23 Ichwan (2006: 15) summarises the concept used by Niewenhuijze (1958) and argues the first *sila*, *Ketuhanan Yang Maha Esa*, and the establishment of the Ministry of Religion were 'the two major elements in what [Niewnhuijze] refers to as the "deconfessionalisation" of Islam in post-colonial Indonesia'. Sukma (2003: 19) also uses the term in reference to Soekarno's first formulation of *Pancasila*.

to the failure of the nation's political elite to 'negotiate and reconcile' the different discourses on the ideological basis of the state.

Faith and the dasar negara *question*

The constitutional, legal and administrative framework in Indonesia is the product, in part at least, of a long, and ongoing dialogue on the prominence that should be given to religious adherence, and specifically to Islam. The debate around the foundations of the state (*dasar negara*) has centred on the level of recognition afforded to Islam, with proponents of Islamic law striving for its formal recognition. Whilst the debate may have been framed only indirectly in terms of religious pluralism, freedom of religion, as seen above, has been adopted multiple times in Indonesian law.[24] The pluralist framework derived from controversial negotiations during the development of the post-Independence constitution and remains contested. The principal point of contention remains the extent to which Islam should be afforded a special place as a source of, or as an inspiration for, national law.

Conflict concerning the role of religion in Indonesia's political life was a feature of debates within nationalist forces before the formulation of the 1945 Constitution (Kahin 2012). Kahin (2012: 192, 200) argues that the major issue dividing nationalists was whether Islam would provide the 'natural tie' to bind Indonesia's diverse societies, which was the view of Mohammed Natsir, the leader of Indonesia's then largest Muslim party active in the nationalist struggle.[25] In the early twentieth century Islam was a significant unifying force that, according to Elson (2102: 308), 'dominated the terrain of indigenous perceptions of self and identity'.[26] Kahin's (2012: 196) study of the debates between

---

24 The nature of the principles underpinning the Indonesian Constitution and the role for religion in this foundation was debated three times. The first debate occurred during the drafting of the 1945 Constitution (Butt 2010: 282; Ichwan 2006: 40–52); the second debate took place during deliberations of the delegates to the Constituent Assembly in the 1950s (Nasution 1992); and the third formed part of the extensive constitutional revision undertaken after the fall of Soeharto (Elson 2010: 332–3; Hosen 2005; Lindsey 2002: 269–271 and 2009: 285).

25 Natsir was associated with the conservative Muslim organisation Persis (Federspiel 2009; Ricklefs 2001: 237–238). See also Lindsey (2012a: 35–36) on Natsir's profile and his promotion of Islam as the *dasar negara*. Persis (*Persatuan Islam* – Islamic Union) is a Modernist and conservative Islamic organisation established in 1923 which opposed secular nationalism (Ricklefs 2001: 222, 238) and which, according to Federspiel (2009: 215), 'formulated many of the arguments against secularism that were taken up by other Muslims'.

26 Cf. Elson's (2010: 329) description of the importance of religious debates underway within Indonesian Islam, with appropriate ritual behaviour being the predominant focus of Islam in the earlier years of the twentieth century. The focus on ritual behaviour took the form of protracted and contentious conflict between Muslim organisations over issues of deviant interpretations of doctrine, and matters of 'innovation' (*bid'ah*), see Fenwick

Soekarno, Indonesia's first President and a leader of the nationalist movement, and Natsir during the pre-Independence years presents the key views of these leaders: Soekarno believed in separating the state from religion so that each would be stronger; Natsir argued against the separation of religion and state, claiming 'the state is the apparatus and instrument for Islam'. Natsir, moreover, claimed that Indonesian Muslims would not be content with independence alone but rather would 'continue their struggle as long as the country continued not to be based, or administered according to the laws and regulations of Islam' (Lindsey 2012a: 36). Moreover, Natsir's vision was for a majoritarian 'Islamic Democracy' and he thought about national unity in sectarian, communal terms (Feener 2014: 11–12).

In the development of the first Constitution for an independent Indonesia at the close of World War II, the initial draft text referred to 'belief in God' (*ketuhanan*) but the original draft prepared by Soekarno had this element in fifth place, with 'Indonesian nationalism' (*kebangsaan*) as the first element of what was to become *Pancasila* (Ichwan 2006: 48–49; Kahin 2012: 201). Soekarno proposed this framework 'to overcome conflict between proponents of a secular state and those of an Islamic state' (Nasution 1992: 10). He also promoted the notion of pluralism, pointing out that an Islamic state would disenfranchise non-Muslims; indeed, he went further and urged that there be no 'religious egoism' (Nasution 1992: 63). The issue quickly became more controversial due to the ongoing negotiations in constitutional drafting in which some sought a home for Islamic law. The so-called 'Jakarta Charter' emerged as a compromise, and it comprised the preamble to the Constitution with a statement of Belief in Almighty God (*Ketuhanan Yang Maha Esa*)[27] elevated to first position in the *Pancasila*, and the inclusion of an obligation for Muslims to carry out Islamic law. Ultimately the reference to Islamic law was dropped, a move that has been considered by some to be highly controversial (Butt 2010: 282; Ichwan 2006: 40–52). Indeed, the 'see-sawing' on formal recognition of Islam was considered by Muslim representatives as a deceit and betrayal

---

(2011b). The influence of these doctrinal issues will be taken up in Chapter 4. Elson (2012: 308, 304) also concludes that 'Islam remained remote from the levers that guided the flow of political events', and 'failed to interrupt or divert' secularised thinking about the emerging Indonesian state, a view challenged by Menchik (2014: 593).

27 This is a difficult phrase to translate which, as noted above, appears in other formulations. Despite the significant change in wording – from 'godliness' (*ketuhanan*) to 'Belief in Almighty God' – scholars appear to have paid little attention to the origin or meaning of the words, and few comment at all on the shift. Nasution (1992: 106) reports that the wording was supplied by Hadikusumo, a leading Islamic figure in the independence struggle and senior Muhammadiyah figure. Cf. Hosen (2007: 63–64), who reports that Hadikusumo had to ask for an explanation of the choice of the phrase and was told that it reflected the Islamic monotheistic concept of *tawhid*. See also An-Na'im (2008: 259) who quotes the late Indonesian Islamic scholar Nurcholish Madjid as revealing that several elements of *Pancasila* were deliberately 'Islamicised'.

(Nasution 1992: 103–106). It has been proposed that this deletion was prompted by the desire to remove the possibility that Christian regions in the East of the archipelago, then under the command of the Japanese Navy, might refuse to join the new republic (Kahin 2012: 202; Nasution 1992: 103–106), and fears that the West might be less supportive of the new republic.[28]

The second debate about formal recognition of Islamic law took place during the 1950s in the work of the Constituent Assembly – a body elected to develop a fully revised constitution (Butt 2010: 283; Elson 2010: 330, 332–333). Nasution (1992: 32–34) relates that the debates between November 1956 and June 1959 reflected the 'ideological polarisation' between Islamic and non-Islamic parties in the 1955 general election, resulting in near equilibrium between the major voting blocks in the assembly.[29] The leading Islamic party figure, Natsir, urged rejection of secularism (and *Pancasila*). Only Divine Revelation, he argued, could provide the guidance required for resolving issues at the state level (as opposed to the merely social level) (Nasution 1992: 107).[30] The debates were not, however, entirely characterised by entrenched conflict. Nasution remarks that while the debate on the *dasar negara* was 'centrifugal' in nature, the debate on human rights, in contrast, was 'centripetal' and 'there was a conspicuous consensus on the paramount significance of rights including freedom of religion' (Nasution 1992: 42). The assembly was dissolved before a new constitution was adopted, as dissolution seemed to be the only way to resolve the ongoing deadlock over the place of Islam. It was a way to 'bypass the intransigence of the Islamic parties' (Ricklefs 2001: 322).

The most recent period of constitutional reform following the downfall of President Soeharto was marked by a very public and heated debate both inside and outside the DPR about the role of Islam in the state (Hosen 2005: 425). Amendments to the 1945 Constitution took place in four rounds across the years 1999–2002 (Lindsey 2002: 254) and in the second round of amendments in August 2000 a comprehensive bill of rights was introduced as a new chapter, Chapter XA, consisting of articles 28A–J. This was 'perhaps the most radical change' to the Integralist State notions underpinning the 1945 Constitution, which embodied an inherently authoritarian state model (Butt & Lindsey 2012: 7–8; Lindsey 2002: 253–254).[31] The authoritarian 1945 Constitution was therefore

28 Nasution (1992: 106) also records that the notion of a potential schism or split in Indonesia along religious lines was proposed by a Japanese Naval officer.
29 The *Pancasila* block commanding 274 votes, the Islamic block 230, and the Socio-Economic (broadly left-wing) block 10 votes (Nasution 1992).
30 Secularism, in Natsir's view, 'essentially relativised all philosophy of life' (Nasution 1992: 107).
31 As seen in Chapter 1, this was a 'romanticised union of state and people' (Lindsey 2002: 253) and Bourchier (1999) deals at length with the philosophical sources of the Constitution.

'tempered' with a wide range of rights borrowed from the Universal Declaration of Human Rights (Lindsey 2002: 254), which will be considered further below.

The Fourth amendment in August 2002 saw the rejection of a proposal to amend the existing art 29 (the original provision protecting freedom of religion) to include reference to an obligation on Muslims to practice Islamic law (Hosen 2005: 428; Lindsey 2002: 269–270). According to Hosen (2005: 420, 429) the debate was of a different order to those earlier in the century, in that there was no longer a focus on altering the *dasar negara* and arguing for the establishment of an Islamic state. The proposal was advanced by two Islamic political parties (accounting for only 12 per cent of parliamentary seats) but the initiative lacked the support of Indonesia's largest Muslim organisations, Muhammadiyah and NU, driven by concerns to maintain national unity (Hosen 2005: 425; Indrayana 2008: 314).[32] Ultimately the lack of consensus over wording (four different formulations were under consideration) and inability to muster parliamentary numbers meant that the proposal was not put to a formal vote (Hosen 2005: 427). The fact the proposal was made at all, however, reflected continued disappointment at the defeat of the Jakarta Charter in earlier constitutional debates (Hosen 2005: 440).

Islam and the law in contemporary jurisprudence

The implications for the legal system of the constitutional framework and the ongoing debates as to the place of faith have been explored thoroughly by scholars writing with particular reference to Islam. Jimly Asshiddiqie (2005: 55), the first Chair of the MK, who has written extensively on Indonesian constitutionalism, and the late Rifal Ka'bah (1999: 77), a former Supreme Court Justice and expert in Islamic law, both argue that the Constitution prevents the state from passing laws inconsistent with belief in God, and, for Ka'bah, *Pancasila* forms a '*grundnorm*' of Indonesian law. Ka'bah (1999: 77–78) proposes, further, that the constitutional protection of religious freedom in art 29 requires the state to take responsibility for implementing Islamic law for Muslims – and respective religious laws for other faiths (if they possess such laws) – and to make laws that promote a sense of faith and prohibit denigration of religious

---

32 Lindsey (2008: 41) observes that national unity was a key factor, but proposes that other 'more influential' reasons also existed. These were that: in Muslim majority nations it is not easy to reach consensus on what syariah means given the divergent views among Muslims about their faith; the two largest Muslim organisations – NU and Muhammadiyah – feared that syariah would provide a 'political weapon' to smaller, more radical Islamic groups; and, it was not clear how securing the amendment would add significantly to the existing framework of Islamic legal institutions, including the Religious Courts (Lindsey 2008). On the position of the two parties concerned (the PPP – United Development Party, and PBB – Crescent Moon and Star Party), and their broader 'syariah first' agenda in the post-Soeharto era, see Hefner (2011a: 294).

teachings. While 'Islamic law has significant scope to become part of Indonesian national law' (Ka'bah 1999: 82), for these scholars it appears clear that Islamic law cannot itself be a source of law, but must be incorporated through specific democratic and legislative action (Ka'bah 1999: 83; Asshiddiqie 2005: 131–132).[33] This is consistent with Hefner's (2011b: 21) observation that there is a global trend toward syariah being 'a standardised code to be enforced by the state' rather than being identified, as in the past, with religious scholars.[34]

Asshiddiqie (2005: 74–82), however, hints that there is by no means a consensus on the approach outlined above. He identifies three prevalent viewpoints on the place of Islam in the Indonesian legal system: a 'pragmatic' approach, in which the positive obligation to implement Islamic law is avoided in order to maintain unity; an 'idealist' approach, taken by groups which desire to struggle continuously for Islamic law; and, a 'realist' view, which sees Islamic law as an obligation, but also sees no need for political struggle to implement it since it is, in any event, the way of life for adherents (Asshiddiqie 2005). The views of the second, 'idealist' group can cause alarm in non-Muslim members of society and raise practical problems about the implementation of Islamic criminal law or adultery, both of which require clear rules to operationalise them (Asshiddiqie 2005: 79).[35] Once a concept is transformed into national law, it no longer needs to be identified with the particular faith from which it is sourced (Asshiddiqie 2005: 81). This does not, for Asshiddiqie (2005: 131–132), remove from Indonesian law the primary association with religiosity, as the concept of *ketuhanan* serves to establish one of three sources of sovereignty that operate simultaneously – sovereignty of God, of law, and of the people.

Issues of religion and religious freedom have come before the MK on a number of occasions. In three prominent cases the Court has considered elements of the legal framework established to implement aspects of Islamic law, and the 'blasphemy' regime. The first two cases involved challenges brought by Muslims questioning the validity of law permitting polygamy, and challenging the jurisdiction of Indonesia's Religious Courts. In the challenge to the polygamy law (handed down in 2007) it was argued that the stipulations established for a valid polygamous marriage breached the applicant's rights to

---

33 Ka'bah (1999: 59–61) however distinguishes those elements of Islamic law touching on custom and worship (*ibadah*), which do not require state power to be enjoyed, and those in which the interests of other people are engaged (*muamalah*), which do require state power. The challenge, he writes, is 'understanding and implementing Islamic law in the context of national law' (Ka'bah 1999: 65–66).

34 Asshiddiqie (2005: 81) describes three distinct periods commencing with the period of religious law, where law was coincident with divine revelation, the period of *ijtihad* (the Islamic concept of applying independent thought) where religious law no longer applied directly, and the period of 'enactment or legislation'.

35 An example being the adoption in Aceh of Islamic legal standards and corporal punishment, see above.

religious freedom under art 28E of the Constitution (Butt 2010: 292).[36] The Minister for Religious Affairs in his submission to the Court proposed that Islam favoured monogamy on the basis that the Qur'an 4:129 states that man is unable to be 'fair and just as between women and, further, that Islam does not provide an unqualified right to polygamy (Qur'an 4:3)' (Butt 2010: 293). The Court considered the Qur'anic references provided by the Minister as well as expert evidence on historical practice in Islam and the views of Islamic scholars (Butt 2010: 294–295). It then found that polygamy is capable of regulation by the state as it does not fall within the category of *ibadah* (matters related to worship) but rather relations between humans (*muamalah*) 'so Islam does not prohibit the state from imposing preconditions upon its exercise' (Butt 2010: 295–296).

In a 2008 challenge to the jurisdiction of the Religious Courts the applicant argued that confining the matters over which the Courts have jurisdiction breached his rights to religious freedom (Butt 2010: 296).[37] The Court determined that it lacked jurisdiction to expand the powers of the Religious Court and that the legislature was constitutionally entitled to grant jurisdiction to the Religious Courts at its discretion (Butt 2010: 297). The Court also made observations about the place of religion in the state, asserting the view that the Indonesian state is neither secular nor religious. Butt (2010: 298) notes that the court also held:

> Indonesia is a state which is based on Almighty God. The state protects [the right of] all religious adherents to carry out the teachings of their respective religions . . . it can be said that Islam is indeed a source of national law. But it is not the only source of national law.

Thus the Court simultaneously labels the state with an indeterminate status somewhere between secular and religious, and provides explicit recognition of a religious foundation to the state, and of Islam as a valid source of national law. In relation to the status of Islamic law, Butt argues (2010: 298–299) the Court's approach demonstrates that it acknowledges the 'inherent conflict between the authority of the state and Islam' but the conflict is resolved in favour of the state, because Islamic doctrine is not a direct source of the rules to be applied.

36　Constitutional Court Decision 12/PUU-V/2007. The Marriage Law (Law No 1 of 1974) and the Compilation of Islamic Law (Presidential Decision No 1 of 1999) require that consent to a polygamous marriage be obtained from the Religious Courts; that existing wives provide agreement, or the existing wife or wives be unable to perform their duties as a wife; and that there be guarantees to provide for all wives and children (Butt 2010: 268)

37　Constitutional Court Decision 19/PUU-VI/2008. Article 49 (1) of the Religious Courts law sets out the various arms of its jurisdiction including marriage, succession, payment of alms (*zakat*) and syariah economy matters.

Judicial review of the Blasphemy Law

In late 2009 a challenge was brought in the MK to the validity of the so-called Blasphemy Law.[38] The applicants included seven leading human rights and legal aid non-government organisations, as well as several prominent individuals including the former President, the late Abdurrahman Wahid. In addition, a group of fifty-four lawyers, known as the Freedom of Religion Advocacy Team, were identified as applicants. The Court recognised a total of twenty-four related parties comprising a wide range of religious organisations and inter-faith groups. Eleven of these were Islamic, including MUI, FPI and *Hizbut Tahrir Indonesia* (HTI). In support of the review case the application refers in outline to several case studies, including those of Yusman Roy and the whistling prayer case noted above.[39]

All of the Islamic bodies opposed the application, as did the Hindu, Buddhist and Confucian religious parent organisations. The court heard from a large number of expert witnesses called by the parties, related parties and the government, and the Court itself called seventeen expert witnesses. Written submissions were made by the related parties and submissions were made by the Minster for Religious Affairs and the Minister for Law and Human Rights and the DPR. The hearings of the Court were marked by protest action by Islamic groups, who displayed banners outside the Court, attended hearings, interjected during evidence, and at times allegedly intimated witnesses in and around the court (Margiyono et al. 2011 28–33; Menchik 2014: 612–613). A large group (possibly 500 strong) conducted a demonstration at the MK during the course of the review, and representatives of *ulama* from Madura submitted a petition personally to the Chair of the MK, who also appeared together with them in a press conference in the court building (Margiyono et al. 2011: 34–37).[40]

A substantial amount of expert evidence was received criticising the content of the various provisions constituting offences. The prominent Catholic priest, Frans Magnus Suseno (for the applicants), gave evidence as to the difficulties of interpreting and applying the law, discussing in his evidence the distinction between what does or does not amount to an act disgracing a religion, or

---

38 Constitutional Court Decision 140/PUU-VII/2009.
39 Due to the nature of judicial review in Indonesia, constitutional challenges proceed separate to any individual cases as there is no nexus between the general courts, which hold jurisdiction for trials and appeals, and the power of constitutional review. The MK is thus not an appeal court on constitutional issues for matters arising in the general courts. Instead, it hears 'in principle' applications regarding provisions of statutes claimed to be contrary to the Constitution. See Butt & Lindsey (2012: 87–88) and Fenwick (2009).
40 Prior to the release of the Court's decision, the Chair of the MK released a statement on his personal website declaring that the Court was independent and its ruling would be made solely on constitutional and legal grounds (Margiyono et al. 2011: 37).

deviating from its fundamental teachings.[41] He proposed that practising a religion or teaching not in accordance with fundamental principles of a faith did not amount to disgracing religion. This was because there is, in such cases, no intention to disgrace. He also suggested that the question of deviation suggested a deviation from the 'right path' (*jalan yang benar*), which was a relative concept: each party to a dispute would claim the other to be deviant because each would feel that their position was correct. The witness also noted that it was not within the competence of the state to consider whether a teaching was deviant; this was within the competence of the relevant religion.

Only one witness provided the MK with any comparative information about the issue of interpretation. Jalaluddin Rakhmat[42] referred to the application of the concept of disgracing a religion in Pakistan, and stated that what was required in that country was an element in the act that was contemptuous, reviling, scurrilous and ludicrous; spreading hatred was not enough, what was needed was the offending of religious sensibility. He stated that in Australia (without specifying by state) offending words must be harmful, and that there needed to be an element of vilification, the lowering of respect for religious figures such as through ridicule, or not showing respect for what was respected by that religion. For this reason, he suggested the Court should revise or provide a new interpretation of the law which protects all parties, permitting freedom for all to reconstruct religious thought. The Court later endorsed this view and adopted it in what it described as taking a 'middle path' (*jalan tengah*) approach to the case.[43]

MUI submission

Given its prominence as a national Islamic organisation, and the role of subnational branches of the organisation in the Roy case, it is valuable to consider its submission to the Court, which is quoted in full in the judgment, in detail.[44] The submission opened with the observation that the field of religious freedom in the *Reformasi* era presented both opportunities and challenges. It considered the promotion of Islam (*dakwah*) had progressed well but that numerous sects

---

41 Paragraph 2.2. The Court identified no fewer than nine expert witnesses, called by the Court itself, who agreed on the need for revision of the law so that its provisions were clearer and did not lead to errors in interpretation and practice.

42 Paragraph 3.31. Jalaluddin Rakhmat is an academic and a leading figure in Indonesia's Shia community.

43 Paragraph 3.71. The phrase is also used by the witness Yusril Izha Mahendra in a different context (paragraph 3.31). This witness, a former Minister for Law and Human Rights and prominent conservative Muslim figure, argues that Indonesia occupies a middle path between being a secular or religious state by adopting the notion of *ketuhanan* and rejecting constitutional recognition of the obligation of Muslims to implement Islamic law.

44 Paragraph 2.6.

had arisen promoting approaches that conflict with Islamic teaching, and there had been many cases of the abuse and 'disgracing' of Islam. Accordingly, it noted that MUI was obliged to take an active role guarding Islamic values and protecting the Islamic community (*umat*).

The submission went on to consider Islam and human rights. It stressed the influence of Western thinking and philosophy in international human rights instruments, and observed that Western beliefs on religion are generally influenced by 'secular thinking'. Human rights, in an Islamic perspective, on the other hand, cannot be separated from the responsibility to respect the rights of others. The MUI submission then noted that freedom of religion under the Constitution can be restricted by law under article 28J. In connection with this, MUI submitted that Indonesians held the view that human rights had to possess 'Indonesian characteristics', and that any right had to be balanced with the responsibility to respect the rights of others.

The submission further observed that in the fulfilment of human rights in Indonesia, as a democratic rule of law state (*negara hukum yang demokratis*), there were no absolute freedoms – absolute freedoms give rise to extraordinary danger and disorder, especially because religious matters carry significant sensitivity. According to MUI, the revocation of Law 1/PNPS/1965 could give rise to even more extraordinary turmoil. The law, in MUI's opinion, does not generally restrict interpretations of faith and religious activities, it only addresses that which deviates from fundamental religious teachings for the sake of creating order in society, the nation and the state, and to protect religion itself. Unrestricted, people would promote religious interpretations or conduct activities deviating from fundamental religious teachings and this would destroy the religious calm (*ketentraman beragama*) of Indonesian society. Should this be destroyed, it followed that the result would be the destruction of public order.

Court's decision

In its opinion,[45] the Court dealt at length with the relationship between the Constitution, the state and religion. It commenced by noting that the philosophical basis of the Indonesian state is the result of a compromise between two streams of thought – secular and Islamic, neither of which have been adopted as the basis of the state. The Court observed that the Indonesian concept of the *negara hukum* is not the same as either *rechstaat* or the concept of the *rule of law*.[46] This is based upon the fact that the Constitution places

---

45 Paragraphs 3.34–3.74.
46 The concept of the *negara hukum* (literally 'law state', or a nation of law) is often used in Indonesia in place of the phrase 'rule of law'. The 1945 Constitution in fact employs the other word referenced by the Court, the Dutch *rechstaat*, which conveys the concept of a state based on right, rather than might (*machstaat*); see Lindsey (1999: 13) and Lubis (1999: 171).

Ketuhanan Yang Maha Esa as the leading principle which, together with religious values, underpins the life of the people and state.[47] The Court further concluded that the Constitution does not allow for a campaign for freedom to not hold a religion (atheism), nor an anti-religion campaign. As a result, the Court determined that in the conduct of matters of state, formation of the law and the conduct of government business including justice, the basis of *ketuhanan* and religious teachings and values are the yardstick for ensuring good law or bad law, and for ensuring constitutional or unconstitutional law.[48]

The Court concluded its consideration of the *dasar negara* with a reference to the significance of religiosity in framing the whole conception of law:[49]

> The acknowledgement by the Indonesian people of the power of God and the foundation of *Ketuhanan Yang Maha Esa*, constitutes an acknowledgement that does not change whether from a philosophical or normative perspective.

The MK held that the *Pancasila* is a 'fundamental state norm' (*staatsfundamentalnorm*) (the Court cites the Indonesian philosopher Notonagoro on this point); it includes *Ketuhanan Yang Maha Esa* and cannot change (as opposed to a *grundnorm* which the MK stated is open to change).

On the question of the human rights provisions in the Constitution, the Court noted that freedom of belief cannot be forcibly restricted, nor adjudicated, but also observed that article 28J (2) provides for limiting rights, including on the basis of religious values.[50] The freedom to express thoughts and attitudes consistent with one's conscience can be restricted, as it concerns relations with others in society, but only by law, and solely with the objective of guaranteeing the recognition and acknowledgment of the freedom of others.[51] The Court remarked that while the case involved religion (a matter 'sacred to Indonesians') it also took note of the fact of the expanded affirmation of human rights following the Constitutional amendment process, which brought to the surface a new discourse concerning the relationship between the state and religion.[52]

---

47 'Prinsip Negara hukum Indonesia harus dilihat dengan cara pandang UUD 1945, yaitu negara hukum yang menempatkan prinsip Ketuhanan Yang Maha Esa sebagai prinsip utama, serta nilai-nilai agama yang melandasi gerak kehidupan bangsa dan negara . . .'; paragraph 3.34.10.

48 'dalam pelaksanaan pemerintahan negara, pembentukan hukum, pelaksanaan pemerintahan serta peradilan, dasar ketuhanan dan ajaran serta nilai-nilai agama menjadi alat ukur untuk menentukan hukum yang baik atau hukum yang buruk, bahkan untuk menentukan hukum yang konstitusional atau hukum yang tidak konstitusional'.

49 Paragraph 3.72.

50 Paragraphs 3.51, 3.34.11.

51 Paragraph 3.34.11.

52 Paragraph 3.36.

The Court went on to state that although interpretations of faith are a personal matter, they must be consistent with fundamental religious teachings using appropriate methodology based on relevant religious sources, such as the respective holy books.[53] Interpretations not based on 'recognised methodologies' can give rise to reactions that threaten security and public order if pronounced or conducted in public – the Court identifies this position as consistent with art 18 of the ICCPR, which allows for such limitations to freedom to manifest religion or belief as are necessary to protect public safety, order, health or morals or the fundamental freedoms or rights of others.[54]

The Court further stated that determination of a deviation in interpretation is to be based on the opinion of relevant religious authorities.[55] When an interpretation considered deviant is publicly promoted, this can disturb the religious peace in the relevant religious community, leading to unrest because that community feels stained (or disgraced) (*dinodai*). The Court concluded that the state would not be fulfilling its responsibility to create security and order in society by allowing reactions to arise in religious communities. Thus, legal provisions which prohibit publishing interpretations of religion that differ from those commonly adhered to are a form of preventive action against the possibility of horizontal conflict in the community.[56]

The Court stated that religious parent organisations (*organisasi keagamaan yang induk*) – without identifying any by name – are capable of becoming partners with the state in creating order in religious society. Indeed, the Court also observed that not only are the boundaries of religious values as communal values constitutionally valid, religious tradition in Indonesia is unique and is something in which the state cannot intervene.[57] Indonesia is not a nation where religious beliefs are separate from the state, and the state is assisted in monitoring developments in religion by the Department of Religion. The state did not act autonomously in this regard but determined the fundamental teachings of a religion as intended by Law 1/PNPS/1965, based on the agreement of those inside the religion itself (*pihak internal*).[58]

Almost in passing, and in response to an argument raised by the applicants, the Court considered the question of whether Indonesian law recognises only six religions (Islam, Protestantism, Catholicism, Hinduism, Buddhism and

---

53 Paragraph 3.52.
54 Paragraph 3.52.
55 Paragraph 3.55.
56 Paragraph 3.58.
57 '*pembatasan mengenai nilai-nilai agama sebagai nilai-nilai komunal* (communal values) *masyarakat adalah pembatasan yang sah menurut konstitusi. Tradisi keagamaan di Indonesia memang memiliki kekhasan dan keunikan yang memang tidak dapat dintervensi oleh negara . . . organisasi keagamaan yang induk . . . yang pada akhirnya mampu menjadi mitra negara dalam menciptakan ketertiban masyrakat beragama . . .*'.
58 Paragraph 3.53.

Confucianism). Turning to the clarification (*penjelasan*) to the Law, the Court noted that the Law does not prohibit the recognition or protection of any more than these six religions but rather recognises all religions that are practiced in Indonesia.[59] The clarification to the law observes that even Judaism, Zoroastrianism, Shintoism and Taoism are fully protected, so long as they do not breach the provisions in the law. Equally, the Court clearly acknowledged the rights of belief groups under art 28E (2) – but did not see discrimination suffered by them as stemming from errors in legal norms, only from administrative errors in the application of the law.[60]

Dissenting opinion

Justice Maria Farida delivered a separate, dissenting opinion.[61] She observed that while the Law in question was a product of the past, it was valid but contains several weaknesses as a result, particularly, of the human rights amendments to the Constitution made after the Law was passed – and, indeed, conflicts with those provisions. In particular, she referred in her conclusion to 'the occurrence of several problems which frequently give rise to arbitrary action in the implementation of the law'. These problems include the fact that, while in practice the law does not restrict the number of religions or beliefs, in reality, assistance and protection is only provided to six religions (as seen in the administration of identity cards, death certification and marriage registration).[62]

Justice Farida conducted a detailed study of the legislative history of Law 1/PNPS/1965 and noted that in the process of rendering the original Presidential Decree into legislation (under Law 5/1969) it was specified that the elevation to the level of legislation came with the stipulation that the decrees must be subject to 'improvements in the sense that the substance of the [decrees] is to be accommodated or to become material for the composition of new laws'. Justice Farida noted that the amendments to the Constitution provide constitutional protection for freedom of religion and for individuals to worship according to their faith, together with freedoms of belief and expression. These rights are further guaranteed in the Law 39/1999 on Human Rights and the legislation ratifying both international human rights covenants:

> From a juridical perspective the guarantee of freedom of religion and belief in the Indonesian legal regime is stated with a very firm foundation, so that accordingly the Indonesian Republic also holds the constitutional

---

59 Paragraph 3.54.
60 Paragraph 3.73.
61 Paragraph 6.2.
62 The majority agreed with Justice Farida on this point, holding that the requirement for notification of religion on identity cards is discriminatory.

responsibility and obligation to ensure the fulfilment of these rights, especially the right of all people to freedom of religion and belief.

The Constitution – compromise or compromised?

The role of the Constitutional Court forms perhaps the most important dimension of current efforts to analyse the nature of the Indonesian state and understand contemporary constitutionalism. For the first time since Independence, the nation has a high court of review that has the authority to interpret and apply the Constitution.[63] The MK dealt in the Blasphemy Case with notions of the rule of law and sought to distinguish the Indonesian *negara hukum* from 'Western' notions of the concept, while at the same time explaining the place of religion, or perhaps more accurately, religiosity, in Indonesian law and human rights. This decision adds to previous cases in which the Court has addressed directly the place of religion in the legal system, although in this case it did not need to address the scope for recognition or acknowledgement of syariah as such.

There is clear consensus on the primacy of religion as a leading source of guidance, but the jurisprudence is not clear on how to balance this with a comprehensive human rights regime or with a fully conceived democratic system. Most significantly here, the validation of administrative measures and sanctions under Law 1/PNPS/1965, which are void of any connection with legal procedures or review mechanisms, seems anomalous at best. There is also a degree of artificiality about the process of review, as while several case studies were identified in the application before the MK, the Court was interpreting the law in the abstract, and not in the context of an actual prosecution or set of facts. This renders discussion of the definition of key terms, or discussion of the impact of elements of offences, virtually impossible. Despite this, the MK was not operating in a vacuum, as evidenced by the protest action accompanying the hearing and the unusual sight of the Chair of the MK appearing in a press conference with religious scholars. The views, particularly of Islamic organisations were, in any event, evident from submissions which uniformly opposed the reading down of the Blasphemy Law.

The human rights dimension

As observed by Justice Farida in dissent, freedom of religion is heavily protected in Indonesian law, through two articles in the Constitution, human rights legislation and, arguably, also through Indonesia's accession to the ICCPR. The

63 See Fenwick (2009) for a review of the development of judicial review in Indonesia and the formation and role of the Constitutional Court.

majority in the MK drew upon art 18 of the ICCPR to reinforce its interpretation of the interaction between art 28 J (2) of the Constitution and the protection of religious freedom. The Court rested its decision entirely on the importance of maintaining public order, when public unrest arises in response to 'deviant' practices or teachings. The Court also refers to the importance of religious values as communal values when discussing the 'special place' of religious tradition in Indonesia. A single justice of the MK, Justice Harjono (who delivered a separate concurring opinion), dealt directly with the latent conflict between the protection of religion and the promotion of human rights, but without himself proposing a solution.[64]

In taking this approach, the Court implicitly rests blame for public disturbances upon groups that have themselves been the subject of sometimes violent protest, as seen earlier in the analysis of a large number of case studies of alleged blasphemy or deviant religious behaviour. In doing so, it fails to seek to balance, or in some way rationalise, the impact of its reasoning with the rights of the adherents to minority faiths. Indeed, despite stating the significance of communal rights, there is no attempt to consider the rights of 'deviant' faith groups themselves. The result is, in effect, the prioritising of majority rights, or what the Court must be taken to infer are majority rights, which it defines as being the rights of adherents to any religion recognised by the Indonesian state as formally established. Moreover, the Court makes special mention of the important role of religious parent organisations in assisting to distinguish between mainstream and 'deviant' doctrine.

The Court's reasoning could have been augmented by reference to the international and comparative commentary on the right to religious freedom. It has been observed, for example, that international instruments hold 'inviolate' the '*forum internum*' or the right of an individual to their particular form of belief (Durham & Scharffs 2010: 165). The Court adopted the distinction between the internal forum of belief and the external forum of expression or the manifestation of belief, but its reasoning reveals uncertainty – or confusion – as to the practical application of this concept. For example, it explained that the interpretation of faith is part of the internal forum but held: 'this interpretation must be consistent with the principle teachings of religion through correct

---

64 Paragraph 6.1: 'when the existence of [the law under challenge] is related to the amendments to the 1945 Constitution clearly there are two provisions, that is the protection of religion on the one hand and the freedom to hold a faith on the other hand. In the Indonesian law state, the relationship between these two provisions needs to be combined in a formula that doesn't negate one or the other provision. The application of the law in question in a literal fashion whether from the perspective of the arrangement of the words or the clarification and without reference to the contemporary context can give rise to an imbalance when devising a formula that does not negate either provision'.

methodology based on relevant religious sources . . . freedom to interpret religion is not unconditional or absolute'.[65]

Durham and Scharffs (2010: 205) state that there is no doubt concerning the validity of restrictions on religious freedom – the issue that arises is how the limitations are to be drawn. The United Nations Human Rights Committee General Comment No 22 on art 18 of the ICCPR addresses this directly.[66] Thus restriction is only allowed for the reasons stated in art 18 (3) (public safety, public order, health or morals, or the rights and freedoms of others). They must be applied only for the purposes they are prescribed; must be directly related and proportionate to the specific need; and may not be imposed for a discriminatory purpose or in a discriminatory manner. Public order is taken to mean a measure that protects against disturbance or disorder that threatens 'concrete harm' (Durham & Scharffs 2010: 232–233). The European Convention on Human Rights art 9 includes a further provision that any limitations must be 'necessary in a democratic society' (Durham & Scharffs 2010: 233).[67] This provision has been interpreted by the European Court as requiring a proportionate response to the aim to be pursued, and that state responses must be neutral and impartial and not arbitrary or burdensome (Durham & Scharffs 2010).[68]

A further element of the General Comment is of particular interest in the light of the approach taken by the MK, particularly its emphasis on the central, guiding role played by religion in all aspects of law and policy. The committee states in the General Comment:

> If a set of beliefs is treated as official ideology in constitutions, statutes, proclamations of ruling parties, etc., or in actual practice, this shall not result in any impairment of the freedom under article 18 or any other rights recognised under the Covenant nor in any discrimination against persons who do not accept the official ideology or who oppose it.

More broadly, the United Nations Special Rapporteur on Freedom of Religion has observed that the right to freedom of religion and belief 'does not include

---

65 Paragraph 3.52.
66 General Comment Adopted by the Human Rights Committee Under Article 40, Paragraph 4, of the International Covenant on Civil and Political Rights, Addendum, General comment No 22 (48) (art. 18), CCPR/C/21/Rev.1/Add.4, 27 September 1993.
67 Sezgin (1999: 15), writing about personal status systems, observes that it is not always clear when a democratic state should intervene in order to save citizens from 'the oppression of her community' – the point being that they should have options 'especially when there is a direct and imminent threat by communal norms and institutions to the constitutionally protected rights and freedoms'.
68 McLaughlin (2010: 420–425) considers the European standard in the context of the question of defamation of religion and suggests it is 'a workable benchmark' for national laws and discusses how the test might apply in particular country settings.

the right to have a religion or belief that is free from criticism or ridicule' (Blitt 2010: 16). This comment has particular relevance for cases such as those involving the publication of material considered derogatory of Islam (of which there have been several).[69]

Article 28J (2) provides a source of weakness for potentially every human right adopted in the Constitution and Indonesian law.[70] It negates the non-derogable status assigned to specific rights including the right to freedom of religion. Moreover, while it reflects the principle, established in both the UDHR[71] and ICCPR, that states may lawfully place some restrictions on enjoyment of human rights, art 28J (2) extends the permissible grounds in an important way. That is, in addition to being able to establish lawful restrictions on rights such as on the grounds of public order, the Indonesian state may restrict rights – including the right to freedom of religion – on the ground of 'religious values', a ground not adopted in art 18 of the ICCPR.[72] This presents the unusual situation of faith itself being a potential basis for restricting the experience of religious freedom.[73]

The internationally accepted grounds for limitations to rights of morality and the fundamental rights and freedoms of others are arguably sufficient to provide a measure of special protection (if required) for religion and belief. Indeed, groups claiming offence in the conduct or words of another might argue that their enjoyment of their religious freedom has been affected by an alleged act of blasphemy, or that moral standards have been adversely affected, and that regulation is justified to manage such situations. Nevertheless, the additional ground puts beyond doubt the authority of a government to provide special measures to protect faith. It is a critical counterpoint to the primary acknowledgement of religiosity in the preamble and, as a substantive provision in the

69 See the case studies examined by Sihombing (et al. 2012) and discussed above.
70 The Court has on two occasions adopted a similar approach to another non-derogable right under the Constitution, the right to life. In two instances it has rejected challenges to the existence of the death penalty on the grounds that art 28J (2) permits restriction to constitutional rights, although in one of the two challenges a minority of the Court agreed with the applicants (Butt 2014).
71 Article 29 (2) of the UDHR substantially repeats the same exceptions.
72 Blitt (2010: 17–18) notes that resolutions of the UNGA and Human Rights Committee in the context of religion and the right to freedom of expression have been similarly extended with the addition of 'respect for religion and belief' as among the objectives for valid exceptions or modification to rights, a development he attributes to the lobbying of the OIC, the Organisation of the Islamic Conference.
73 Hefner (2011: 26–27) observes that there is tension between the liberal principles of the UDHR and some Islamic approaches to freedom of expression which reflect a classical approach to syariah. This has also been seen in communitarian and Catholic critiques of the 'individualistic features of liberal philosophy' as the UDHR 'says little about the need for individuals or institutions to uphold any specific idea of the good' (Hefner 2011).

body of the Constitution, may arguably have more legal potency than the reference to *ketuhanan*.

The law reconsidered

As seen above, the text of the Blasphemy Law was criticised by numerous experts. The analysis of those experts called by the applicants was more specific, and addressed the terms of the provisions in some detail. The MK, and experts called by it, noted the problems arising from the drafting and linked this to practical consequences of interpretation, a point raised by the dissenting Justice. The majority in the Court, however, did not take the opportunity to provide any guidance, relying on a strict interpretation of its role and stating that it does not have the authority to make editorial changes or of a kind relating to content, this being the role of lawmakers as part of the normal legislative process.[74] The MK is not incorrect in defining its role in this way, but it is hard to see how the Court could not accept any role for interpretation of the words of a Law under challenge. The Court's practice in this respect is not consistent. It has, for example, determined statutes to be 'conditionally constitutional' in cases where it considers language to be vague or open to interpretation, requiring certain interpretations to be applied (Butt & Lindsey 2012: 133–134). The Court has also attempted to remedy constitutional defects by effectively issuing instructions to the government and legislature (Butt & Lindsey 2012: 115–118).

The provisions of the Criminal Code are most relevant for this research, as they were the basis of the prosecution of Yusman Roy. The elements of the offences established by arts 156a and 157 will be discussed at greater length in the context of the case study in Chapter 6, however it is important to review briefly the notion of blasphemy or offences against religion. There are several key terms in art 156a but, broadly, both this provision and art 157 address hostile or offensive behaviour or statements. Article 156a includes the additional term 'disgracing' (*penodaan*), which appears to be too broad to be capable of consistent or clear interpretation and application (Lindsey 2012a: 407, 428). Added ambiguity arises from the lack of a preposition between the two sub-paragraphs of the article. This raises the question as to whether both parts of the offence are required for a conviction – does the behaviour have to meet the test of offensiveness or disgrace, and also be directed at encouraging godlessness? If so, this element suggests a very high threshold of conduct to be capable of being captured by the provisions, and a quite particular form of conduct, which would also appear to include a mental element of intention (which would require a clear evidentiary basis).

---

74 Paragraph 3.71.

Neither provision necessarily addresses 'blasphemous' conduct unless the abusive, offensive of contemptuous acts or expressions are specifically grounded in some issue of doctrine or practice. Demonstrating this in reality may be problematic – recall above the evidence of Frans Magnus Suseno, who queried the competence of the state to determine matters of deviancy. The broad term 'disgracing' might be capable of encompassing the acts or expressions that are hostile or offensive, but it is only the provisions in the original Decree forming the basis of administrative action and sanction that appear to come close to an inherently religious issue. Deviant behaviour, in the sense of moving away from central teachings, clearly has the potential to include blasphemous conduct, although the concept seems more closely aligned with the notion of apostasy or withdrawal from the faith.[75]

Fundamentally the question arises as to whether Indonesia has a 'blasphemy' law or does it maintain a de facto blasphemy regime?[76] None of the criminal provisions use the Indonesia word for blasphemy, *penghujahan*. Blasphemy has been equated with 'direct criticism of God and sacred objects' and with sacrilegious behaviour,[77] and also with the protection of institutions, including the state itself. A challenge to the Christian faith in England, for example, was, in the past, condemned as a subversion of the law (Blitt 2010: 5–6; Mirza 2003: 351).[78] The law, as it developed in England, appears in fact to have permitted certain forms of 'dissent or denial of Christian doctrine' so long as it was expressed in ways that did not insult the deepest feelings and religious sentiments of the 'great majority' (Mirza 2003: 351). Pringle (2011: 321) notes that it has since been seen as desirable in liberal democracies to address religious

---

75 This notion is, however, found in the regional regulations in Aceh, as noted above.

76 I describe the legal framework in this way in Fenwick (2011: 513). The concept of a de facto blasphemy or apostasy regime has also been raised by Marshall and Shea (2011) in their coverage of religiously based prosecutions in Egypt. In that case, a key provision is contained in art 98 of the Egyptian Penal Code, which prohibits 'ridiculing or insulting a heavenly religion' (Marshall and Shea 2011: 62). The law is deployed against Baha'is, but Pink (2003: 430) argues it is 'vague' and is used against those said to exploit religion to 'sow discord, weaken national unity or to deride revealed religions'. Islamic law does not apply in these instances to Baha'i, argues Pink (2003), but 'this does not mean, however, that religion is not an issue here'. Arrests of Baha'is are 'at least, outwardly, driven by the intention to protect "true religions" and to exclude from the public sphere religions that are not recognised by Islam as revealed religions' (Pink 2003: 430). For a more detailed discussion of the deployment of criminal law in Egypt in cases of alleged blasphemy including art 98F see Freedom House (undated).

77 The Oxford Dictionary of English defines 'blasphemy' as 'the action or offence of speaking sacrilegiously about God or sacred things . . .' and 'sacrilege' is defined as 'violation or misuse of what is regarded as sacred'.

78 See Crouch (2012) for further references on this question and Blitt (2010) for more discussion of the history of the offence in the common law world. Mirza (2003: 351) notes that 'attacks on God were viewed as attacks on the state' and the offence was moved from trial in the ecclesiastical courts to the common law courts in the seventeenth century.

insult or outrage 'in terms of such neighbouring categories as offensiveness or obscenity', draining blasphemy of its (religious) meaning. As a consequence, '*specific* protections for godly persons' effectively disappears, and the category of religious insult is neutralised by its incorporation into more general provisions (Pringle 2011: 316, 322).

Indonesian commentators have previously identified very clearly the limitations of the offences in the criminal law, and a government legal research team was tasked in the early 1970s to review religious influences on criminal law. Its report (LPHN 1974: 9) considers the 'interrelationship between state and religion' which arises from the influence of religion in the establishment of criminal legal norms. The report (LPHN 1974: 12) proposes a theoretical framework for the establishment of criminal offences, arguing they should be based on one or a combination of three theories, depending on which legal concerns (*kepentingan*) are sought to be protected:

a   Protection of the peace, which considers public order as the legal concern that must be protected;

b   protection of feelings/emotions, which aims to protect religious feelings; and

c   protection of religion, which sees religion as the legal concern that must be protected.[79]

The report (LPHN 1974: 13) goes on to distinguish 'religious offences' and 'offences relating to religion'. The former include offences in relation to God, religious organisations, the Prophet, Holy Book, the *umat* (or congregation of believers), and proposes that it is not important for the offence to endanger or breach the public order but 'their criminalisation must be based on Divine Truth/its essence' (LPHN 1974). Ideally, it is argued, these offences should be contained in a separate Chapter of the Criminal Code, rather than being 'sprawled' among general crimes (LPHN 1974).[80] Turning directly to art 156a, the report (LPHN 1974) notes that this provision does not include acts which ridicule or insult God, and the provision:

> does not contain a criminal offence such as in the Netherlands and Germany known as 'blasphemy' [*Godslastering*] (for example individuals stating that Jesus is a false prophet, which has occurred, individuals trampling on the Qur'an or the Bible etc.).

---

79 The report ascribes to each of these the following German terms: *Friedensschutz-theorie*, *Gefuhlsschutz-theorie* and *Religionsschutz-theorie*.

80 The report (LPHN 1974: 28–30) goes on to recommend twelve specific offences which endanger or attack religion such as ridiculing the name or attributes of God and impeding or undermining acts of worship, and several offences that relate to religion such as attacks on houses of worship.

For this reason the research team recommends (LPHN 1974) the Criminal Code be amended to include a provision specifically to accommodate the criminalisation of 'blasphemy'.

In a longer exploration of the same issues, Omar Seno Adji (1984: 68)[81] agrees that the primacy of religion in the *Pancasila* state effectively mandates the creation of religious offences. Adji (1984) holds that religion can play a role in the establishment of moral offences, and in his view:

> it does not cause the slightest problem for our legislative efforts, when religious elements become the central and vital point in the creation of such offences, harmonised in their relationship with our legal consciousness.

According to Adji (1984: 69) the criminal offences found in the chapter of the modern Code dealing with public order are similar in both Indonesian and Dutch law, and reflect earlier Indonesian criminal provisions. In some cases they demonstrate a different formulation but a similar spirit, 'whereas the well-known law named 'Blasphemy' [*Godslasteringswet*] . . . [introduced in the Netherlands in 1932] . . . was regarded as less suitable for the legal reality of the earlier Indonesian criminal code' (Adji 1984). While 'blasphemy' did not find a home in Indonesian law, pre-independence Indonesia 'hate-speech' articles [*haatzaai-artikelen*] were introduced in the modern Code in the 'unpopular' art 156 in order to combat the nationalist and independence movement (Adji 1984). He argues art 156a is not independent of these other 'hate-speech' provisions and is of an 'undemocratic' character due to its colonial roots (Adji 1984: 74). In Adji's (1984) view, such provisions were not tolerated in the Netherlands itself, as they offend against freedom of expression. Adji (1984: 84–85) observes that the provisions found in Chapter 5 of the Code (arts 156, 156a and 157) are aimed at protecting public order, and that this is a form of secularising of offences against religion as they are not directed at religion itself. Like the MK, Adji (1984) suggests that pronouncements or statements captured by art 156a can endanger public order by disturbing religious adherents, an interpretation which potentially shifts the onus against the person expressing their faith in favour of those claiming to be 'disturbed'.

Observations on the dasar negara

There is, on one view, nothing particularly remarkable in the recognition that Islam, or Islamic values, may be transformed into law in a democratic process. Islam, strictly speaking, remains outside the formal boundaries of the

---

81 The late Omar Seno Adji was Minister for Justice between 1966 and 1974 and Chief Justice of the Supreme Court between 1974 and 1982. He was also a member of the research team that produced the government report (LPHN 1974).

constitution in Indonesia. Repeated attestation, and judicial reinforcement, of the singular importance of religion in the Indonesian way of life provides, however, a critical launching place for faith. This place is occupied by Islam, which functions as a source of inspiration for law-making, interpretation and application, and in certain circumstances as an indirect source of law. This is because given the priority accorded to godliness and the context of a pious Muslim society, when religious issues arise for consideration, Islam will inevitably be seen as offering solutions.

The MK's deferral to communal values and group rights, together with the special place afforded religion, reflects a form of legal or constitutional majoritarianism. Despite the Court's stated approach of taking a 'middle way' in reaching its decision on the Blasphemy Law, the Court has established a new benchmark for religion, making it the touchstone of good or bad, valid or invalid, law. The practical effect of the decision is to make *ketuhanan* 'the axis for the whole Indonesian legal system' (Margiyono et al. 2011: 86).

The Court's determination that those holding faith must ascribe to core teachings restricts both the internal and external dimensions of religious freedom, and ultimately places power in the hands of religious authorities – with the result that any member of any faith can potentially suffer discrimination with no certainty of redress or protection. The dual objectives of protecting religion and promoting religious freedom are not necessarily in conflict. It could be argued, for example, that, absent provision in the law preventing hostile or offensive attacks on faith, the right to religious freedom lacks substance. As currently interpreted, however, the legal framework does little to promote genuine freedom, or to provide appropriate limitations on state power or on the influence of religious organisations. Religious pluralism is advanced through the legal protection of religious freedom in Indonesia, but its fulfilment is truncated through the pursuit of 'godly nationalism' (Menchik 2014).

Conclusion

It is not surprising that, in a Muslim majority nation, most of the legal and administrative effort under the blasphemy regime is against Muslims. The rulings of the MK maintain, however, that the Constitution allows the prosecution in certain circumstances of those that pursue and promote 'deviant' interpretations of the majority faith. Indonesian jurisprudence stresses the supremacy of religiosity – and the Constitution is interpreted as virtually mandating the adherence to religion among Indonesians. The MK also reinforces the important role of religious parent organisations which, in the case of Islam, means that MUI has a special place in the promotion of Islam.

The MK decision is unsatisfactory for its failure to come to grips with either the simple issue of the interpretation of elements of offences and legal terminology, or the more complex problem of balancing contradictory provisions in the Constitution. Human rights cannot be both non-derogable and subject to lawful limitation. The Court relies on a formulaic interpretation of key human rights provisions and does not explore international or comparative material in arriving at its decision. An individual's experience of faith is confined by reference to orthodox interpretations of religious doctrine and by broader community expectations (or what the court considers such community standards to be). The priority accorded to national stability moreover reflects a pre-*Reformasi* (authoritarian) concept of governance in which the interests of security and stability are promoted in preference to individual rights. At the same time as preferencing state control, formal acknowledgement has been given by the MK to the function of religious authorities not only as guardians of faith but also as partners with government in promoting religiosity and – thereby – social harmony.

There remain questions about the way Indonesian law mediates between the two key fields of promotion of religion and protection of the right of religious freedom. There is agreement that current law requires redrafting and, as criticism of the blasphemy regime is longstanding, this issue is capable of resolution. Scholarly commentary suggests, however, that any reform of the law would result in a legislated blasphemy regime that would not satisfy the critics of the status quo. For the moment, a de facto blasphemy regime is in place which provides a vehicle for potentially arbitrary law enforcement action. Arbitrariness arises from the absence of clarity regarding the interpretation and proper application of key terms and provisions in the law, and the MK's literal application of the Constitution's human rights provisions. The Court's 'middle road' position reflects in many respects the historic stalemate between proponents of a liberal constitution, and proponents of an Islamic basis for law-making.

4 MUI – The institutionalising of Indonesian Islam

This chapter considers some elements of Islamic law and practice particularly relevant to the case study, with a particular emphasis on the way in which Islam has developed, and is currently experienced, in Indonesia. Emphasis is given to MUI which, while not the only significant Muslim organisation in Indonesia's diverse civil or non-state Islam, has adopted a very assertive posture in relation to the promotion of Islamic law. Its evolution during the years following *Reformasi* is an important dimension in Indonesia's democratic transformation. MUI also plays a prominent role through the issuing of *fatawa*, or religious rulings, and its views on what is considered to be deviant religious teaching or activity are important to an understanding of the application of the Blasphemy Law.

More specifically, I try to understand the significance of the concept of innovation – *bid'ah* – within Islamic thought, which was the issue of religious doctrine underlying the prosecution of Yusman Roy. A broader social context will be outlined using the concept of piety as a social marker in Indonesia.[1] This analysis includes a review of the labels or categories attached to Muslim groups based on different approaches to doctrine, focusing on ritual worship and the importance of doctrinal differences in disputes among groups in Indonesian Islam. MUI's evolution sits within broader change underway in this categorisation, and this has implications for the promotion of religion in state law.

The focus in this chapter is on the degree of tolerance that exists, or that has existed in the past, to variation in Islamic ritual. This focus derives from the fact that, as noted in Chapter 1, the performance of worship is a matter of great importance in Islam. The question of innovation involves a consideration of the evolution of Islam in Indonesia, and its historical and contemporary practice. There is clear evidence in Indonesia of variation in practice, including interpretations of Islamic ritual obligations that vary from mainstream or orthodox requirements. I do not seek to attempt to resolve the theological arguments that arise

---

1 Hirji (2010: 7) notes that 'for many Muslims today, religion is a critical marker of personhood and community, increasingly overriding other markers such as social status and ethnicity'.

from the case study. However, the discussion of innovation helps to explain the actions and responses of parties in the case, and MUI's reaction in particular. This chapter helps to place Roy's actions in context, and also adds to understanding the place of religious doctrine given the applicable Indonesian law, and the legal process.

Islam in Indonesia

According to Ricklefs (2001: 14), documentary evidence supports the conclusion that 'the Islam of Indonesia has been full of heterodoxy and heresy, a fact which later encouraged major reformist movements in the nineteenth and twentieth centuries'. Worship, in particular, functions as a 'primary sign of Muslim identity' in Indonesia, and can serve to badge Muslim identity as against non-Muslims, or indeed be used to distinguish different Muslim identities (Bowen 1989: 612). Ricklefs' (2007: 11) own research led him to propose that, historically, Javanese Islam was characterised by a 'mystic synthesis' that included a strong commitment to Islamic identity and widespread observance of the five pillars of faith, but combined with an acceptance of local (non-Islamic) spiritual forces. The approach to prayer is a regular subject of discussion in Ricklefs' (2007: 30) research and he identified a divergence of approaches emerging during the nineteenth century, driven by differing approaches to ritual that challenged the established mystic synthesis.[2]

Categories of social and religious identity applied to Indonesian Islam developed particular significance with the publishing of Clifford Geertz's *The Religion of Java*, which advanced a three-way classification of Javanese society (Ricklefs 2007: 85): *santri*, *abangan* and *priyai*.[3] Geertz's social/religious classifications have been criticised for being simplistic, and for confusing religious behaviour and social strata,[4] however the categories *abangan* and *santri* in particular have become familiar tools of analysis to students of Javanese society.[5] The *abangan* were characterised by their failure to behave as 'proper' Muslims by rejecting the pillars of Islam, and by the late nineteenth century they arguably constituted the majority of Javanese (Ricklefs 2007: 85–86). Ricklefs (2007: 103–104) notes, with reference to the elements of his 'mystic synthesis', that Islamic identity (the

2 The case study is situated in East Java. Javanese mystical poems dating to the early nineteenth century, for example, at times ridicule ritual piety and, specifically, the pursuit of worship through fixed prayer times (Ricklefs 2007: 36).
3 The latter identifying the class of Javanese administrative officials (Ricklefs 2001: 168).
4 See Muhaimin (1995). Azra (2005: 1–2) describes the influence Geertz's typology as the 'myth of *abangan*', which led to the majority of Indonesian Muslims being considered only nominal Muslims, and hence contributing the view that Southeast Asian Islam was marginal and peripheral to Middle Eastern Islam.
5 *Santri* is a term used to describe pious Muslims, a group also known as *putihan*, or 'white ones'. *Abangan* is a term derived from low Javanese meaning 'brown ones'.

first element) and observation of the five pillars (the second element) became the territory of the *santri*, with belief in local spiritual powers (the final element), becoming the territory of the *abangan* alone.[6]

Fealy and Hooker (2006: 39) identify four social categories as dominating Indonesia's Islamic community over the past century. These categories include the *santri* and *abangan* groups, with the *santri* further divided into Traditionalist and Modernist Muslims (Fealy & Hooker 2006). 'Traditionalist' and 'Modernist' were terms applied, respectively, to Indonesia's two large 'mass' Islamic civil society organisations, NU and Muhammadiyah.[7] Fealy and Hooker (2006: 40) describe Traditionalist/Modernist division as primarily a 'doctrinal divide', although it also reflects socio-economic, political and cultural elements.

The defining characteristics of Traditionalists are seeking to preserve medieval Islamic scholarship (including reliance upon the four schools of Islamic law) and a tolerance for local custom in religious practice; Modernists, who are also referred to as 'reformists', regard the theology and ritual practices of the Traditionalists as deviation from the original teachings of Islam (Bush 2009: 30; Fealy & Hooker 2006: 40).[8] Abolishing innovation was therefore one of the primary objectives of the Modernist movement, which emphasised a return to the original sources of Islam (the Qur'an and *sunna*), the diversity and heterodoxy found in Indonesia being considered unacceptable (Ricklefs 2001: 213–215; 2007: 221).[9] Modernism has been described as a 'conservative intellectual revolution' and puritan in nature (Ricklefs 2001: 212–213; 2007: 220).[10] It is defined by opposition to un-Islamic accretions and innovations during the medieval and early modern period that 'had corrupted the faith and lead Muslims into error' (Fealy & Hooker 2006: 40). The efforts of reformists, at least in Java, were highly effective and resulted in a 'great transformation' of practice in popular religion (Hefner 1995: 33).

---

6 These tendencies are also reflected in data which indicate that by the 1960s only between 0–15% of Central Javanese villagers prayed (Ricklefs 2007: 104, n39).
7 See Fealy & Hooker (2006: 40–41), Ricklefs (2001: 214; 2007: 221), and Saeed (2005: 6). Federspiel (1970: 57) describes Muhammadiyah as an 'orthodox' religious movement, and orthodox Muslims as obliged 'to establish, whenever possible, community responsibility for fulfilment of religious obligations'. NU was established to 'counter the Modernist aspirations of Muhammadiyah', and defended a 'syncretic Javanese understanding' of Islamic doctrine (Lindsey 2012a: 122). They are described as mass organisations due to their memberships which reportedly reach as high as 30m–40m members each (Lindsey 2012a: 119, 121).
8 Traditionalists accept local beliefs and practices possibly on the basis that suppressing such traditions would weaken devotion among Muslims (Bush 2009: 30).
9 Both organisations were primarily concerned with social development but NU was formed 'in order to protect the traditional rituals and practices they adhered to' such as forms of Sufism, and the visiting of tombs, considered *bid'ah* by Muhammadiyah (Bush 2009: 6–7, 14).
10 Bush (2009: 30–31) notes that the reformist/modernist movement in Islam was influenced by the earlier Wahabi movement originating in Arabia. Wahabism was based upon the objective of ridding Islam of corruption stemming from the integration of Sufi Islam and 'popular Islam'.

The divide between these two groupings – Traditionalist and Modernist – narrowed during the twentieth century, following independence and the adoption of *Pancasila* (Saeed 2005: 7), although scholars only noticed in the late 1980s and early 1990s that the historical gap between the two groups as being bridged (Bush 2009: 11–12). Categories of Muslim identity in Indonesia, however, remain relevant. Bush argues (2009: 11), for example, that following the events of 1965 'it was no longer safe to take a desultory attitude towards religion'. Bush is here referring to the failed coup and the anti-communist violence unleashed subsequently, which brought Soeharto to power and saw the end of the Soekarno presidency.[11] Beside the crucial political changes that took place, the period was also significant for Modernists who had hoped that the fall of Indonesian communism would result in greater power for Islam (Ricklefs 2001: 343). From this critical point in time scholars have identified the emergence of 'Neo-Modernism', whose members demonstrated a capacity to 'synthesise traditionalism with modernism' (Saeed 2005: 8).[12] Doctrine also forms a part of this evolution in categories of Islam, and Saeed (2005: 9–10) notes the approach of Neo-Modernists to Qur'anic scholarship led to claims of *bid'ah* and even heresy from their ultra-conservative opponents.

Key ideas characteristic of Neo-Modernist thought include an emphasis on the fact that the Qur'an was revealed at a certain time and in a particular context and should be interpreted in this light, and that classical scholars interpreted the Qur'an taking their cue from their particular social and political contexts, thus emphasising some parts over others (Saeed 2005: 9–10). Alternative labels for the Neo-Modernist movement include 'contextualism' and 'liberal Islam' (Saeed 2005). Consistent themes in Neo-Modernist writing, in addition to the question of Qur'anic interpretation, have been pluralism and anti-sectarianism (Bush 2009: 12). Saeed (2005: 11) identifies one of the key reasons behind the emergence of the Neo-Modernist movement as being the freedom available to the religious thinkers involved to explore new ideas. He contrasts this with the relative homogeneity in other parts of the Muslim world where 'local

11 See, for example, Ricklefs (2001: 338–341). The links between Indonesian Islamic organisations and the rise of Soeharto's New Order are well documented, including the role of NU's youth wing in the conduct of mass killings in 1965–1966 (Anwar 2007: 197; Bruinessen 2013: 2; Drakeley 2014; Sukma 2003: 43). Communism was widely associated with atheism, and therefore considered antithetical to the interests of Muslim Indonesians, and Drakeley (2014: 202–203) notes the mutual antipathy between communists and groups such as the Islamic Student Association. Conversely, Hefner (2013: 23) observes that 'the scale of the killings led some two million nominal Muslims to repudiate their faith, converting to Christianity or, in smaller numbers, Hinduism'.
12 The leading Indonesian neo-Modernist, Nurcholish Madjid, has been considered above. He is part of a 'long line' of thinkers since the late nineteenth century who 'have argued that the shari'a does not provide a fixed or all-encompassing model for politics' (Hefner 2011b: 7).

orthodoxies' are protected by the state, and contrary views 'might be considered dangerous or heretical' (Saeed 2005). Saeed (2005) comments:

> because of the pluralistic nature of Indonesian society and the absence of a unified religious outlook, it is difficult for a particular local orthodoxy to be imposed. It is impossible even for a centralised institution such as the national Majelis Ulama Indonesia . . . to impose its own views on what is or is not Islamic.[13]

Equally, Bush (2009: 12) identifies Bahtiar Effendy's[14] 'substantialist' Islam as an important body of thought which emerged at a similar time to Neo-Modernism. Effendy noted the development of liberal intellectual thought among Indonesian Muslims from the 1970s onwards, and himself promoted substantialist Islam as a counter to 'scripturalist' Islam (Bush 2009). Substantialist Islam was characterised by a rejection of the formal, legalistic expression of Islam and the ideological and symbolic issues of political Islam (such as an Islamic state), and emphasised religious and political tolerance (Bush 2009).

The most recent categorization of Indonesian Islam is either 'extreme' or 'moderate', and Bush (2009: 13) highlights the argument of William Liddle, who predicted that scripturalist Islam would proliferate in post-Soeharto Indonesia. Liddle proposed (2002) that the relevant distinctions for Indonesian Islam in the future would be 'between non-Muslims, syncretists, traditionalists and liberal modernist Muslims on one side and conservative modernist Muslims on the other', which Bush summarises as the moderate-militant divide (Bush 2009: 13).[15] The Modernist–Traditionalist split is not synonymous – according to Bush – with the moderate–militant divide, because, while the 'overwhelming majority' of both Muhammadiyah and NU reject the militant agenda, both camps include components that were 'variously for or against an Islamist agenda' (Bush 2009: 195). These contemporary developments are entirely consistent with earlier scholarship on the development of Indonesian Islam. Azra (2005: 2) notes that scholars since the mid-twentieth century have remarked on the move over hundreds of years towards a more orthodox form of religion (and the notion of a 'conservative turn' was raised in Chapter 1).

Ricklefs (2008) also addresses at length the contemporary classification of Indonesian Islam. He proposes that the general public discourse post-Soeharto

---

13 This chapter advances a view that MUI is, in fact, successful in imposing its views, particularly as it is able to obtain support of the law and state institutions.
14 Professor at the State Islamic University, Jakarta.
15 Liddle's framework was presented in collaboration with an Indonesian scholar Saiful Mujani. Bush discusses the categories of Indonesian Islam in the context of her own argument that so-called *aliran* politics remains a valid categorisation. *Aliran* ('stream') here refers to the alignment of political parties with religio-social constituencies (Ricklefs 2008: 120–121).

tends to support a simple division between 'liberals and moderates' on one hand and 'radicals and extremists'[16] on the other, but concludes that the reality is 'complex, confused and confusing' (Ricklefs 2008: 122–123, 133). He provides a detailed account of the wide variety of expressions of Islam in contemporary Java,[17] and also records examples of 'infiltration' (a term used by Indonesians) of both Muhammadiyah and NU by 'puritan' elements (Ricklefs 2008: 129–130). The complexity of the contemporary scene is evidenced in part by the fact that these organisations recognise they have been 'infiltrated', which suggests resistance to the attempt by more radical groups to influence their agendas. Ricklefs (2008: 134) ultimately concludes that features of a trend towards ongoing 'polarisation' are clearly identifiable, that is that, in essence, both 'puritan extremists' and their opponents may be gaining strength.[18] The label 'puritan' has been attached to MUI, and it has in fact embraced conservative Islamic voices within its structure. Following consideration of the question of innovation and an introduction to MUI, I will return again to the categorisation of Indonesian Islam.

Innovation and related concepts

It was seen above that among the issues forming part of disputes about doctrine in Indonesian Islam were differences in approach to 'innovation'.[19] The historical discourse in Islam holds that '"illegitimate innovation" (*bid'a*) is not tolerated in acts of *ibadat*', and this thinking leads to an 'overriding concern with

---

16 Azra's (2005: 10) detailed discussion of radicalism associates this term with religiously inspired violence, including terrorism, and he argues that there have been two centuries of Islamic radicalism in Southeast Asia.

17 He includes Muhammadiyah in East Java (considered puritanical and immoderate); the central-Java *pesantren* of radical cleric Abu Bakar Ba'asyir; small independent grassroots movements in central Java; a Sufi order, also based in central Java; a liberal and feminist-oriented civil society movement based in West Java; and the progressive Liberal Islam Network (JIL) based in Jakarta (Ricklefs 2008: 122–132). JIL is described by Anwar (2007: 187) as emerging in response to the rise of 'radical conservative Islam' in the early post-Soeharto years. Anwar's opposing categories of Radical-Conservative Islam and Progressive-Liberal Islam are not quite as stark as the liberal/moderate:radical/extremist divide identified by Ricklefs (2008) but generally reflect the kind of continuing polarisation he discusses. JIL was formed by young, urban and well educated Muslims who believe that 'the entire corpus of Islamic teachings needs to be contextually reinterpreted' (Anwar 2007: 216). JIL is not the sole group in the progressive-liberal camp but Anwar (2007: 217) considers it the most outspoken.

18 'Polarisation' is Ricklefs' (2007) own term, originally used to describe trends in late nineteenth and early twentieth century Javanese Islam.

19 Masud (1993: 55, 61–66) argues that the concept has not been studied properly, particularly when compared with the doctrine of *sunna*, and he provides a thorough review of the history of innovation in *fatawa* literature.

conformity to ritual norms in carrying out central ritual duties' (Bowen 1989: 611). Innovation – *bid'ah* – has been defined as follows:

> Any modification of accepted religious belief or practice. Based on the *hadith* 'Any manner or way which someone invents in this religion such that that manner or way is not part of this religion is to be rejected', the term has a negative connotation in Islam. Conservatives extend the prohibition beyond strictly religious matters to social practice, while more liberal thinkers condemn only innovation judged to substantially alter the core of Islamic teaching.[20]

The SEI, concisely describes *bid'ah* as 'the opposite of *sunna*'.[21] Expanding on the approaches described in ODI, SEI notes that two positions can be taken on innovation: a conservative interpretation holds that the duty of the believer is to follow the *sunna* and not to innovate; a further interpretation holds that there are good and even necessary innovations.

Innovations can be classified into five categories (SEI): forbidden (such as heretical systems opposed to orthodox Islam); disliked (such as the decorating of mosques and copies of the Qur'an); permitted (such as expenditure in eating and drinking); recommended (such as the founding of religious houses and schools); and duties incumbent upon Muslims (such as the study of Arabic philology).[22] Where innovation is claimed to extend to heresy it is said the origin of the innovation is a critical issue: if based only on confusion as to a sound proof, the innovation amounts to heresy; if based in obstinate opposition, it extends to unbelief, or *kufr* (Abd-Allah 2007: 1).[23] Heresy and unbelief are concepts closely related to apostasy, with other related concepts being blasphemy and hypocrisy (Abd-Allah 2007: 1; Glenn 2000: 191; Saeed & Saeed 2004: 35).[24] The positions that can be taken on innovation, reflect a classical approach, and according to Abd-Allah (2007: 10) the nuances of the concept have been 'largely forgotten', with the term now simply denoting 'extreme religious error'.

20 'Innovation' ODI (2003). Available in Oxford Reference Online. www.oxfordreference.com.
21 '*Bid'a*', SEI.
22 See also Zamhari (2010: 31), who references this five-fold categorisation, which he identifies as based in the Shafi'i school of Islamic law.
23 This term is related to the more familiar *kafir* or unbeliever; '*Kafir*', SEI. This source notes that various states of unbelief have been described ranging from neither recognising nor acknowledging God, to outwardly acknowledging but at heart not recognising God, that is, being a hypocrite. Cf. Masud (1993: 63), according to whom *bid'ah* does not extend to heresy or disbelief, but rather is condemned as 'forbidden'.
24 On the close link between apostasy and heresy Glenn (2000: 191) notes that 'by leaving the faith you challenge it and may provide a model for others'.

While the scope of heresy is difficult to define, it has been understood as including questioning the fundamentals of Islam, or advocating actions that may be prohibited in Islam (Lewis 1953; Saeed & Saeed 2004: 40).[25] The claim of heresy has historically been used by rulers to persecute opponents, and by some *ulama* to attempt to eliminate other *ulama* from rival schools (Saeed & Saeed 2004: 40).[26] Unbelief, at a simple level, denotes that a person does not recognise the existence of God, or that Muhammad was not a prophet (Saeed & Saeed 2004: 42). However, while a person subscribing to the key beliefs of Islam will be considered a believer, they are also required to put that belief into practice (Saeed & Saeed 2004).

The Arabic term for apostasy is *riddah*, and apostasy in Islam has been considered punishable by death – a position also held in early Jewish and Christian law (Saeed & Saeed 2004: 35). Apostasy is defined as rejecting Islam or converting to another religion, and there are several means by which this can be said to take place, and numerous 'apostasy lists' that identify behaviour considered unacceptable circulate among Muslims (Saeed & Saeed 2004: 36–37, 44–48). Apostasy lists include such acts as denial of one of the fundamentals of Islam (for example, that there are five daily prayers), or denial that a particular proscribed form of worship is required for a particular prayer session (such as four units of prayer for the late afternoon prayer). Jurists classify apostasy into three categories – belief-related, action-related and utterance-related (Saeed & Saeed 2004: 37). Belief-related offences include making permissible things that by consensus are considered prohibited, or a doubt about a fundamental element of belief, such as doubts about the existence of God. An example of action-related apostasy is prostrating oneself before an idol. Cursing Allah is an example of an utterance-related act of apostasy.

Saeed and Saeed (2004: 43) argue that there is, overall, a 'substantial degree of fluidity' among the terms and concepts reviewed in this section, making specific or clear definitions extremely difficult to formulate. This fluidity has also resulted, historically, in the use of these terms by Muslims against other Muslims, when they held a belief that their position on Islam was the only authentic or true belief (Saeed & Saeed 2004: 43). The following section will address in

---

25 Lewis (1953: 43) observes that in medieval Islam claims of heresy often included accusations of ulterior motives, including 'the recurring theme of a plot to undermine Islam from within in favour of some other faith'. He also notes that medieval Europeans 'shared the fundamental assumptions' of their Muslim contemporaries on this subject (Lewis 1953: 44). Lewis (1953: 51–59) discusses five different Arabic terms (commencing with *bid'ah*) associated with the concept of heresy, and argues that the term heresy is fundamentally a loan word from Christian scholarship.

26 According to Taylor (1967: 201): when theology and its expression are 'held by men with sincerity or even with misplaced fanaticism, they constitute a schism or sect . . . only when a man deliberately and cynically exploits and morally abuses the theological integrity of his group and of his own claims within the group does he constitute a heretic'.

more detail the way in which the concept of innovation has been applied in Indonesian Islam. In particular, it will be seen how this concept has formed part of debates about different approaches to ritual practice, including prayer, providing context-specific background to the case study and the charge of innovation laid against Yusman Roy.

Innovation in Indonesian Islam

Zamhari (2010: 30–35) identifies two broad approaches to *bid'ah* in Indonesia, mirroring in general terms the different approaches identified above. One approach is founded in the Shafi'i school of Islamic law, which establishes that innovation that contradicts recognised sources of Islamic jurisprudence is objectionable, and that which does not contradict these sources may be good or praiseworthy (Zamhari 2010: 31). A second group identifies 'all newly invented activities in religious matters which are believed to be part of religion but in fact [are] not part of religion' as *bid'ah* (Zamhari 2010). This approach is based on the Maliki school, and is grounded in the argument that such innovations amount to an allegation that the Prophet has concealed part of God's message. According to Zamhari (2010), it is the second approach to innovation that is pursued by Indonesian *Salafi*[27] groups in their opposition to Sufi ritual practice.[28] Zamhari (2010) also explores in depth the contemporary application of the concept of *bid'ah* in relation to *Majlis Dhikr* groups (for example arising from their practice of unison recitation).

Federspiel (1970: 64) provides a detailed study of approaches taken earlier in the twentieth century by Muhammadiyah to innovation and quotes a Muhammadiyah committee as defining *bid'ah* as:

> believing that certain behaviour and tenets of faith were sanctioned by the Prophet Muhammad when, in fact they were not. Bidah generally appears because of a desire to increase religious performance, but due to ignorance the action undertaken is not actually that which is sanctioned by Islam. Hence bidah is an unintentional mistake but a mistake which should be corrected.

---

27 *Salafism* can be described as a movement seeking to purify and reform Muslim society (*Salafis* taking as a model the religious and social practices of the earliest generations of Muslims) and has as one of its defining characteristics the active rejection of innovation in Islamic belief and practice (Bubalo et al. 2011: 40).

28 This approach also finds support from Persis. Zamhari (2010: 28) notes Persis maintains its 'radical' rejection of practices that do not meet its puritanical objectives, including 'illicit innovation', and that this coincides with the rise of the Indonesian *Salafi* movement. Persis has coined provocative acronyms to describe the various approaches which it condemns. These include 'TBC' (Indonesian for tuberculosis) which refers to *tahayyul* (for superstition), *bid'ah* (innovation) and *khurafat* (myths), and 'SIPILIS' (Indonesian for syphilis) which stands for *sekularisme* (secularism), *pluralisme* (pluralism), and *liberalisme* (liberalism) (Zamhari 2010).

The term has been applied by Modernist reformers against the Traditionalist use of Islamic jurisprudence and, in turn, Traditionalists condemned Muhammadiyah reformers as 'heretics and apostates' (Federspiel 1970: 65). Federspiel (1970: 65–66) proposes that much of the animosity around innovation was caused by a low level of religious knowledge among religious scholars, and eventually (as noted above) the disagreement between the reformists (Modernists) and Traditionalists narrowed.[29]

The question of innovation has also been applied to aspects of ritual directly relevant to the case study. Muhammadiyah, for example, accepted that the Friday sermon could be delivered in Indonesian despite the fact that 'it was recognised by nearly all orthodox Muslim groups that the general ritual of worship had to be in Arabic' (Federspiel 1970: 66).[30] The use of translation of the Friday sermon from Arabic into Indonesian was a matter of 'intense debates' between the 1930s and 1950s (Hooker 2003: 104). The issue is important because the literalist position was that the sermon forms part of *sholat*, and so should be in Arabic (Hooker 2003: 104). Hooker (2003: 104) observes that the literalist position has never seriously been held in Indonesia, but remains 'a nagging issue in "modernist" circles'. Muhammadiyah has, however, ceased directly challenging innovation because it had 'failed to convince nominal Muslims to set aside rituals seen by reformist groups as *bid'ah*' (Zamhari 2010: 27).

Bowen's work (1989; 2003) includes analysis of variation in ritual practice in Aceh in which allegations of *bid'ah* were made in relation to variations in prayer practiced in villages in the Gayo highlands (2003: 604–606). These debates were driven by confrontation between Modernist-inspired reformists, and Indonesian Muslims defending older practices (Bowen 2003: 601).[31] In exploring these disputes, Bowen identifies different public discourses about the proper form of ritual prayer, and – on a practical level – demonstrates through further international comparisons that disputes about variation in ritual practice are not confined to Indonesia.[32]

---

29 Indeed, Federspiel (1970: 70) notes the official Muhammadiyah position has been that 'no one claiming to be a Muslim should be branded a heretic'.
30 Ricklefs (2007: 223) suggests that Muhammadiyah's early position in relation to local customs was 'tolerant and incremental', due to the influence of its founder Ahmad Dahlan – a Javanese.
31 Zamhari (2010: 26) observes – more broadly – that 'polemical debates' about religious matters have been a characteristic of Indonesian Islam from its formative centuries, up to the present.
32 Bowen (1989; 2003: 613) refers to a number of other specific variations including: the Sasak 'Three Timers' in Eastern Indonesia who observe fewer than the accepted five regulated daily prayer times; a debate in Nigeria in the late nineteenth and early twentieth centuries concerning crossing the arms during prayer (versus letting them hang at the sides); and, a 'major dispute' in the then British frontier region between Afghanistan and India at the turn of the nineteenth century as to the raising of the index finger during worship.

Hooker's (2003: 90) study of contemporary *fatawa* demonstrates that significant attention has been paid to matters of ritual with prayer, in particular, being a matter 'of intense interest in the Muslim community'. Indeed, the volume of rulings in this area is described by him as so 'vast' as to make the scale of the subject almost overwhelming; the question of innovation in prayer appears to be 'perennial' (Hooker 2003: 68, 90, 99). Hooker (2003: 88) notes that at issue is the tension that exists 'between the requirements of dogma and the realities of its practice'. More particularly, the nature of worship as a public act – especially in the context of the Friday congregational prayer – brings forth 'real dissension and difficulty' (Hooker 2003: 91). From his study of a range of *fatawa*, Hooker (2003: 90) notes that the emphasis is on 'exactness and absolute certainty in observance', reflecting a 'preoccupation' with innovation, and its constant rejection.

Hooker (2003: 90) identifies only one MUI *fatwa* on the conduct of prayer,[33] while in contrast more than half the *fatawa* collections of Persis and Muhammadiyah address the practice of prayer. Among Indonesian *fatawa* there are 'plain differences of opinion between . . . sources on quite fundamental matters, most especially in the individual and religious obligations' (Hooker 2003: 237). This principally arises in relation to *sholat*, where 'fundamental differences in opinion and occasionally in practice occur' and is 'most obvious in the forms and formalities prescribed' (Hooker 2003). Hooker (2003: 237–238) observes there is a range of opinion on virtually all dimensions of the procedure: the uttering of the intention to pray; the recitation of the *fatihah*; the prayer cycles (*rakat*); the use of Arabic; the use of repetition in recitation; and the language used in the sermon (*khutbah*).[34]

Majelis Ulama Indonesia and its *fatawa*

It was noted in the preceding section that there are other Islamic bodies in Indonesia that produce rulings on issues of interest to the Islamic community. It has also been seen that there is a diversity of approaches to Indonesian Islam

---

33 This is no longer an accurate figure as there are eight *fatawa* on different aspects of *sholat* in a recent collection of MUI *fatawa* (MUI 2010a).

34 Further on the question of prayer see Weiss (2006: 63–71), who quotes at length from a thirteenth-century *fatwa* of Ibn Taymiyya on the question of innovation in ritual prayer that suggests that this has been a perennial issue, not just in the context of Indonesian Islam as proposed by Hooker, but also in the Middle East. The significance arises because for prayer to be valid it must conform to established requirements, yet validity becomes an issue in a 'setting of sectarian diversity', where the *Imam* and members of the congregation may come from different schools. The *fatwa* states, for example, that if knowledge of what is required in ritual prayer is needed, as opposed to what is recommended, then 'the prayers of most Muslims would be invalid' (Weiss 2006: 65). Ultimately, the *fatwa* holds that 'if the view of another happens to be incorrect but that person sincerely believes it to be correct, God will forgive the incorrectness' (Weiss 2006: 71).

evidenced by the existence of different organisations which have maintained, at times, opposing views on matters of doctrine. In this section I consider the origins and development of MUI, and its character and influence as a *fatawa*-giving organisation. Further, I discuss MUI's policy on and contribution to the development of national law.

MUI was, until relatively recently, considered a creature of government, and there continues to be ambiguity around its contemporary links to government. This ambiguity arises in part from funding arrangements, which are opaque, and from the increasing interleaving of MUI and state administration via law and regulation. What appears clear, however, is that the organisation has taken steps to emerge from the shadow of earlier association with, or perhaps subordination to, the state administration and position itself as an independent voice. This voice is expressed in part through *fatawa*, and MUI clearly identifies the capacity to influence law and policy development as being a matter of high priority.

Historical profile

MUI (2010b), itself, remarks candidly upon the early history of the organisation:

> At the beginning, there was a controversial point of view concerning the existence of MUI. At that time people gave very low appreciation to MUI, caused by the disharmonious relationship between the government and Muslim society . . . the existence of MUI was seen as engineered by the government to limit and steer the role and activities of Islamic organisations and institutions in society.

It is accepted by scholars that MUI was established in May 1975 at the instigation or on the initiative of the government (Hasan 2008: 26; Hooker 2003: 60; Hosen 2004: 149; Kaptein 2004: 9). This followed discussions at conferences during the early 1970s among Muslim scholars on the question of the need for such a body (Hosen 2004: 149–150).[35] Soeharto promoted the concept of a national body, and the Minister for Internal Affairs instructed provincial Governors to establish regional council of *ulama* (Hosen 2004: 150; Ichwan 2005: 48).[36] Subsequently these regional representatives came together in a conference with representatives of Islamic organisations and, in July 1975, MUI

---

35 According to Mudzhar (1996: 236), a former director of the Department of Religion's research and development organisation, Soeharto proposed formation of the national body in 1970 but this went unanswered as *ulama* did not want 'to be used by the government'.

36 Noer (2010: 81–90) provides a detailed history of earlier regional and national *ulama* councils. The earliest regional body identified in this account was established in West Java

was established by declaration.[37] Hooker (2003: 60) describes the government's motive as being to 'establish and control the public expression of Islam under state (here Department of Religion) auspices'; in short, it was the extreme expression of the New Order's bureaucratisation of Islam.[38] The organisation has however always been, at least in form, an independent, non-governmental organisation (Ichwan 2005: 48)[39] and Ricklefs (2008: 122) describes it as being one of the major non-political structures for *santri* Muslims in post-1965 Indonesia.

MUI has also been described as being positioned between government and Muslim organisations, and needing to maintain good relations with both (Hosen 2004: 154). This relationship is 'complicated',[40] due both to government support for MUI, and to the extension of financial support to the organisation (Hosen 2004; Hooker 2003: 60).[41] MUI's main function has been described as supporting, and in some cases justifying, government policy and programmes (Hosen 2004: 154), and it was seen by the Muslim community as a government 'mouthpiece' (Olle 2009: 95).[42] A more nuanced analysis is put by Mudzhar (1993), who concludes from his study of early MUI *fatawa* that the organisation was independent because rulings at times supported and opposed government policy, and both types of ruling may have had the same impact on the *umat*.[43] Olle (2009: 9) also points out that the MUI journal *Mimbar Ulama* repeatedly dealt with two issues throughout the New Order period: concerns over women covering their body and, concerns about heresy. Both of these

---

in 1958 specifically for security reasons, and under the auspices of a military commander, although not all pre-MUI *ulama* councils were government controlled.

37 The Department of Religion (2007: 25–27) supports this account of the formation of MUI.

38 Kaptein (2004: 9) describes it as 'an attempt by the government to involve the *ulama* in its developmental policy in an institutionalised way' and Saeed (2005: 8), similarly, observes that Soeharto's aim was to keep political Islam at bay and nurture an 'apolitical Islam in order to use it as a tool in the economic and social development programme of the New Order'. MUI has also been grouped in one source with other examples of 'state *mufti*' appointed in the Islamic world during the twentieth century (Masud et al. 1996: 27).

39 Lindsey (2012b: 255) is more specific, labelling it a 'quasi autonomous non-government organisation'.

40 Hosen here quotes from Atho Mudzhar's (1993) study of MUI *fatawa* issued between 1975–1988.

41 MUI's sources of funding include its state-sanctioned activities in the syariah economy and *halal* certification, supplemented with funds from the state budget, but MUI does 'not publish or publicly discuss its accounts' (Lindsey 2012b: 262). MUI publications do make brief reference to the receipt of state funds (see MUI 2010c).

42 Another formula offered by Hasan (2008: 26) is that the establishment of MUI was the New Order's attempt to 'domesticate the social force of *ulama*'.

43 Hosen (2004: 155) also refers to arguments raised by Islamic scholars that MUI received requests for *fatawa* because it was seen as trusted, and legitimate (and so not merely supportive of government policy). Hooker (2003: 60) quotes Mudzhar's study as finding that only three out of a total of 22 *fatawa* demonstrate 'any sort of government policy influence'.

issues can be seen as matters primarily of a religious nature, and remain of major interest to MUI.

It appears that relatively early in its life MUI also saw itself as playing a role in monitoring the state legal programme. The third Secretary General, Hasan Basri – who served between 1985 and 1998 – explained that MUI should function as a 'watchdog to ensure that there will be no laws in the country that are contradictory to the teachings of Islam' (Hosen 2004: 154).[44] The fall of Soeharto afforded MUI an opportunity to reflect on its role but according to Ichwan (2005: 46) it was not until the Presidency of Abdurrahman Wahid (1999–2001) that it began to clearly distance itself from the state. This was apparently related to Wahid's suggestion that communism might be legalised and trade relations established with Israel (Ichwan 2005: 46).[45] In his view, MUI's policies as published in both *fatawa* and *tausiyah* (a form of non-legal recommendation or advice) reflect its 'changing position as a mediator between state and society' and that they are mechanisms by which the organisation attempts to 'bring Indonesians closer to its understanding of "orthodoxy"' (Ichwan 2005: 46).

The stance of MUI is also informed not only by the broader political context – the New Order itself and its relations with Islam – but also by relations among Islamic organisations. Hosen (2004: 152) notes, for example, that there was a concern in the early years following MUI's formation that leaders of existing Muslim organisations feared MUI becoming a serious rival. However, this concern appears to have been reflected in MUI's restriction to an advisory role (one accepted by MUI itself), avoiding the conduct of 'practical programmes' such as running schools or other institutions (Hosen 2004: 152; Noer 2010: 90). Traditionally MUI comprised representatives from a range of organisations, including the large NU and Muhammadiyah, but this membership widened after 1998 to include more radical organisations (Ichwan 2005: 49).[46] The result of this willingness to accommodate diverse streams has arguably led to MUI acting as a religious authority in a way that 'triggers tensions and conflicts in society' (Hasan 2008: 44).

The contemporary view

MUI describes itself, in the simplest formulation, as acting as Indonesia's national *Mufti*, although this term appears in parenthesis, and following on from the statement that its role is to deliver *fatawa* and act as religious adviser to the

44 Hosen here quotes Mudzhar (1993).
45 President Wahid was an NU leader and Islamic scholar prior to taking office and his presidency was characterised by 'pluralism and openness' (Lindsey 2012a: 121; Ricklefs 2001: 419). However, some of his thinking was potentially threatening to established policies on religion, such as a threat to close the Department of Religion (Lindsey 2012a: 107).
46 Radical organisations joining MUI at this time included HTI and FPI, and this move was based on a deliberate programme to bridge radical and moderate Islam (Ichwan 2005: 49 n9). See further, below.

nation (MUI 2010b: 31; MUI 2010c). Its establishment reflects the existence of similar councils in other parts of Southeast Asia with roles as 'supreme advisers on religious affairs to the government' (MUI 2010c). MUI also claims the role of being the external face of Indonesian Islam (such as representing Indonesia in international forums, and in meeting foreign religious figures domestically), the bridge between the government and 'Muslim society', and a consultative forum among Muslim scholars. Indeed, MUI claims to have become the 'umbrella organisation for the central levels of more than 63 Islamic organisations, ranging from moderate to extreme' (MUI 2010c).

Further detail on these functions is found in the Decree issued at MUI's Eighth National Conference in 2010 (MUI 2010b: 1–19). MUI sees itself as playing a key strategic role in coordination, through consultation, among Muslim scholars and organisations. As the 'meeting place' (*rumah besar* – literally, 'big house') for Muslim society in Indonesia, MUI cooperates with Islamic organisations and institutions 'without distinction based on orientation and type of movement (*pola pergerakan*) whilst not including categories of mass organisation and institutions that deviate from the core teachings of Islam'.[47] MUI has established a special forum for this 'horizontal' coordination among Islamic bodies, known as the *Forum Ukuwah Islamiah* (Forum for Islamic Community Brotherhood), attended not only by Islamic organisations but also by representatives of government, legal and political circles and some radical groups (MUI 2010b: 14).

The conduct of the *Kongres Umat Islam Indonesian* (Congress of the Indonesian Islamic Community), convened by MUI on 17–21 April 2005, appears to have marked an important stage in MUI's development. One outcome of the conference was a renewal of MUI's earlier decision in 2000 to deal with heresy as a matter of priority, and following this conference there were a series of attacks against Islamic groups accused of being heretical (Olle 2009: 95–96). Olle (2009: 6–11) further describes MUI as one of at least three Islam-based organisations playing central roles in an 'Islamic authoritarian movement', in which attacks on heresy form a core approach. The importance of the Congress was that it was the fourth in a series that spanned a significant period of time: the first two were held in 1947 and 1952, the second two in 1998 and 2005 (Olle 2009: 95). Olle argues (2009) that MUI was thereby claiming the inheritance of the earlier pre-MUI conferences, and that this amounted to a politicisation of Islam due to the long hiatus between the conferences. The fourth Congress, in 2005, attracted a wide range of participating groups including radical groups such as the FPI and HTI, in addition to Muhammadiyah and NU (Olle 2009).[48]

47 As noted in the Chapter 1, representatives of liberal Islamic groups are not part of the MUI family, and this proscription against including liberal Muslims extends from the national level down to the provincial and district offices of the organisation (Ichwan 2013: 64).

48 This year also saw a key shift in the make-up and agenda of Muhammadiyah, with its 2005 conference ushering in a new, conservative, agenda in comparison to its earlier resistance

In relation to its internal affairs, MUI asserts that a 'consultative' relationship exists between its national and regional levels (MUI 2010b: 14). This relationship between the national/central and regional levels has both coordinating/aspirational and structural/administrative dimensions, and this relationship is aimed at ensuring the national strategy is implemented at the local level, and that there is appreciation of the national-level issues identified by MUI (MUI 2010b). It also appears that in 2010 MUI announced the establishment of an additional level, so MUI representation now extends down to the lowest administrative level in Indonesia, being the village/subdistrict (2010b: 12).[49] While the national MUI is theoretically in control, the lower, regional-level MUI tend to 'go their own way' and provide advice in their own areas, a tendency also exhibited by the Jakarta-based branch of MUI (Hooker 2003: 230). This reflects MUI published policy, which acknowledges that *fatawa* at central and local levels are of equal status, one cannot override another even if they contradict each other (Lindsey 2012a: 131). Lindsey (2012b: 261) therefore concludes there is no clear national hierarchical relationship between levels of MUI, and so the nature of the relationship is 'sometimes obscure'.

Operational guidelines endorsed at the 2010 national conference also dealt with MUI's approach to advocacy in the field of national law and policy. Accordingly, MUI (2010a: 31) claims the role of *Mufti* in the following terms:

> *fatwa*-giver to the Islamic community whether requested or not requested. As a *fatwa*-giving institution MUI accommodates and provides an outlet for the aspirations of Indonesia's Islamic community that comprises a very diverse range of streams of opinion and thought together with their religious organisations.

MUI's Broad Outline Programme for 2010–2015 includes both a *fatwa* programme, and a programme for the development of law and legislation (MUI 2010a: 73–74). The first stated objective of the *fatwa* programme is to spread syariah activities among scholarly circles and provide both guidance and legal guidelines to the Islamic community. Moreover, MUI also seeks to do everything in its power to ensure (*mengusahakan agar*) 'every MUI fatwa whether at the central or local level becomes positive law' (MUI 2010a). Objectives of the law and legislation programme include preparing draft laws and regulations, urging or motivating (*mendorong*) national legal agencies in law enforcement in Indonesia, and, preparing legal advocacy teams to represent MUI in and outside of court (MUI 2010a).

---

to the promotion of syariah (Burhani 2005; Ichwan 2013: 8). There was also an awareness by both NU and Muhammadiyah at this time that they 'were vulnerable to infiltration and takeover of assets by radical Islamist movements' (Ichwan 2013: 9).

49 At the time of the case study the lowest tier was the District level.

MUI also passed a set of more specific recommendations (*tausiyah*) for law reform (2010a: 150–151). This particular set of recommendations in fact far exceeds a law reform proposal and commences with a statement expressing MUI's views on Indonesia's political and legal system:

> There has lately been a tendency of disloyalty [among] society and law enforcement figures (*oknum*) towards law and legislation among other things caused by a legal system impartial as to religious values, [and] weaknesses in the supremacy of law enforcement. . . . Because of this MUI urges:
>
> a   the government and parliament that in the process of constructing laws and regulations that aim for living Islamic values and teachings along with being guidance to society . . .

This part of the recommendation continues by addressing the flaring up of 'porno-action' and pornography. It urges the government to implement Law 44/2008 (Law on Anti-Pornography), and encourages parliament to pass the revised Criminal Code in a form consistent with the spirit and teaching of Islam, particularly in the field of morality. The recommendation also notes that there is a lack of guidance for notaries executing a range of syariah transactions and suggests collaboration with the Supreme Court and Department of Law and Human Rights to this end.

Evidence suggests that MUI's objective of influencing the state legal programme is effective. In a presentation to a conference celebrating MUI's thirty-sixth anniversary in 2011, the Director-General of Law and Legislation Dr Wahiduddin Adams,[50] discussed the clear impact of both MUI *fatawa* and advice since its establishment in 1974. Eleven national laws passed between 1974 and 1999 reflect in some way Islamic needs (such as the marriage law from 1974 and the establishment of the Religious Courts in 1989), and Adams identified 18 laws or regulations which have absorbed Islamic legal principles or which protect the interests of the *umat* (such as narcotics legislation from 1976 and the 2008 pornography law). The Director-General stated that MUI *fatwa* and advice 'occupy an increasingly strong position as a resource and reference in developing law and legislation'.

Several pieces of legislation indeed make direct reference to a role for MUI: the Companies Law (Law 40/2007, art 109) requires corporations carrying out activities on the basis of syariah principles to establish a Syariah Supervision Council which includes an expert nominated by MUI; under syariah securities legislation (Law 19/2008, art 25) the relevant Minister must request *fatwa* or declarations of conformity with syariah from MUI; and, under the Syariah Banking Law (Law 21/2008, art 26) business activities and products and services

---

50 In 2014 Adams was appointed a Justice of the MK. This section draws on Adams (2011).

must be consistent with syariah principles as established in MUI *fatawa*.[51] The Director-General also observed that (at the time of the conference) there were eight draft laws before parliament to which MUI might offer a contribution by way of Islamic legal thought (including draft legislation on *halal* products, and the prevention of child trafficking).[52] He concluded with the invitation that MUI formulate clear and concrete input 'in order that it can be adopted directly as raw material (*materi muatan*) for the relevant laws and regulations'. The draft law on *halal* products was passed into law in late 2014, as Law No 33 on *Halal* Product Assurance. While establishing a government agency to manage halal labelling, it establishes a key role for an MUI *Halal Fatwa* Committee which will issue decisions determining the status of products (art 10) and regulate categories of unacceptable foods through *fatawa* (arts 18, 20).

Olle's (2009: 105) research on the opinions of provincial representatives of MUI about the organisation and its role indicate that MUI members think of it as a 'partner' with the government. Indeed, Olle (2009) notes that some MUI actors see that action against heresy is felt to be 'in seamless continuity with a tradition that sees heresy as a threat to national security', drawing on both colonial era arrangements between the state and representatives of the *umat*, and on the New Order's 'deliberate conflation' of political and religious dissidence. Moreover, in its relationship with the state, MUI clearly sees itself having special authority to deal with heresy, an authority that extends *over* state institutions (Olle 2009: 106). This is reflected particularly in the development and deployment of *fatawa* (for example those against Ahmadiyah, most recently issued in 2005) and reference to the potential for 'anarchy' to break out should deviations from Islam not be suppressed, as a means to put pressure on the state to accept MUI's authority (Olle 2009).[53] This is confirmed by the national chair of MUI's *fatwa* commission who has stated publicly that the government is obliged to follow MUI's *fatwa* in the case of Ahmadiyah (Olle 2009). Olle (2009) proposes that rather than speaking for the state (as MUI arguably did earlier in its existence) it now 'claims priority over other state institutions'. In short, MUI has developed a 'platform of expansion' in a clearly political move (Olle 2009: 107).

MUI fatawa – *an overview*

The structure and content of the *fatawa* in the case study are described in more detail in Chapter 5. However, briefly, it can be noted that MUI *fatawa* do not follow a traditional format (see further below) but rather follow a set pattern that gives them the appearance almost of a government-issued

---

51 See Lindsey (2012b: 264–265) on MUI and Islamic finance.
52 MUI has had a virtual monopoly over the process of *halal* certification (Lindsey 2012b: 269).
53 Overall, the campaign against heresy, suggests Olle (2009: 116), creates a fear that 'leads to enforced uniformity in the field of religion and beyond it'.

document, such as a regulation (Hosen 2004: 169; Kaptein 2004: 9).[54] Whether or not contemporary Indonesian *fatawa* are considered binding on members of the issuing institution varies, and MUI rulings have never been considered binding upon members of other Muslim organisations (Hooker 2003: 229–230; Ichwan 2005: 49). In its earliest charter, MUI claimed the role of *fatwa*-giver 'on questions of religion and society to the Government and community' (MUI c.1995: 38). This charter changed following *Reformasi*, with the reference to the government removed, and the additional comment that *fatawa* would be given to the *umat* 'whether requested or not' (Ichwan 2005: 50). This remains the stated policy on *fatawa*, as seen in MUI's operational guidelines quoted above, together with a new acknowledgement of the variety of views within the *umat* (MUI 2010b: 31).

In its traditional form, the *fatwa* is presented in a question and answer format (Weiss 1996: 63).[55] The *fatawa* of MUI can be distinguished both on this basis and in their being institutional products, rather than being written by individual scholars. Mudzhar (1996: 230) suggests that the issuing of *fatawa* by individual scholars was a feature of the pre-modern era, and that in modern times they have come to be issued by groups of scholars or by an institution. It is certainly the case that the institutional *fatwa* is a feature of Islam in Indonesia, and Kaptein (2004: 7) identifies this form as emerging at the beginning of the twentieth century.[56] There are many bodies in Indonesia that issue *fatawa*, with four main institutions being responsible for the majority of them and MUI being the youngest member of this group (Hooker & Lindsey 2002: 286; Mudzhar 1996).[57]

An indication of the position MUI takes on the significance of deviant sects can be found in the title of a recent MUI collection of *fatawa* on this subject. Titled *Mengawal Aqidah Umat* – Guarding the Faith of the Islamic Community – the publication (MUI c.2007) clearly associates the existence of groups it defines as deviant to threaten adherence to the fundamentals of the Islamic faith (*aqidah*) among the Muslim community. The publication follows the establishment in 2007 of guidelines for the identification of deviant sects, and surveys a total

---

54 This can be distinguished from Hooker's (2003: 62–63) category of 'bureaucratic' *fatawa* which he applies to Islamic rulings on medical ethics issued by the Ministry of Health over many years. According to Masud et al. (1996: 24), *fatawa* 'assume a variety of local forms, differing in language and literary style, conventions of inclusion and exclusion, and usage of characteristic rubrics'.
55 See also Hooker (2003), where in the many quotations from *fatawa* a clear question and answer are frequently identified, often labelled as such in the text of the ruling.
56 Kaptein (2004: 2–7) describes *fatawa* following a traditional style dating from the nineteenth century and being requested by Muslims form Southeast Asia of scholars in the Middle East, and others issued in the early twentieth century in Indonesia and also following a question and answer format.
57 The others are NU, Muhammadiyah and Persis.

of 14 *fatawa* issued between 1971 and 2007.[58] This collection is of relevance because it focuses on Islamic sects or, in the words of MUI, religious sects operating 'in the name of Islam' (MUI c.2007: i).

MUI rulings on deviant sects

One of the challenges arising from freedom of religion in the *Reformasi* era, according to MUI (c.2007: 1), is the voicing of thoughts and opinions, and activities by sects or groups, that conflict with *aqidah* and syariah:

> Thoughts, opinions and activities that conflict with *aqidah* and syariah clearly cannot develop that way in the midst of society because this will surely give rise to the disturbance of the *umat* besides which it will create victims among those of the *umat* who are misled. Because of this, it is necessary to strive to the utmost to ward off and put a stop to these sects and convince them to return to the correct path.

MUI (c.2007), as the umbrella organisation for *ulama*, considers it important to play an active role in guarding Islamic values, and protecting the *umat* from deviant sects, and the guidelines were developed to support this objective. The guidelines distinguish between an error (*kesalahan*) and deviancy (*kesesatan*) (MUI c.2007: 4). An error is described as a 'confusion in understanding or practice related to a matter of syariah the consequences of which is only sin (*maksiyat*)' (MUI c.2007). Deviancy is defined as a 'confusion in understanding or practice related to a matter of *aqidah* or syariah but that is believed to be the truth, the consequence of which is unbelief (*kekufuran*)' (MUI c.2007).[59] These distinctions reflect the approaches to innovation discussed above.

The 2007 (MUI c.2007: 8) guidelines set out ten criteria by which to judge whether thoughts, opinions or acts are deviant, and it is considered sufficient to satisfy only one of these criteria:

1 Denying one of the six pillars of faith being belief in God, the Angels, the holy books, the prophets, the Day of Judgment, the *Qadla dan Qadar*[60] and the five pillars of Islam . . .

---

58 Some *fatawa* in the collection clearly predate the establishment of MUI, and include the prohibition of a sect by the government.

59 Prior to a ruling (*penetapan*) on deviancy being issued, the guidelines require research into the activities or teachings concerned, and that MUI engage with the leadership of the group or sect (MUI c.2007: 4–5). This includes a process of validation or clarification, together with the provision of advice so that those concerned will abandon the incorrect thoughts, opinions or acts and return to the right path. As will be seen in Chapter 5, these procedures were not followed in the Roy case, presumably as the guidelines were not yet in effect.

60 The principle of predestination of God.

2 Belief in or following a creed (*aqidah*) that is not in accordance with argumentation based in syariah (the Qur'an and *hadith*).
3 Belief in the descent of revelation after the Qur'an.
4 Denying the authenticity of the contents of the Qur'an.
5 Producing interpretations of the Qur'an not based in rules of interpretation (*kaidah-kaidah tafsir*).
6 Denying the position of the *hadith* of the Prophet as a source of Islamic teaching.
7 Defaming, belittling and or disparaging the prophets and apostles (*para Nabih atau Rasul*).
8 Denying the Prophet Muhammad as the final Prophet and apostle.
9 Changing, adding to or reducing the fundamental tenets of *ibadah* that have been established in syariah, such as the *hajj* isn't conducted to Mecca, the obligation of *sholat* is not five times, etc.
10 To consider another Muslim to be an infidel (*mengkafirkan*) without support in syariah, such as considering a Muslim an infidel only because they are not of the same group.

A recent collection of *fatwa* produced by MUI (2010a) comprises a total of 120 rulings issued since the organisation's establishment. This collection is divided as follows: *aqidah* and religious sects (14 *fatawa* – thus comprising just over a tenth of the collection); *ibadah* (30 rulings – making up one quarter of the total); 'social and cultural' (47 *fatawa*); and a group dealing with food, medicine and science and technology (totalling 29 rulings, or approximately one quarter of the total).

Of the *fatawa* concerning *ibadah*, eight deal with matters arising in *sholat* and the majority provide simply guidance; only one incorporates the concept of innovation. This *fatwa* is the ruling issued by the national-level MUI concerning Yusman Roy (those issued at the provincial and district level are discussed in the following chapter). As a preliminary matter the timing of this *fatwa* is of interest. The *fatwa* was issued on 7 May 2005, a Saturday, and the day following Roy's arrest. This postdates the *fatawa* issued in the Roy case at the local level, which were issued in January 2004 and February 2005. The national-level *fatwa* – No 3/2005 – is titled '*Sholat* Accompanied with Translation' (*Shalat Disertai Terjemah Bacaanya*) and refers in its preliminary paragraphs, in passing, to the existence of the practice of using translation in *sholat*, without referring to Roy specifically, and also briefly to the 2005 provincial-level *fatwa*. In its three operative paragraphs the *fatwa* declares *sholat* a pure form of religious observance that must be performed according to the guidance of God, as conveyed and exemplified by the Prophet; declares the practice of dual-language prayer to be invalid; and, specifically categorises the practice of *sholat* at Roy's *pesantren* to be an innovation that is deviant and rejected.

The breakdown of *fatawa* by category in this latest MUI resource (2010a) can be compared with the compilations used by Hooker (2003) in his study of

Indonesian *fatawa*.[61] There are some inconsistencies apparent in the numbers of rulings in each category which may be a result of the research methodology.[62] Nonetheless the evidence suggests that the emphasis on *aqidah* and religious sects (described by Hooker as 'religious teaching') has not changed significantly over time. Thus between 1995 and 2011 the proportion of *fatawa* on this subject remains steady at 9–11 per cent of all MUI *fatawa*. In contrast, the number of *fatawa* addressing *ibadah* increased slightly over time from 20 to 25 per cent of all rulings. Greater changes can be seen in the rulings on social/cultural matters with the proportion falling from 50 per cent in 1995 to 40 per cent by 2011.[63] The final category of science and technology (including *fatawa* on food and drink) follows a different pattern rising from 20 per cent to 29 per cent and then falling to 25 per cent of all MUI *fatawa*. Based on the dates of *fatawa* included in the most recent collection, several years saw a heightened level of activity in the fields of religious teaching and *ibadah*. In 1980 MUI issued six *fatawa* across both categories (three in each); in 1981 it issued five rulings on *ibadah*; and, in 2005, a total of six *fatawa* were issued (three on religious teachings and three on *ibdadah*).[64] Attention to matters of religious observance, including prayer, has accordingly been seen regularly in MUI *fatawa* over recent decades. Its approach to the Roy case, therefore is not outside the norm. MUI, however, went on to attract significant attention by issuing a ruling that sought to control a much wider range of conduct and religious thought, both inside Islam and beyond.

Fatwa *on Pluralism, Liberalism and Secularism in Religion*

Launched at its July 2005 National Conference, this national-level *fatwa*[65] was issued in response to concern in the community about the rise of plural, liberal

---

61 Hooker (2003: 253–254) refers to two compilations published by MUI: a 1995 collection of 53 rulings; and, a 1997 collection of 76 rulings. Mudzhar (1996: 236) notes that a total of 39 *fatawa* were issued between the founding of MUI in 1975 and 1988.

62 For example, in the compilations identified by Hooker (see above) the 1995 collection contains 13 *fatawa* on *Ibadah* and the 1997 collection contains 19, suggesting that six *fatawa* may have been issued on this subject between 1995 and 1997. In contrast, however, MUI's 2010 collection of *fatawa* indicates that only two new *fatawa* were issued on this subject between 1995 and 1997 (MUI 2010a).

63 In contrast, Masud (1993: 59–60) records a much lower rate of references to *bid'ah* (innovation) and concerns about ritual practice in a detailed study of South Asian *fatawa*. In a database of 13,232 *fatawa* only 301 mention *bid'ah* and, of these, 56 dealt with aspects of ritual prayer (Masud 1993).

64 Mudzhar (2011) notes that in recent years the number of *fatawa* issued by MUI has reduced, but their impact has – correspondingly – increased. This comment reflects specifically the growth in *fatawa* issued in the area of syariah economy, which alone generated 35 *fatawa* between 2001 and 2006.

65 MUI Fatwa Number 7/MUNAS VII/MUI/11/2005 on Pluralism, Liberalism and Secularism in Religion, 28 July 2005 (MUI 2010a: 92–97). Ichwan (2013: 82) observes that

and secular religious thoughts. It is expressed as having been requested by an element of the community as a result of these views causing disturbance (*men-imbulkan keresahan*). The ruling commences with a number of Qur'anic references, and is accompanied by a clarification which expands upon the social context rather than on the relevant issues of doctrine.[66] The *fatwa* in its operative parts is relatively short, comprising four paragraphs of definitions and four paragraphs described as 'legal provisions' (*ketentuan hukum*).

The *fatwa* defines pluralism in religion (*pluralisme agama*) as:

> a view (*paham*) which teaches that all religions are the same and because of that the truth of all religions is relative; as a result of this, every follower of a religion cannot claim that only their religion is true while other religions are wrong. Pluralism of religions also teaches that followers of all religions will enter and live together in heaven.

In contrast, it goes on to define plurality of religion (*pluralitas agama*) as 'a reality (*kenyataan*) that in a state or specific region can be found followers of various religions living together'. Liberalism in religion (*liberalisme agama*) is defined as 'understanding the Qur'an and *sunnah* using free forms of reasoning,[67] and only accepting religious doctrine that is specifically consistent with such reasoning'. The *fatwa* defines secularism in religion (*sekularisme agama*) as:

> separating worldly affairs from religion; religion is only used to arrange private relations with God (*Tuhan*), whilst relations amongst humanity are arranged only on the basis of social agreement (*kesepakatan sosial*).[68]

The *fatwa* goes on to state that pluralism, secularism and liberalism in religion 'are views that conflict (*bertentangan*) with Islamic religious teaching'. It declares that the *umat* is prohibited from following this approach (declaring it *haram*). It also states that in respect to *aqidah* and *ibadah* the *umat* must remain exclusive – that is there can be no blending (*mencampuradukkan*) with *aqidah* or *ibadah* of other religions. Where there is plurality of religion, and in social matters not related to *aqidah* and *ibadah*, the *umat* can take an inclusive approach, in the sense of conducting social relations with members of other religions, so long as there is no mutual harm (*tidak saling merugikan*).

---

some scholars neglect to include reference to religion in the title of the ruling, presenting the *fatwa* as being against 'all forms of pluralism, liberalism and secularism'.

66 MUI (2010a: 98–100).

67 '*dengan menggunakan akal pikiran yang bebas*'.

68 This last term could perhaps be understood also as 'social contract'.

The clarification to the *fatwa* explains that the *umat* in Indonesia is in the midst of a non-physical war of thoughts or belief (*perang pemikiran*).[69] This conflict has a wide scope including teachings, beliefs and the religiosity of the *umat*. It describes secularism and liberalism in religion as being of Western origin, deviating (*menyimpang*) from the fundamental teachings of Islam, and destroying the beliefs and opinions of the community towards Islam. The clarification describes secularism and liberalism as having distorted (*membelokkan*) Islamic teaching, giving rise to doubts in the *umat* concerning *aqidah* and Islamic law. The free interpretation of religion without the guidance of proper rules (*kaidah penuntun*) has given birth to '*Ibahiyah*' – or the endorsement of various acts (*menghalalkan segala tindakan*) – related to ethics and religion.

On the issue of pluralism in religion the clarification states that this gives rise to the view that all religions are the same, and states that this approach 'clearly can trivialise belief in *aqidah*'.[70] It is proposed that this approach emerged from the religious dialogue in Indonesia in the 1970s, led by Professor Dr Mukti Ali,[71] in which pluralism was viewed as 'agree to disagree', and the existence of different truth claims of the various religions was dissolved via 'syncretism', or the 'mingling of religious teachings' (*penyampuradukan ajaran agama*): 'that all religions are true and good, and religion is capable of being changed, like a change of clothing'.

The clarification states that the advocates of pluralism, liberalism and secularism of religion have gone too far (*telah bertindak terlalu jauh*) in thinking that many verses of the Qur'an are no longer relevant – such as the prohibition against marriage among those of different religions. It is stated that the same advocates believe that the Qur'an is not the word of God (*firman Allah*) but merely constitutes an ordinary text. The clarification supports this with reference specifically to material on the website of the liberal Islamic organisation JIL.[72]

69 According to Ichwan (2013: 82), MUI issued the clarification some time after the publication of the *fatwa*, after the emergence of controversy over the intended scope of the ruling.

70 '*dapat mendangkalkan keyakinan akidah*'.

71 Appointed Minister for Religious Affairs in 1971 by Soeharto, Mukti Ali launched a project emphasising harmony in religious life (Hasan 2008: 26). Saeed (2005: 8) also identifies Mukti Ali as contributing to the development of Neo-Modernism; see also Afrianty (2011) for an explanation of his role in contributing to the introduction of 'western social methodology in understanding Islamic knowledge' in Indonesia's Islamic higher education institutions.

72 Ulil Abshar Abdallah is a key figure in this network, and, as noted in Chapter 1, he was an expert witness in the trial of Yusman Roy. The clarification to the *fatwa* goes on to include a quote from JIL which is said by MUI to expresses the view that the majority of Muslims believe that the Qur'an is the word of God transmitted verbatim to the Prophet but that this belief is a formulation constructed by *ulama* as part of their formalisation of Islamic doctrine. There has been longstanding enmity between MUI and Islamic liberals, including, in particular, Ulil (Gillespie 2007: 237–239). There was 'severe' criticism of the *fatwa* from among liberal-progressive Muslims, including Ulil (Ichwan 2013: 82).

The clarification closes with the observation that the *fatwa* is intended to refute the growth of the view of relativism in religion (truth in religion is relative, not absolute).

Orthodoxy entrenched

A number of issues arise from the foregoing summary, including the influence of piety on Islamic identity in Indonesia, and MUI's place in the contemporary spectrum of Islamic identity. Following from this, it is valuable to consider the manner in which innovation is deployed in the process of constructing these shades of Islamic identity. The existence of sects and consistent argumentation about deviancy and heresy are hallmarks of Islam, while scholars have also noted that the faith in Indonesia has long been characterised as plural and diverse. Further, some commentary on the policies and posture of MUI is relevant to the case study. I outlined in the previous chapter key developments since the 2005 trial (principally the decision of the MK in the Blasphemy Case) which highlight the ongoing entrenchment of MUI as a key contributor to national level law and policy making. Therefore, some consideration needs to be given to the transformation of MUI from its original incarnation as a creature of government, and its drive to advance the cause of Islamic values. The Roy case demonstrates the organisation's capacity to influence law and administration not only at a policy level, as seen in this chapter, but also at a practical (and individual) level, as will be seen in in the next two chapters.

In this chapter I have concentrated on issues that reinforce the observation by Bush (2009) raised in the Chapter 1 that dispute about the Islamic faith in Indonesia is characteristically an intra-Islamic debate. It is valuable then to revisit, briefly, issues about Islam raised in the opening chapter that highlight some of the essential qualities of the faith which are themes in the research. The notion of an Islamic community – *umat* – is a key feature of the faith, yet there is no clear answer as to how this community is defined for any time or place. The existence of major divisions within the faith, including particular schools of legal thought, and the tensions between orthodox and more accommodating forms of local Islam, as well as the emergence of 'liberal' Islamic thought, reinforce that fact that the *umat* is a complex phenomenon. Religious guidance, for example through *fatawa*, is a means of assisting the faithful to orient themselves in relation to particular aspects of faith and towards (or within) particular forms of teaching.

What the review of Indonesian Islam in this chapter demonstrates is that the coherence of the concept of the Islamic community and its unity is, and has been, a major preoccupation of Muslim organisations. Rulings or commentary on deviancy and innovation (or, ultimately, heresy) arguably deal with the question of membership of the *umat* and its overall unity. This is, in respect to the application of doctrine, a spiritual concern. However, as seen in the preceding chapter, questions of blasphemy are also of interest to the state. This is clearly the case in Indonesia where the question of deviancy, or innovation, within the *umat* is regulated by law and, accordingly, very much an issue within the secular domain. Indeed, there is a distinct accord between, on the one hand, the orthodox Islamic concern with managing the spread of deviancy and, on the other, the state's concern with national unity. The challenge is to understand the link (or perhaps collaboration) between the two, as both tend toward the imposition of order and control, and to consider their influence within (or upon) Indonesia's liberal constitutional order.

It is important to note that reference has been made to policies and publications of MUI which postdate by several years the events of the case study. This material is included to provide a more contemporary account of MUI's doctrinal stance. It shows that the events of 2005 are not only consistent with this stance, but also foreshadow these more recent pronouncements. This assists in delineating the trajectory followed by MUI as it evolved from its origins as a government-sponsored organization to a proponent of what has been described as 'puritanical moderate Islam' (Ichwan 2013: 61).

Piety as a social marker

There is value in assessing both the contemporary approach to classifying approaches to Islamic faith in Indonesia, and in attempting to characterise MUI itself using such a system. Categories expressed in the literature are a useful reference because they have traditionally reflected, or had at their heart, theoretical viewpoints on matters of religious doctrine in Islam. This exercise is not intended to be conclusive and is somewhat problematic. For example, policy statements of MUI at the national level have been referred to in this chapter, but the case study involves also sub-national levels of the organisation. Further, the review of *fatawa* above concentrates on one area of doctrine most closely related to the case study – innovation in matters of *ibadah* – and so does not amount to a comprehensive study of MUI's approach to Islamic doctrine. There is ample evidence of doctrinal contestation in Indonesian Islam. In the twentieth century major organisations were established (Muhammadiyah and NU), and their existence (and doctrinal differences) were defined in important ways by their approach to innovation. Historically, this was evidenced – at least in Java – by Ricklefs' 'mystic synthesis' and variation from orthodox religious practices in this part of Indonesia.

The decline of serious, doctrinally based conflict among the Modernists and Traditionalists in Indonesia took place in the second half of the twentieth century, and was accompanied by other important developments. These include the watershed of the 1965 coup and subsequent purge of Indonesian communists which – in Bush's analysis – led to making a 'desultory attitude' to religion being no longer an option for Indonesian Muslims (piety has very much become the norm). Indonesian Islam was also marked in the 1960s and 1970s by the emergence of Neo-Modernist and so-called substantialist thought, which included critical liberalising elements in Islam. It should be noted that a demonstrable increase in public piety is important to an understanding of

Islam in contemporary Indonesia. While the focus here is on institutional approaches to doctrine, there is well-documented evidence of strong endorsement for the notion that 'the state should implement shari'a law for all Muslim citizens' (Hefner 2011a: 304).[73]

Zamhari's study of the critique of Sufi practices by *salafi* Muslims and MUI's opposition to Roy's teaching and practices show that innovation continues to play a role in religious disputation. The weight of scholarly focus has been on the emergence of 'extremist' Islam, and this can be seen in part in the replacement of the Modernist/Traditionalist classifications with a Moderate/Radical classification. There is some reluctance on the part of scholars to fully adopt this new classification, in part a result of the fact that radical Islam cuts across the existing institutional structures and traditional classification scheme, rendering the process of analysis more complex. This may also be a sign that classifying or categorising Islam in this way is becoming less meaningful.

MUI functions as an umbrella organization and embraces a wide range of Islamic organizations, including those considered extreme, an approach not previously taken by the mainstream organisations NU and Muhammadiyah (Azra 2005: 15). In relation to its engagement with more extreme versions of Islam, Olle suggests abandoning the application of terms such as 'conservative' and 'radical', proposing that MUI – together with extremist groups – be seen as an 'Islamic authoritarian movement'. This proposal is consistent with Azra's (2005: 13) observation that radicalism is primarily a political posture, rather than a religious one. These perspectives appear apposite given MUI's public posture and influence on Indonesian law and society. That is, while doctrine remains a key part of its agenda, and is deployed through *fatawa*, it is clear that MUI has a wider programme, and aspires to have real impact in the field of policy and politics.

As noted above, MUI rulings against dual-language prayer are not definitive of its doctrinal position more generally, but its *fatwa* on pluralism, liberalism and secularism in religion speaks clearly of its views. This ruling takes issue specifically with the approaches to doctrine advocated by contemporary liberal Muslims in Indonesia, who carry on the project initiated by Neo-Modernism. MUI's development and promotion of guidelines determining what amounts to deviancy in Islam, and its rulings over time on deviant sects, also demonstrate that MUI seeks to express and uphold specific doctrinal standards. Taken together, these public statements lead to the conclusion that MUI is a key advocate of orthodox Islamic doctrine, and the leading mainstream national

---

73 Public surveys show an intriguing commitment to both syariah and democratic governance (Hefner 2011a: 304–306). Surveys have also indicated significant religious intolerance, including against religious deviancy, and a 'strong sense' that religious identity rather than nationality is the foundation for identity (Elson 2010: 336).

organization challenging the expression of liberal Islamic thought in Indonesia. MUI does not directly command large numbers of individual members as is the case with the mass organizations, NU and Muhammadiyah. Its authority derives instead from its claim to represent and channel the collective views of Islamic scholars and organisations, both publicly and to government.

Condemning deviancy

Based on the documentary record of MUI *fatawa*, rulings explicitly invoking the concept of innovation are relatively infrequent, if not rare. This does not mean that debate or conflict over ritual, including prayer, is uncommon, as ritual has been frequently raised in the rulings of *fatwa*-giving organizations in Indonesia (and over a relatively long period). It would appear that application of the concept of innovation reduced over the twentieth century, certainly in the context of conflict between Muhammadiyah and NU. It has also been proposed that Muhammadiyah ceased its efforts to combat innovation because they were proving unsuccessful. This indicates the persistence of variation in practice in Indonesian Islam, although whether this reflects choice, or ignorance, on the part of the *umat* would be difficult to determine.

It was seen that MUI has been concerned from its earliest days with establishing appropriate standards for ritual through its rulings. Indeed, MUI has arguably stepped into the role left vacant following the reduction in the intense conflict between Modernists and Traditionalist over ritual in the mid-to-late twentieth century. Its approach to the innovation of *sholat dwi bahasa*, and the views relating to innovation documented by Zamhari, suggest that Indonesia's experience mirrors that in other parts of the Muslim world. That is, a narrow, and classically more conservative interpretation of the concept of innovation, has become common.

The consequences of condemning innovation depend upon the particular social and political context. Scholarship indicates that, historically, charges of innovation and heresy have been deployed for 'political' purposes. The experience in Indonesia shows that for a large part of the twentieth century such charges were a part of the institutional politics among the major Islamic organizations (which were coloured also by '*aliran*' politics, in which piety and religious affiliation were factors in national political alliances). This framework was shattered by the violence in and around 1965, which had a particular impact on less-committed Muslims, and changed the dynamics around piety in a significant way. As has been seen, the administration and regulation of religious freedom through the New Order period captured and channelled doctrinal issues for the purposes of state security. This alliance between state and religion continues today in Indonesia, but with the relative weighting or priority of the factors of security and doctrine altered – if not inverted. Previously, the dominant paradigm was state security, with religious doctrine called on by the state apparatus in a supporting role to justify state action. Now it is arguably the case that security and stability are called upon as justification for declarations of deviancy; that is, that a desire to instil religious conformity forces a supporting response from the state.

Transformation of MUI

The key Islamic organization in this alliance between state and religion is MUI. Having highlighted the link between state and security, an important factor in the case study, it must be noted that the relationship between MUI and the state, and between state and Islam in Indonesia, extends well beyond this field. One of the clearest indicators of this is the rapid rise in the volume of *fatawa* issued on the syariah economy. Another indicator is the high proportion of MUI rulings dedicated to subjects other than deviancy and ritual observance. What is interesting about the transformation of MUI is that it has worked consistently since *Reformasi* to establish itself as independent of government, yet it has not in any way sought to yield its role as the acknowledged advisor to government. A critical feature of MUI's relationship with government has been its return to a close association with government but with a transformation in the mode of engagement. Traditionally, MUI was seen as a representative of government, supportive of policy (although the degree of this support has been debated), or perhaps, more simply, as a creation of government. Now the position is rather more of MUI as an advisor to government, and – in the views of MUI members – as a body that expresses views on Islamic doctrine to government, which it expects to be recognised, or implemented.

The infiltration of puritan elements into the mass organisations Muhammadiyah and NU demonstrates that MUI's embrace of more extreme elements within Islam is not unique. What distinguishes this engagement, however, is the apparently deliberate move by MUI to embrace organizations without distinction as to their orientation (provided, that is, that they are what MUI considers sufficiently orthodox). This research has not sought to describe or interrogate MUI's internal dynamics, including the mechanisms by which *fatwa* are developed. Therefore, it is difficult here to assert – for example – that the embrace of these groups has led to the issuing of certain rulings. There has not been an obvious rise in the number of *fatwa* dealing with deviancy, for example, and heresy has been a focus since the organization's founding (as noted earlier). Nonetheless, MUI's actions in reviving national Islamic community meetings in 2005, also a 'peak' year for rulings on core matters of doctrine, show its willingness to assert itself with confidence.

There are questions outstanding about MUI's internal dynamics, specifically the nature of the links between national and regional branches. Hooker has identified this is a subject requiring further study, and this research is to an extent a contribution to this agenda (I deal in some detail with the events at the regional level in the case study). It was observed above, however, that MUI at the central level does not insist on uniformity in *fatawa*. The following chapter demonstrates the way in which MUI at the local level functions in practice, and, according to Olle (2006: 10), local Islam may reveal an even more deep-seated conservatism than that seen at the elite level.[74] The fact that a third, national-level, *fatwa* was issued in the Roy case, indeed on the day following his night-time arrest, is of interest, but it is difficult to determine what this reflects about relations between the local and national level.

Advancing the role of Islam

MUI's policy is to influence legal reforms, and *fatwa* and recommendations are directed toward this aim (senior government officials also openly acknowledge this fact). The desire to influence state law is not a new trend as was seen in the views of its third Secretary General Hasan Basri, who said that MUI should seek to ensure laws passed in Indonesia did not contradict Islam. In its current publications, MUI adopts for itself the classic descriptor for the 'official' voice of Islam in a Muslim country – state *Mufti*. The state has become increasingly receptive to this role and the recent developments in constitutional interpretation mean that the consequences of this role are more far reaching than ever. Thus, it is now accepted that MUI has a role to play in policy proposals for legislation, and in supporting the state in law enforcement under the blasphemy regime: MUI plays a defining role in establishing appropriate religious standards for public policy. This, argues Olle (2006: 6), reflects the renegotiation of who is the arbiter in Indonesia of religious 'truth' and 'who has the political and cultural legitimacy/power to regulate social life'.

This drive for pre-eminence extends MUI's influence beyond the limitations described by Saeed (2005) for establishing a 'local orthodoxy', and its partnership with government places it in a unique position to influence – and perhaps determine – the character of Indonesian Islam. This institutional posture is married with a doctrinal posture that reflects a drive towards a singularity of doctrine, and one that is characterised, in the context of innovation, by a conservative approach. Moreover, MUI has a will and capacity to influence the state on matters of religious standards previously unseen in Indonesia.

Conclusion

The case study reflects the fact that matters of ritual are of 'intense interest' in Indonesian society (Hooker 2003: 90). The ongoing need for *fatawa* to explain doctrine to the *umat*, and to seek to reinforce 'exactness and absolute certainty in observance' (Hooker 2003), speaks of the reality of diversity and pluralism in Indonesian religious society. The traditional breadth of the subject of innovation

---

74 Considering the number of provinces in Indonesia (in excess of 30) and districts (numbering in the hundreds) there are potentially a very large number of sub-national components of MUI, which may operate to a greater or lesser extent in conformity with national policy.

and its relationship to more serious charges of violation of Islamic religious doctrine suggests that the subject should be approached with caution. Doctrine is important, of course, because 'perceived purity of doctrine is crucial for Islam whatever the time, place and circumstance' (Hooker 2003: 63). Yet Islam is a universalistic faith, which encounters diverse 'ecologies, languages and cultures' that differ significantly from the point of origin in the Arabic Middle East (Hooker 2003). With the persistent move towards increasing conservatism seen in Indonesian doctrine, its interpretation and application therefore plays a critical role in the interaction between tradition and change.

MUI's response, through *fatawa*, is characteristic of the Modernist rejection of innovation seen earlier in the twentieth century in Indonesian Islam and described above. Its rulings – and stance on deviancy more generally – reflect the more confined and limited orthodox interpretation of *bid'ah* that has become prevalent in Islam. This doctrinal approach, combined with MUI's active role in the legal process, suggests a desire to advance a sectarian position using state legal mechanisms. This reinforces a growing view that MUI has positioned itself as the legitimate face of conservative Islam in Indonesia.

Claims relating to innovation are important because of their close association with notions of blasphemy and apostasy. I do not seek to determine the validity or significance for Muslims of claims such as these, and indeed the more severe claim of unbelief. The question that arises – rather – is the nature and extent of the consequences of such fundamental issues of faith. MUI policy reflects a conscious and clear agenda to access available legal mechanisms to pursue Islamic doctrinal agendas. This reflects dissatisfaction with, and contestation of the boundaries between, Islam and the state. But this contestation sits within a social setting that constantly reminds us that tensions arise 'between the requirements of dogma and the realities of its practice' (Hooker 2003: 88). Religious pluralism and variation in beliefs and ritual practices are a fact of life. The question raised here is the basis upon which MUI has become elevated to the position of being able to dictate what the requirements of 'dogma' might be in any given situation. MUI is in a unique and unrivalled position to determine when any – or all – of the potentially vast number of variations in ritual practice should be classified as deviant. Further, it works to gain the support of the state in ensuring this classification is sanctioned via the legal process. Criminalising minority expressions of faith extends the consequences that deviancy might otherwise attract well beyond the realms of the (merely) spiritual or social. Declarations of innovation (and deviancy) are not new in Indonesia, but their criminalisation under MUI's guidance expands in a critically important way the engagement between Islam and state law.

5 Case Study Part 1 – The language of devotion

The previous chapters established the theoretical framework and broader legal and social context for religious freedom in Indonesia. This chapter, and the one following, examine a particular case study based on the experiences of Yusman Roy in pursuing and promoting his interpretation of Islam in a village in East Java. It has been seen how diversity in Indonesian Islam has been the subject of doctrinal debate, and I have also indicated the extent to which variations in approach to matters such as ritual prayer have been one key area of contestation not only in Indonesian Islam, but more widely. I address the Roy case in two parts to thoroughly examine both the circumstances of the case and the legal process. This chapter deals with diversity in practice and the challenges it raises for the state, for MUI and other Islamic organisations, and for individuals such as Roy. Looking closely at his actions and the reactions of other parties provides insight into the experience of religious freedom in reality.

The focus in this chapter is on events leading up to Roy's arrest. The information presented here is based on a study of primary documents, including correspondence, the *fatawa* issued by branches of MUI at the local level, and records of police interviews.[1] This rich collection of material allows a clear timeline to be developed from the first emergence of Roy's particular teaching, and permits quite detailed analysis of the conduct and opinions of the different parties. In this way, it is possible to understand more fully the context in which a typical blasphemy prosecution against an Indonesian Muslim unfolds. In particular, it illuminates the role of MUI as an important counterpart to state legal institutions in the implementation of the blasphemy regime. This reinforces the value of the case study as a means of appreciating the prominent place that can be played by Islamic doctrine in regulating the experience of the right to religious freedom.

---

1 References to primary sources found in footnotes; all referenced documents are on file. See Hosen (2012) for a detailed account of Roy's teachings and the doctrinal issues in question.

Pondok Itikaf Jamaah Ngaji Lelaku

Roy established *Pondok Itikaf Jamaah Ngaji Lelaku* in February 1996, and its nature and location were outlined in Chapter 1. Roy claimed to lead a group of up to 300 *santri* or religious scholars at the *pesantren*, although a former student claimed a significantly smaller number of around ten to fifteen, with between fifteen and thirty attending Friday prayers.[2] Roy first employed his approach of dual-language prayer in 1995 during private worship with his family, and he described the concept as being his own creation. In January 2005, sometime after distributing leaflets to publicise and promote his teaching (discussed below), Roy released a brief 'Mission and Vision' statement.[3] This one-page document stated the principal mission of the *pesantren* to be the 'development of the noble character[4] of the Muslim faithful with the guidance of the Qur'an and hadith'. The *pesantren*'s role was to 'resolutely assist the government's program in the education sector of noble character/national moral development' with the objective being to 'make – God-willing – the unitary state of Indonesia safe, calm, secure and prosperous'. The statement went on to observe that 'morality depends entirely upon the quality of *sholat*, as intended by the word of God . . . "Recite what has been revealed to you of the Book and perform the prayer . . ."' (Qur'an 29:45). Accordingly, the *pesantren* took the initiative to:

> pioneer and concentrate [on] improving the performance of leading congregational worship appropriately. That is [by] using the method of reciting the Arabic verses in the two prayer cycles delivered to the congregation for repetition, always accompanied by translation into *bahasa Indonesia* or into a common language in order that its meaning can be effectively received by lay members of the congregation/especially by those who have limited/ no understanding of Arabic.

The publications

Roy's teachings were published in leaflets produced in February 2002 and August 2003, and in a VCD recording of a presentation given by Roy. The written publications are interspersed with Qur'anic references, and are characterised by variations in font and presentation, including sections appearing in smaller type, and other sections underlined, with other sections capitalised. The

---

2 See Indictment, Attorney-General's Office Kepanjen; Kepanjen District Court Decision.
3 'Mission and Vision of *Yayasan Taqwallah, Pondok I'tikaf Jama'ah Ngaji Lelaku*', 3 January 2005. References in the section immediately following this note are from the mission statement.
4 *Budi Pekerti Yang Luhur.*

documentary evidence does not provide a great deal of detail to confirm with any accuracy the times or locations for the distribution of the handouts. The VCD was played at a seminar at the State Islamic University *Sunan Ampel*, Surabaya, in April 2005 (see further, below).

February 2002 leaflet

In this two-page handout, Roy set out his thinking on the question of Arabic as the language of formal prayer. Carrying the title 'The Authentic and Correct Method of Worship and Leading Congregational Worship', this leaflet questioned how Indonesian Muslims could understand the meaning of Qur'anic verses – particularly younger Muslims with a limited grasp of Arabic. It opened as follows:

> **and people that maintain their sholat.** QS 23 Verse 9
>
> Are you already among those that can maintain worship?
>
> Upholding that which is referred to in the broadest sense possible, in this matter we intentionally focus only on the sense of upholding *sholat* with *efforts to comprehend the meaning of each recitation which is in Arabic, so that it can be applied and also used for answering questions which arise in our daily lives* . . .
>
> are you able to comprehend the meaning of each recitation which is in Arabic, let alone apply it, *if basically you do not understand the Arabic language to begin with?* And this also includes the moment you are engaged in communal prayer led by an *Imam*, how would it be possible for you to gain understanding [of it] if an *Imam* who recites God's instructions during communal prayer *always uses the Arabic language ONLY and does not want to ADD an Indonesian translation?*

Support for this view was found by reference to the Qur'an 14:4 – 'We did not send any messenger unless it is with the language of his own people, so that he is able to give clear explanations to them'.[5] The leaflet repeated this key theme throughout, with additional commentary and argumentation at various points. For example, the leaflet noted that a good Indonesian Muslim should stand out not only for their knowledge of Arabic (which it encouraged the Muslim community to master) but also for their honourable character. It also proposed that an *Imam* who refused to provide an Indonesian translation was concealing revelation, stating 'the perpetrator who

---

5 It is interesting to note the commentary of Madjid (1994: 70) on this verse, which, he explains, shows that just as the Islamic message was adapted to the 'imperatives of the Arabian Peninsula. . . . Therefore it must also be adaptable to the environment of any culture of its adherents, any where and at any time'.

leads that sholat is clearly cursed (*terlaknat*)'. This position was supported by reference to the Qur'an 2:159: 'Surely those who conceal the clear proofs and the guidance that We revealed after We made it clear in the Book for men, these it is whom Allah shall curse, and those who curse shall curse them (too)'.

Further Qur'anic references were used to support the argument that 'normal' people had a right to clarity in communication, Qur'an 41:44: 'If we had made it a foreign Qur'an they would have said "If only its verses were clear! What? Foreign speech to an Arab?"'; Qur'an 26:198, 199: 'If we had sent it down to someone who was not an Arab, and he had recited it to them, they would still not have believed in it'. Numerous other Qur'anic references were provided 'to increase your steadfastness and judgment in choosing a quality technique for communal prayer' (*sholat berjama'ah berkualitas*). The leaflet asserted that the teaching was founded on a 'legal standpoint *which shows that one is obliged to include a translation in the language of the people of the one who recites God's decrees . . .*'. It closed with the invitation to challenge the arguments raised in the leaflet, with the note that '*deliberations will not be accepted without the legal grounds of the Qur'an and valid hadith*'.

August 2003 leaflet

The theme of quality prayer also appeared prominently in this second publication, but the overarching theme in this leaflet is that of independence. Carrying the title 'To Preserve the health of your life and soul, Therapy with the Formula of the Qur'an', this leaflet also carried the word 'Independence!!!' (*Merdeka!!!*) as a subtitle. This reflected the fact that it was published on Indonesian Independence Day, 17 August 2003. The publication stated:

> we of the *Yayasan Taqwallah Pondok Itikaf Jama'ah Ngaji Lelaku* have already been able to taste our freedom. . . . The happy and good news to be known by the Muslim community wherever they are, is mainly for the friends who desire *improvement in the quality of performing their communal prayer*.

The leaflet went on to claim that the failure to provide translations of the Qur'an 'rendered us unable to understand its meaning, and caused us to become even more unjust and often committed wickedness against God'. The problem, it was claimed, is well known, being 'due to the fact that the *Imam* of the communal prayer who is unprofessional in reciting the guidance of God, does not want to include a translation'. The concepts of independence and understanding were then further developed:

> Freedom! Freedom! Freedom! Think, my friends, devout Muslim men and women everywhere, you must not get to the point where you – in reciting the Qur'an – are only able to recite the Arabic, but have no idea about its

meaning and objective, as well as its further application. Because of that, surely there will occur wickedness or treachery against the truth of Islam when you do not understand the meaning of every recitation in Arabic, just like our fate in the past, before liberation, while being dominated by people who were not responsible towards the truth of Islam.

The leaflet repeated several of the propositions and Qur'anic references presented in the first publication. It also presented a new perspective on the validity of the teaching stating: 'It is known that there is no argument/ evidence in the Qur'an, as well as the Hadith which prohibit the recitation of the holy verses of the Qur'an from being accompanied by a translation into any language'.

VCD

The contents of the VCD was described in the indictment as lectures (*ceramah-ceramah*) by Roy, with 300 copies produced and provided to his *santri* for distribution in the region.[6] The Indictment includes several quotes from the VCD including:

No one can enter heaven if they only speak Arabic, there is no law that prohibits *sholat* accompanied by translation . . .

If there is anyone who states that *sholat* is not valid if accompanied by a translation, that is extremely stupid thinking [*pemikiran yang goblok pol*], they are not aware that doing that is misleading itself and misleads good people . . .

I curse [*saya melaknat*] every *Imam sholat* who deliberately does not want to accompany [it] with language that is understood by his followers, that leads to his followers being misled . . .

I urge all to begin sending out the message [*siar-siarkan*] together, from the city to the far reaches of Indonesia to begin conducting *sholat* accompanied by a translation.

The *fatawa*

One of the key aspects of the case study is the formalisation of critiques of Roy's teaching in two *fatawa* issued first in January 2004 by the District branch of MUI and, later, in February 2005, by the Provincial branch. I considered the nature of *fatawa* in contemporary Indonesia in Chapter 4, noting that MUI is one of several Islamic organisations in Indonesia that issues *fatawa*, and its work is distinguished by the provision of rulings on religious matters for general

6 See Indictment. A copy of the VCD was not located during fieldwork.

public consumption. The reasons for, and timing of, the issue of these doctrinal rulings will be explored in this section.

The *fatawa* followed a similar format, appearing on MUI letterhead, carrying the title '*Fatwa* Decision of [relevant MUI branch]', together with a document reference number. Both *fatawa* also include a sub-title referring to the matter addressed in the document, and consist of several sections commencing with a set of recitals and a set of numbered paragraphs under the sub-heading 'Deciding' (*Menetapkan*). The recitals include 'considerations' ('Considering that' – *Menimbang bahwa*), and various references to documents or events ('In light of' or 'In view of'). In appearance and style the *fatawa* therefore conform to the 'bureaucratic' model and, indeed, closely resemble Indonesian laws and regulations. That is, no specific question is posed, and the situation giving rise to the opinion provided must be derived from the recitals and the text of the decision.

January 2004

The first *fatwa* carries the title 'The Propagation of Deviant Teaching [*Penyiaran Ajaran Sesat*] at *Jalan Sumberwaras Timur* No 136, Kalirejo Sub-District, Lawang District' (the street address of the *pesantren*).[7] Its considerations section refers to the circulation of 'a leaflet' by Roy (not specifying which one was being referred to), claiming that this had 'upset society, particularly the Muslim community' (*telah meresahkan masyrakat*), obliging it to make a determination of the legal issues involved. The *fatwa* also refers to a letter from the Lawang branch of MUI of 11 September 2003, and an undated letter from a group described as the 'Religious Scholars' Communication Forum'. The recitals make it clear that the *Fatwa* Committee made a 'survey' in the field, and met to discuss the matter on 30 September 2003.

The *fatwa* includes two references to sources of Islamic guidance, found in the closing parts of the recitals. The first reference is to Qur'an 59:7: 'accept that which the Messenger gives you, and abstain from whatever he forbids you'. The second reference, following the verse above, is to a *hadith*, which the *fatwa* translates into Indonesian:

> Truly in *sholat* there can be nothing from the utterances of human beings, these may only be the counting of prayer beads and the recitation of the *takbir*[8] and of the Qur'an.

7 *Fatwa* No, Kep.02/SKF/MUI/KAB/I/2004, *Majelis Ulama Indonesia Kabupaten Malang*.
8 The pronouncement 'God is Great' (*Allah u akbar*), a component of the prayer ritual.

The *fatwa* then:

1) determines (*menetapkan*) that the teaching disseminated by Roy through two leaflets [titles of leaflets] is deviant, and causes the Islamic community to deviate [*adalah sesat dan menyesatkan . . .*] and damages Islamic law as taught by the Prophet;
2) determines (*menetapkan*) that those who have followed this teaching whether consciously or otherwise should immediately show remorse;
3) urges the Islamic community not to be inducted into this deviant teaching;
4) relies on *Ulama* to give counsel and guidance to those who wish to repent;
5) urgently invites the government take clear steps to prohibit teaching that deviates from Islamic law.

The document indicates that copies were distributed to a range of government representatives in the area, from both national and local government: the Regent of Malang (*Bupati*); the Malang District Police headquarters (*Polres*); the District Military Command (*Dandim*); the head of the District Prosecutor's Office; the Chair of the District Court of Malang; the Chair of the Malang District Parliament; and the head of the District office of the Department of Religion.

February 2005

The second *fatwa* issued by the Provincial-level *fatwa* committee of MUI on 12 February 2005 is more extensive, and a nine-page elucidation or clarification (*penjelasan*), including extensive religious commentary, is attached.[9] The relevant considerations set out in the opening paragraphs of the document include the observation that using a language other than the revealed language:

> obviously creates a new model for the implementation of *ibadah* outside the guidance of Islamic law, particularly with reference to the guidelines on performing *sholat* as practiced by/exemplified by the Prophet. The creation of new matters in the implementation of *ibadah mahdlah* (pure) are categorised as *bid'ah haqiqiyah* (*bid'ah senyatanya*) or *bid'ah dlalalah* (an innovation that is erroneous and rejected).
>
> The creation of a new model in the implementation of *ibdadah* is a fact of deviation from Islamic law (*syariat Islam*), which leads believers astray and at the same time disgraces the sanctity of Islam.

---

9 *Fatwa* No Kep-13/SKF/MUI/JTM/H/2005, *Majelis Ulama Indonesia Jawa Timur.*

Included in the preliminary considerations is a reference to the Blasphemy Law (Law 1/PNPS/1965), and the *fatwa* committee also notes that the primary role of MUI is, among other things, 'being a movement for the compromise (*ishlah*) and purification of Islamic teaching including instruction in commanding right and forbidding wrong (*amar ma'ruf nahi munkar*)'.[10]

The *fatwa* determines the following:

1) The legal status of compelling the use of translation in leading Qur'anic recital by an *Imam*, in connection with communal prayer as taught/ disseminated by . . . [Roy] . . . is classified as a practice that is a deviant innovation [*bid'ah sesat*] and is rejected. The aforesaid legal status is based on consideration that there is no guidance from Syariah argumentation [*dalil syariah*], principally the *sunnah* of the Prophet.

2) Worship that includes as a component deviant innovation clearly violates *syariah* guidelines, and as a consequence it causes the communal prayer led by an *Imam* and [of his/the] entire congregation to be corrupted (its legitimacy is rejected).

3) Efforts to entrench and spread procedures for group prayer according to the first finding are classified as *fasiq* (sinful acts) because [of] the publication of violations against Islamic teaching (inciting disobedience) in the form of deviant innovations in the midst of believers.

4) Appeals to the community *Ngaji Lelaku, Yayasan Taqwallah*, to realise their error, repent their mistake and return to observing the correct teachings of procedure for communal prayer in accordance with the guidance of Islamic law as exemplified by the Prophet and practiced by the Islamic community in general.

5) This *fatwa* is conveyed to the relevant parties, in particular to the Guardian and Manager of . . . [the *pesantren*] . . . to provide the necessary guidance. . . .

The accompanying clarification, of more than a dozen pages, contains seven sections:

- The basis of obligations for prayer;
- Readiness for the execution of prayer;
- Recitation during prayer;

---

10 This particular role is one of six which includes the role of *mufti* (*pemberi fatwa*) (MUI 2010b: 31–33). MUI (2010b: 32) describe this role as including the objective of changing the condition of society 'from conditions which are not consistent with Islamic teaching in order to become a quality (*berkualitas*) society and nation'. Interestingly, this reflects Roy's own objective of achieving 'quality devotions'. This Islamic concept is not considered further here but is the subject of a lengthy study in its own right, see Cook (2004).

- Translation of the Qur'an and communal prayer;
- The function of the Qur'an;
- On clarifying the significance of the Qur'an; and
- On concealing the truth.

The clarification opens by stating that because *sholat* is a pure form of religious observance the method of carrying it out must follow guidelines established by the Prophet through the Qur'an or *sunna*. In support of this a *hadith* is quoted: 'perform the *shalat* just as you all observed my method of performing the *shalat*'. It goes on to state that a claim for rationality – the ability to receive things intellectually – does not necessarily have to be fulfilled, especially in the field of worship.

In regard to the conduct of prayer, the clarification states there should be tolerance for the possibility that people cannot yet understand the symbolic meaning of all the components of prayer nor the meaning of all the readings used, including verses of the Qur'an. In this case the agreed standard is the ability to utter the Arabic text of the readings. Although it is proposed that all Muslims should try to understand the meaning of prayer readings, it is not through the use of translation when conducting prayer, rather through studying Arabic.

On the subject of recitation from the Qur'an, the clarification states that all readings are sourced from the teachings of God and the Prophet. It goes on to advise that the Qur'an is the word of God, God spoke Arabic to the Prophet, and the meaning (therefore) comes from God. It then quotes Qur'an 43:3 – 'surely we have made it an Arabic Qur'an so that you may understand'. It concludes that translations of the Qur'an cannot be identified as the Qur'an and so cannot be used to replace it during prayer.[11] The existence of the Qur'an in Arabic cannot be forgotten – even if the reader does not understand the meaning of the text, this does not remove the 'Qur'anic-ness' (*sic*) of the verses in question.[12]

In short, the capacity of the reader to understand the text is not able to be used as support for the use of translations of the Qur'an: the reading of the Qur'an is an effective means of communication between a servant and their Lord if it is composed of His words. This is consistent with His will, and separate from whether or not the servant understands the meaning of the words. This communication consolidates the place of prayer as the entitlement of God (*hak Allah*), and not for the benefit (*kepentingan*) of the servant.

The clarification states that use of translations outside prayer is not in issue, but it reinforces that requiring the use of translation in prayer is firmly

---

11 This is the key doctrinal issue underpinning the case study. It will be addressed further in Chapter 6 where the views of religious experts as relayed during the trial in the District Court will be considered.

12 '*tidak menghilangkan jatidiri ke-Qur'an-an ayat yang bersangkutan*'.

prohibited. Relying on *hadith*, the clarification states that firm legal sanctions are to be imposed on those who utter a single word or sentence of personal interest, or instruct other people to do things that have no relationship with guidance on reading during prayer, except where there is clear guidance from the law (*dari syaria'at*) for such a pronouncement.

The clarification also addresses a Qur'anic reference raised in the publications. The Qur'an 14:4 reads in part: 'and We did not send any apostle but with the language of his people'. The clarification states that this reference cannot be interpreted as a requirement that *ulama* use the local language when they lead prayer, because the method for conducting prayer has already been clarified by the Prophet.

Key events

The events of the case study span approximately four years, from the time that Roy released his teaching on dual-language prayer in February 2002, to the rejection of his appeal by the Indonesian Supreme court in January 2006. A complete study of Roy's experience as a *kyai* or Islamic scholar/teacher would span a longer timeframe, including the years from the establishment of his *pesantren*, and conduct of the *hajj*, or pilgrimage to Mecca, in 2000. The main focus in this chapter is, however, on the period during which Roy actively promoted his teaching prior to his arrest in May 2005. Key events and significant pieces of correspondence gathered in field work will be relied upon to illustrate the social and religious conflict in the local community, and to establish the particular positions of Roy and MUI on the religious issues in question.

The teaching in the community – disturbance

Allegations of causing a public disturbance were to be central to the case study, however police statements do not reveal in any great detail information about the times or circumstances of key events. Distributions of Roy's pamphlets were made at various locations both nearby and at further distances from the *pesantren*. These include at Lawang itself; Singosari; the Malang bus interchange at Arjosari; Bantur; and Tulungagung, although the witnesses do not provide dates.[13] The distribution of leaflets outside a mosque in the town of Singosari, which lies on the road between Lawang and the District capital of Malang, in 2003, resulted in assaults upon Roy's *santri* as they handed out the information. A brief

---

13 Evidence of Diono, Ridwan and Mukti Ali, Kepanjen District Court Decision. Witnesses Dion and Bambang Sutejo (both *santri* at the *pesantren*) confirmed in their evidence at trial being detained by a mob and beaten at Singosari; Indictment. Both Bantur and Tulungagung are some distance from Lawang and Malang, to the South and West, respectively.

description of this event is found in a publication produced by MUI Malang after Roy's arrest and in a later publication by the head of the MUI Malang *fatwa* committee (Bashori 2006; MUI 2005). This event took place at the Hizbullah mosque in Singosari on 11 September 2003, and several members of the congregation 'spontaneously' caught and assaulted those distributing the leaflets, before handing them over to the local police.

Ultimately it is difficult to determine how widespread or severe such encounters may have been. However, by early January 2005 the situation was described by Roy in correspondence to state officials as 'conflict prone' – *rawan konflik*.[14] The description of the potential for conflict in this letter is specifically to intra-religious tension: 'conflict-prone conditions amongst the Islamic community'.[15] Later in the same month Roy reminded the regional police that the situation was 'very urgent and conflict-prone'.[16] Correspondence in early February to the National Chief of Police also appears to demonstrate that Roy felt insecure. It states that 'the situation and conditions very urgently demand that all parties be able to feel justice and security'.[17]

On 26 January 2005 an event described by Roy as a 'disturbance' (*keributan*) took place at the Malang office of the Department of Religion, when he attempted to provide the 'Mission and Vision' statement to the Department.[18] The officials did not respond positively (*tidak merespon dengan baik*) and delivered a firm statement emphasising that Roy was of a different opinion to MUI Malang.[19] MUI officials and police were also present and, according to a description of the event published by MUI (MUI 2005), Roy allegedly threatened to kill the Departmental officials and MUI representatives, as well as the signatories to the *fatwa*. These accounts are not necessarily inconsistent, but do place a different emphasis on the exchanges that took place. Whether or not this particular allegation is accurate, the material indicates that there was a significant degree of tension between the parties at this time.

The head of the MUI Malang *fatwa* committee, Bashori, told police that on 5 April he received a telephone call from an Islamic community leader (*tokoh Islam*) from the town of Pasuruan.[20] The caller advised that 'if [the] Malang

---

14 Letter from Roy to Minister of Religion 3 January 2005, copied to the President, Vice-President, and KomnasHAM.
15 '*kondisi rawan konlik antar sesama Umat Islam*'.
16 '*Mengingat situasi yang sangat mendesak dan rawan konflik*'; letter from Roy to Malang Police Chief, 13 January 2005.
17 '*mengingat sikon yang sangat mendesak menuntut keadilan dan keamanan agar dapat dirasakan oleh semua pihak*'; letter from Roy to National Chief of Police, 3 February 2005.
18 Letter from Roy to Department of Religion East Java, 29 January 2005.
19 '*bahkan telah memberikan ketegasan pada kami yang __dapat ditafsirkan maksudnya__ itu demikian, bahwa: apabila selama kami masih berbeda paham dengan MUI Kab Malang*'.
20 Pasuruan is approximately 40 km to the Northeast of Lawang, nearly twice as far as the District capital Malang.

people can't handle this then we from Pasuruan will jump in'.[21] The same person called again at around 2.00 pm on 6 May after arriving at Lawang with a group from Pasuruan, but was prevented from taking any action due to a police presence at Roy's *pesantren*.[22] Word was apparently received by MUI from the community at the neighbouring towns of Sukorejo,[23] Kepanjen and several other locations that they too planned to follow the lead of the mob from Pasuruan (MUI 2005: 3).

Two key witnesses had both served as head of the neighbourhood association[24] in the area surrounding the *pesantren*, and informed police in their statements that they saw a group of fifteen people arrive at the *pesantren* 'so far as I know, to stop Roy's teachings'.[25] The statements of these two individuals were taken one hour apart by the same police officer, and besides the personal details found in the opening questions, the statements are identical in content, word-for-word. Another witness, the head of MUI Lawang, claimed at trial that the group was of around 100 people from Pasuruan and Surabaya, and that he reported their arrival to police.[26] No information explains how witnesses determined the origin, make up or intentions of this group. These witnesses also confirm the general sense of insecurity at least among those neighbouring the *pesantren*. They stated that they were afraid to be considered among Roy's followers and increased their guard duties, fearing that 'unwanted' events (*tidak diinginkan*) might take place, following the publication in print and electronic media of strong statements by Roy (see further below).[27]

An important allegation about the protestors was later made by Roy's defence team in the defence statement (*Pleidooi*) filed at trial.[28] The statement noted

---

21 Police Witness Statement, 6 May 2005.

22 '... *saya ditelephone lagi oleh* [caller] *bersama rombongan sudah di Kec. Lawang Kab. Malang akan tetapi sudah dicegah oleh aparat Kepolisian Polsek Lawang sehinggah kembali ke Pasuruan'*.

23 Sukorejo is approximately 40 km to the South.

24 Identified in the documents by the Indonesian 'RT 03/RW 04 Kelurahan Kalirejo'. *Lurah* or village is the abbreviation for the lowest level administrative units in Indonesian towns. Roy's *pesantren* in Jalan Sumber Waras was located in this *lurah* of Lawang: Decision of Malang Regent. RT stands for *Rukun Tetanggah* or 'neighbourhood association', RW for *Rukun Warga* or 'citizen's association'. Individuals are expected to play active roles in neighbourhood coordination and security through these associations. For a brief history of the development of the RT/RW system, see Walker & Tinker (1975).

25 '*Sepengetahuan saya untuk menghentikan ajaran-ajaran yang dilakukan oleh Roy*'; Police Witness Statement, 7 May 2005.

26 Surabaya, the Provincial capital, is approximately 70 km to the North.

27 '*benar-benar sudah resah dengan ajaran [Roy] sehingga masyarakat meningkatkan kewaspadaan dan merasa takut karena dikira sebagai pengikut ajaran dari pada [Roy] bahkan dengan stetmen [Roy] yang keras di media cetak dan media elektronik masyrakat bertambah resah dikwatirkan terjadi hal-hal yang dinginkan*'.

28 Defence Statement, 23 August 2005.

that it was not Roy himself that disturbed the community but the arrival of others from outside (*dari luar kampung*), coming in the name of the Islamic community (*Ummat Islam*). The statement claimed that this group was the *Forum Umat Islam* (Islamic Community Forum), and that its pressure and threats (*tekanan dan ancaman*) caused concern in the neighbourhood. The statement also alleged that this group was organised by MUI Malang, but did not provide any specific evidence in support of this claim.[29]

According to the police statement of Bashori, national television stations TVRI and Trans TV carried interviews with Roy between 3 and 5 May.[30] One witness, Achwan, a member of a neighbouring branch of MUI, reported that Roy claimed in his media statements that his teaching was valid, and that he planned to report MUI Malang to the police and the central office of MUI.[31] One witness described these media statements as 'strong' (*keras*), thereby creating increasing concern among the local population, fearful that unpleasant acts would take place.[32] At trial it was later claimed that after Roy's teachings had been exposed in the media, the community was concerned that a mob would try to attack the *pesantren* and that many journalists and officials arrived to be on the alert (*berjaga-jaga*) for this eventuality.[33]

Roy's teachings were also disseminated in another public forum, some days prior to the events of early May. On 30 April, the State Islamic University *Sunan Ampel* in Surabaya (the provincial capital) hosted a seminar during which the VCD was played. This event appears to have replaced a proposed public debate sponsored by the Islamic affairs journal *Tabloid Nurani*.[34] MUI East Java wrote to the journal on 29 April opposing the debate on the basis that it would contribute to the dissemination of deviant teaching, and that MUI had received complaints from members of the public about the event.[35] Zubaidi of MUI Malang claims to have attended the seminar and viewed the VCD. He is the only witness to report having seen the VCD.[36]

---

29 International Crisis Group or ICG (2008) describes FUI as a hardline Islamic civil society organisation established to uphold MUI *fatawa* against the Ahmadiyah sect. ICG claims that FUI is comprised of some thirty Islamic organisations, and was established in August 2005. This postdates the events of May 2005, therefore possibly throwing doubt on the claim raised in the defence statement. Alternatively, it demonstrates the difficulty of tracing the evolution of new movements.

30 Police Witness Statement, 6 May 2005.

31 Police Witness Statement, 6 May 2005.

32 Police Witness Statement, 7 May 2005: '*masyrakat bertambah resah dikwatirkan terjadi hal-hal yang dinginkan*'.

33 Indictment, p 7.

34 *Nurani* – conscience.

35 Letter from MUI East Java to *Tabloid Nurani*, 29 April 2005.

36 Police Witness Statement, 6 May 2005.

Encounters with the state and with MUI – 'legalisation'

It is not clear when issues first arose about the status of Roy's teachings, but by late 2003 the question was raised through correspondence between the *pesantren* and the provincial government. In late September of that year a request was made to the East Java government to 'permit and facilitate'[37] dissemination of the teaching, stating that the *pesantren* would take responsibility for any legal consequences that might arise.[38] It is not made explicit in what way there may have been legal issues with the leaflets or teaching. The provincial government subsequently turned to the Department of Religion for assistance with this request, and the office forwarded the request for authorisation to its research department for advice.[39]

The request for authorization was still pending more than twelve months later, when Roy sought information from MUI Malang in December 2004. This request came nearly a full year after the release of the District-level *fatwa* (January 2004), however Roy claims not to have been aware of the release of the *fatwa* until advised about it by a member of the DPR.[40] Roy therefore wrote to MUI Malang seeking 'guidance and *fatwa* concerning genuine *sholat* procedure' – that is, it appears Roy was not seeking confirmation of the incorrect procedure, but positive instruction as to correct procedure.[41] There is evidence to suggest that Roy wrote repeatedly to MUI Malang without receiving any reply to his approaches.[42]

Owing to the delays in receiving a response to his request of late 2003, Roy wrote to the Minister of Religion in January 2005, clearly referring in this instance to his request for the 'legalisation' of the leaflet.[43] Copies of this correspondence were provided to the President (then Susilo Bambang Yudhoyono) and Vice-President and Indonesia's National Human Rights Commission (KomnasHAM). Roy followed this indirect approach to the President with a further letter seeking his recommendation that the Minister of Religion respond to the legalisation request.[44] Roy again wrote to the President in March 2005, outlining his teaching and seeking a meeting. This request was forwarded to

37 '*diizinkan dan diberi kemudahan*'.
38 '*Apa bila ternyata dikemudian hari terjadi penyimpangan-penyimpangan yang melanggar hokum, kami siap untuk mempertanggungjawabkan tuntutan hokum*'; letter from *pesantren* to the Head, Agency for National Unity and Protection of Society (BAKES-BANGLINMAS) 30 September 2003.
39 Letter from Department of Religion East Java to Department of Religion Research and Development Agency, 7 October 2003.
40 Letter from Roy to Malang Police, 29 November 2005. This letter is discussed further below.
41 Reference to this approach for guidance is made in the opening parts of the second *fatwa*.
42 Letter from Roy to Malang Police, 13 January 2005.
43 '*permohonan legalisir selebaran*'; letter from Roy to Minister for Religion, 3 January 2005.
44 Letter from Roy to President, 5 January 2005.

the Minister of Religion, and there is no evidence that the President or a representative responded to Roy.[45]

Late in January 2005 Roy expressed concern to the provincial office of the Department of Religion over the lack of responses to earlier requests for information from the district office of the Department in Malang. At the same time Roy expressed his objection to the fact that the secretary to MUI Malang was simultaneously a staff member of the Department of Religion – a situation he described as 'arbitrary discrimination'.[46] Shortly thereafter Roy received a reply from the provincial office of the Department on the subject of the 'Mission and Vision' statement of the *pesantren*.[47] The response made the point that, as the official mission statement contained an error according to syariah, the Malang office was obliged to honour and give effect to the district-level *fatwa* as material in its considerations.[48] Referring to Law 1/PNPS/1965 regarding the propagation of deviant teachings, it noted that MUI East Java was considering Roy's case,[49] and closed with the observation that in relation to maintaining stability in regional security, the religious problems under consideration could precipitate social unrest, and so should cease.[50] Within a further few days, a reply was sent to Roy by the Department's research agency stating that 'the Department of Religion does not legalise brochures/printing produced by the public'.[51]

The Department also received from MUI East Java around the same time advice in writing confirming its opinion that Roy's teaching was in error.[52] This correspondence was sent in response to an earlier request from the Department for MUI's observations about the *pesantren*'s 'Mission and Vision' statement. MUI however went further and also expressed its desire that there be a

45 Letter from Roy to President, 7 March 2005, and letter from Presidential Secretariat to Minister of Religion, 31 March 2005.

46 '*discriminatif sewenang-wenang*'; letter from Roy to Department of Religion East Java, 29 January 2005. Research and field work were unable to identify evidence of earlier approaches to the district office of the Department, but this assumes that these were documented in correspondence, which may not be the case.

47 Letter from Department of Religion East Java to Roy, 7 February 2005.

48 '*Menyangkut masalah kebenaran Syariah Agama Islam, maka Departmen Agama Kab. Malang memang seharusnya menghormati dan menjadikan Fatwa MUI Kb. Malang sebagai bahan pertimbangan*'.

49 Although how it came by this information is not clear. The second, provincial-level *fatwa*, was issued five days after the date of this correspondence, on 12 February. The implications of this statement are discussed further below.

50 '*Dalam rangka menjaga stabilitas keamanan di daerah, maka permasalahan-permasalahan agama yang dianggap dapat menimbulkan keresahan dalam masyrakat seharusnya dihindari*'.

51 Letter from Department of Religion Research, Development and Education Agency, to Roy, 17 March 2005.

52 Letter from MUI East Java to Department of Religion East Java, 21 February 2005. The date of the incoming request for advice is not specified, but was sent earlier in 2005.

'coordination meeting' (*rapat koordinasi*) between the Department, the Attorney-General's Office (identifying PAKEM as the appropriate agency),[53] and MUI itself. The purpose of this meeting would be:

> in relation to anticipating/and or taking preventative or repressive steps in order that teachings or opinions of the sort that can mislead the religious community or moreover that can lead to disgracing of a religion do not break out.[54]

A copy of MUI's 12 February *fatwa* accompanied the letter with a request that it be distributed to appropriate parties via the Department's offices across the province:[55]

> in order to be made known to the extent necessary and at the same time to prevent the possibility of the outbreak of other similar teachings, or at least which can be categorised as religious harassment, whether based on incorrect opinions concerning religious teaching that are 'wanting' or not ruling out the possibility that there are elements of other parties that would knowingly engage in regional destabilisation, and the like.[56]

A range of officials received copies of this correspondence: the provincial Governor; the Speaker of the provincial Parliament; the head of the provincial police; the Chair of the Provincial High Court; and, the Malang office of the Department of Religion.

Two other key state agencies were engaged, one directly and the other indirectly. As has been noted, KomnasHAM received copies of correspondence regarding Roy's teachings and on several occasions replied directly to Roy. Thus in January 2005, following Roy's complaint to the Minister of Religion about the delay in legalising his leaflets, the Commission advised Roy that it had no authority to make any form of evaluation about the teachings of a religion or belief system.[57] In February the Commission described briefly the legal basis for religious freedom in Indonesia, and proposed that if it should be alleged

---

53 PAKEM is a version of *Bakorpakem*, discussed in Chapter 3, being the inter-agency group established to manage the emergence of religious sects or beliefs.

54 *'dalam rangka antisipasi dan/atau mengambil langkah-langkah preventif maupun represip agar tidak sampai timbul "Ajaran atau Faham" serupa yang dapat menyesatkan umat beragama atau bahkan dapat menjurus kepada "Penodaan" terhadadap agama'.*

55 *'sebaiknya . . . [fatwa] diinformasikan/disebar luaskan . . .'.*

56 *'untuk diketahui seperlunya dan sekaligus untuk "menangkal" kemungkinan-kemungkinan akan timbul ajaran lainnya yang sejenis, atau paling tidak dapat diketagorikan sebagai pelecehan terhadap agama, baik karena kesalah fahamnya terhadap ajaran agama yang 'kurang' atau tidak menutup kemungkinan ada unsur-unsur dari fihak lain yang sengaja ingin mengacaukan daerah, dan sebagainya'.*

57 Letter from KomnasHAM to Roy, 13 January 2005.

that there were actions in conflict with Indonesia law, the government, police or Courts would handle this in the course of any legal action.[58]

Direct approaches were also made by Roy to the Indonesian police commencing in 2004, when he was told about the existence of the first *fatwa*. In late November that year Roy wrote to the Malang police making a formal complaint alleging that the *fatwa* constituted defamation (*pencemaran nama baik*) and seeking the intervention of the police.[59] Some six weeks after sending this complaint Roy wrote again to Malang police, seemingly prompted by the urgency of the situation which had become 'conflict prone', as noted above. In late January 2005 the Malang police advised Roy in writing that the defamation complaint would not be pursued on the basis that the alleged defamation was found in a *fatwa* issued by an institution and that the object of an offence of defamation must be an individual, advising him to pursue other legal avenues.[60] The response raises some questions about how the police view MUI as an organisation because the reply refers to 'acts committed by a public servant in the valid exercise of their duties',[61] which suggests that the police assume MUI holds state or quasi-state authority.

Action by the state – enforcement

The events under consideration culminated in enforcement action by representatives of the state in May 2005. The key events are the conduct of a meeting led by the *Muspida*, or Regional Leadership Council,[62] and subsequent issuing

---

58 Letter from KomnasHAM to Roy, 14 February 2005.
59 Letter from Roy to Malang Police, 29 November 2004. The letter refers to '*pencemaran nama baik*', which translates as 'contaminating the good name', a form of defamation which is a criminal offence under art 310 of the Criminal Code.
60 Letter from Malang Police to Roy, 24 January 2005.
61 '*Bahwa perbuatan yang dilakukan seseorang pegawai negeri pada saat menjalankan pekerjaanya yang sah . . .*'.
62 *Muspida* is an acronym derived from the Indonesian *Mu̱syawarah* (Consultation/ Meeting/Council) *P̱impinan* (Leadership) *Ḏaerah* (Regional). Although this body is under the authority of the local government, it has a long history in Indonesian governance as a vehicle for managing security issues. It originated in coordination meetings between the military and administration at the local level post-Independence. Its formal status stems from a decision of Soekarno in 1964, and evolved at this time to include the local prosecutor (representative of the Attorney-General's office) with the head of the local police and District Court added later. In the Soeharto era the body is said to have played a role in the overarching national security mechanism *Bakorstanas*, with membership evolving further to include the local legislature and intelligence agencies. Under Soeharto the dominant member of the body was the local military commander, although under a 1986 Presidential order, the body is clearly intended to be under the direction of the local civilian authority (Presidential Decree Concerning the Regional Leadership Council, 10/1986, art 5); see Walker & Tinker (1975) and Kingsbury (2003). Presidential Decree 10/1986 specifies the membership of the body to include four individuals on an *ex officio*

of a decision of the *Bupati* (Regent – local senior official) purporting to shut down the *pesantren*; the filing by representatives of MUI of a complaint with the police; and Roy's arrest shortly thereafter.

On the morning of 6 May 2005 a 'coordination meeting' took place between the *Muspida* under the direction of the *Bupati*, and representatives of MUI, religious leaders (*tokoh agama*) and the Regional Intelligence Community.[63] Around thirty people are reported to have attended the meeting which took place at the Malang *pendopo*,[64] with attendees described as agreeing that Roy's teaching was disturbing the community and had the potential to lead to mass riots (Bashori 2006: 93). A decision was issued on the same day by the *Bupati* of Malang closing the *pesantren*, suspending its activities, and requiring its leadership to implement the *Bupati*'s decision, failing which 'orderly steps and firm action consistent with prevailing laws and regulations would be taken'.[65]

The only specific power referred to in the *Bupati*'s decision is art 27 (1) of Law 32/2004 on Regional Government, said to provide the local administration with the authority to 'maintain peace and social order, where peace and security along with order constitute things desired by the public'.[66] A number of other laws and instruments are also referred to in the 'considerations' section of the recitals to the instrument issued by the *Bupati*, including Law 1/PNPS/1965. In its recitals the decision also 'takes note of' (*memperhatikan*) a range of documents already referred to in this chapter including the *fatawa* and correspondence from the Department of Religion and MUI, and the outcome of the coordination meeting.

---

basis: the civilian authority (*Bupati* in this case, and the Governor at the Provincial level); the local military commander; the head of the local police; and, the prosecutor (art 4). In this case, the decision itself was copied to the following parties: Head, Regional Office, Department of Religion; Chair of MUI East Java; Head of Police, Malang; Commander of Regional Military District Malang; Head, State Prosecutor's Office; Chair, District Court, Malang; Chair, Regional Legislative Assembly; Head, Department of Religion, Malang; and Chair, MUI Malang. This distribution list suggests that in practice the membership extends to a broader group than the four members referred to in the 1986 decree.

63 Decision of the Malang *Bupati*, 6 May 2005. According to Roy's defence team, the Regional Intelligence Community consisted of the *Bupati*, Police, Commander of the Regional Military District, and the Head of the State Prosecutor's Office (LBH Surabaya 2005: 34). It may be that the involvement of this 'intelligence' group explains the apparent inconsistency in the identity of members of the *Muspida* identified above.

64 A pavilion for conducting public meetings.

65 '*akan dilakukan langkah-langkah penertiban dan tindakan tegas sesuai ketentuan peraturan perundang-undangan yang berlaku*'.

66 '*memelihara ketentraman dan ketertiban masyarakat, dimana keamanan dan ketentraman serta ketertiban adalah merupakan hal yang diinginkan masyarakat*'. Article 27 does include an obligation, among others, to maintain peace and order in the implementation of a regional head's responsibilities under the Regional Autonomy Law.

In the afternoon of 6 May, at 4.00 pm, representatives of MUI Malang filed a complaint with the local police.[67] The police report was made by a member of the local MUI *fatwah* committee; Roy is listed as the offender (*pelaku*) and the 'Islamic community' (*Umat Islam*) is identified as the victim (*korban*) of the crime. The crime is identified as a breach of art 156a of the Criminal Code:[68]

> The accused instructing the learning of prayer accompanied by translation in *bahasa Indonesia* the aforesaid teaching considered to constitute deviant teaching because it deviates from the law concerning prayer (*syariat sholat*).

The evidence (*barang bukti*) produced is Roy's second leaflet dated 17 August 2003. The summary of events repeats the description of the crime (above) and cross-references the *fatwah* issued on 21 January 2004, and the decision of the *Bupati* Malang to close Roy's *pesantren*:

> Since 2003 at . . . [the *pesantren*] . . . Roy taught a doctrine of prayer accompanied by a *Bahasa Indonesia* translation wherein the said teaching deviates from Syariah teaching on prayer and this situation constitutes a deviant teaching, with the result that on 21 January 2004 MUI Malang issued a *fatwa* which by its contents prohibited the deviant teaching referred to . . . and the *Bupati* Malang produced a decision prohibiting the activities referred to . . .

In the early evening, following lodging of the complaint with the police, Roy was arrested and questioned through to the early hours of Saturday, 7 May 2005.[69]

---

67 Police Report NO. POL.: LP/143/V/2005/Polres, Malang, 6 May 2005.
68 See Chapter 3; art 156a of the Criminal Code reads as follows:

Whoever intentionally publicly expresses sentiments or commits an act:

a   that fundamentally and by its nature is hostile, abuses or disgraces
b   a religion practised in Indonesia
      with the intention that persons should not practise any religion at all that is based on Belief in Almighty God

will be subject to a jail sentence of five years.

69 The arrest warrant (*Surat Perintah Penahanan*) is dated 7 May 2005, and from the police statements it appears that Roy's interrogation commenced at 1.45 am, continuing at 5.30 am. The relevant provision of the Code of Criminal Procedure (*KUHAP*) is a little ambiguous, stating in art 50 that an accused has the 'right to be interrogated immediately' (*segera*), and this is interpreted as a requirement for immediate questioning (Fitzpatrick 2008: 506).

Public debate

Less than two weeks after Roy's detention his case gained a significant profile at the national level. On 17 May a joint statement was issued by The Wahid Institute and a group of civil society organisations in support of Roy, defending his teachings and criticising the government for 'criminalising' dual language prayer.[70] The Wahid Institute is a think tank founded by the late former President Abdurrahman Wahid, and the organisations that adopted the statement were The Wahid Institute and JIL, and individuals including Wahid and Ulil Abshar Abdalla of JIL signed the statement (who was to go on to give evidence at the trial). The statement declared that the Roy case amounts to persecution, and that MUI should not act as a sole arbiter of religious doctrine, and it called upon the state not to intervene in matters of worship. The former President also mounted a defence of Roy on his website www.gusdur.net, rejecting measures to monopolise religious interpretation (*menyatakan menolak tindakan monopoli tafsir keagamaan*). He also stated that prayer in languages other than Arabic was permitted, and that there was no problem with the use of Indonesian during prayer.[71]

Not long after these pronouncements on 20 May 2005, the MUI Malang *fatwa* committee, represented by Luthfi Bashori, published a pamphlet titled 'Chronology [of] Why Yusman Roy Was Detained', in which Roy is described as acting arrogantly, asserting that his arrest was the direct result of his provocation (MUI 2005: 8). This document highlighted the 'disturbance' in the community resulting from the distribution of leaflets, referring to the incident at Singosari. This incident is used by Bashori to explain the strength of the feelings engendered by Roy's assertion that those who failed to use translation when acting as *Imam* – something done by thousands of Muslims across Indonesia – were 'cursed', a claim which 'inflamed their emotions' (MUI 2005: 2). Moreover, it suggested that the measures taken by the authorities were in order to prevent the occurrence of events similar to those in Poso.[72] This appears to be a reference to the intense horizontal conflict between Muslims and Christians in this province in the years immediately following *Reformasi*, leading to thousands of deaths (there continues to be social tension) (ICG 2002).

---

70 'The Wahid Institute, NGO's Reject the Criminalization of Two Languages in Sholat', together with 'Joint Statement: A Rejection of Criminalizing of the Use of Two Languages in Performing the *Sholat*', 17 May 2005, www.wahidinstitute.org/v1/Agenda/Detail/?id=336/hl=en/The_Wahid_Institute_NGOs_Reject_The_Criminalization_Of_Two_Languages_In_Sholat.
71 Defence statement.
72 '*agar tidak terjadi peristiwa SARA sebagaimana yang terjadi di Poso*' (MUI 2005: 8). SARA is the Indonesian acronym used when referring to inter-group tension referring to: ethnic group (tribe – *suku*), religion (*agama*), race (*ras*) and sectarian (inter-group – *antar-golongan*).

Bashori also related that the publication of a photograph of Roy with a German Shepherd he kept at the *pesantren* 'enraged' neighbours, and was further evidence that Roy was 'abusing' the institution of *pesantren* (MUI 2005: 3).[73] The publication noted support was received for the MUI *fatwa* from a range of sources including those among the most conservative Muslim organisations – HTI, FPI, MMI – as well as the Bomb Bali Legal Team and the Islamic political parties PKS (Prosperous Justice Party) and PBB (Crescent Moon and Star Party) (MUI 2005: 7). The publication (MUI 2005: 3) also offered a conclusion about the motivations behind the state enforcement action:

> Based on several factors, along with the fear of anarchical actions by the community, accordingly [state] agencies cooperated with the Malang Regional Government to take security steps in relation to Yusman Roy.

Bashori went on to use this material regarding the Roy case as part of a book released in 2006, titled 'The Grand Enemy of the Islamic Community' (*Musuh Besar Umat Islam*). In this later publication Bashori (2006: 93) sought to convince the reader of the independent and apolitical nature of MUI's actions, observing that the *fatwa* was not related in any way to the regional elections for regional heads, or *Pilkada*:

> It must be understood by the public that the Roy case, from the beginning, was not connected with any political interest including the Elections for Regional Heads (Pilkada). MUI is a religious organisation that looks after the religious community (*mengurusi keumatan*). . . . This case is purely an affair of the insult (*ketersinggungan*) to the religious community from Yusman Roy's provocation.

Direct election for regional heads commenced for the first time in Indonesia in 2005 (Bush 2008: 187) and the election for the Malang *Bupati* was held in September of that year.[74] However Roy was not the primary focus of Bashori's writing, but rather liberal Muslims, particularly those associated with NU. Bashori (2006: x) focuses on NU's 'young intellectuals that have changed and become secular, and are devoted to Western ideology, leaving Islamic ideology behind'. Among chapters dealing with misleading liberal Islamic thinking (in which the Roy case study is found), the book addressed syncretism; the difference between Mujahadeen and terrorists; September 11 (which Bashori proposed be declared

---

73 '*merasa institusi pondok pesantren telah dilecehkan oleh Yusman Roy*'. The picture was carried by *Tabloid Nurani* the journal associated with the public seminar held in April 2005. Dogs are widely accepted in the Muslim world to be impure.

74 Authoritative records are difficult to identify, but a contemporary election schedule on the website of 'Cetro', the Centre for Electoral Reform (http://aceproject.org/about-en/regional-centres/cetro) provides this information (accessed June 2016).

'International Anti-America Day'); and a critique of the work of Ulil in the form of a chapter titled 'Ulil Abshar Abdalla Insults Islam' (*Ulil Abshar Abdalla Menghina Islam*).

Reactions and resonances

The information set out above allows some conclusions to be drawn about the sequence of events, and the contributions of the various actors. I do not propose to develop a detailed view of developments in Indonesian political Islam or society more generally, but broadening the frame of reference beyond the local level provides important context. Specifically, the local events need to be considered in the context of the unfolding political and security situation in Indonesia post-9/11.

The first publication was developed within six months of 11 September 2001, and the events at the Singosari mosque took place on the second anniversary of 9/11.[75] Given the central place of MUI, it is also reasonable to consider the evolving profile of this organisation nationally during this time. I observed in the previous chapter that in 2005 MUI released a *fatwa* at the national level rejecting pluralism, liberalism and secularism in religion, and that recent scholarship has identified credible links between MUI and conservative and militant Islamic organisations. These links appear to be confirmed through the acknowledgment by a key actor in the case study – Luthfi Bashori, MUI Malang – of his own links with conservative Muslim organisations (Bashori 2006: 192), and also in the support claimed for the *fatwa* from similar conservative groups.[76]

Bashori's reference to a link between the events of 2005 and the looming regional election for *Bupati* must be presumed to reflect commentary or observation to this effect (although no documentary evidence has been located to support this). The *Bupati* – Sujud Pribadi – was indeed returned in the election in late 2005.[77] It is not possible to determine from the evidence available whether or not the election was a motivating factor for the *Bupati*, or indeed whether MUI or the community saw the upcoming election as an opportunity to place pressure on the regional government. However, religious factors played an important role in regional politics in the years leading to the 2005 elections,[78]

---

75 Significant terrorist incidents also occurred in Indonesia in parallel to the events unfolding in Lawang. The first Bali bombing occurred in October 2002, and the Australian Embassy (or Kuningan) bombing took place in August 2004.

76 In cataloguing his *dakwah*, or missionary, activities Bashori notes, for example, that he has been an adviser to MMI and FPI.

77 Pribadi was a member of the PDI-P party established by former President Megawati Sukarnoputri. See 'Closer to the Malang Bupati on the Occasion of the Turn of 1249 [Islamic year]', *Malang Post*, 28 November 2009.

78 The number of religiously inspired laws adopted at the regional level across Indonesia is one measure of the prominence of religion (and morality more broadly) in local politics. See, for

and there is no reason to expect that local politics in the Malang Regency would not reflect this pattern.

Innovation in context

There is no evidence that Roy had any affiliation with a larger organisation, including any of the recognised religious organisations in Indonesia, such as NU or Muhammadiyah. There is also no reference in the publications, or elements of his teaching, to indicate that he derived any part of his teaching from the work of another individual or religious organisation. Roy's *pesantren* was therefore independent and relatively small. In fact, if the evidence of his former students is accepted over Roy's own estimate, the *pesantren* was indeed very small. The result is that Roy cannot readily be categorised in terms of the distinctions identified above in relation to degrees of piety or interpretation of doctrine. The fact that no party or commentator sought to do this, according to the evidence identified in field work, reinforces the conclusion that Roy's work was an authentic and local reaction to the questions of faith and religious observance identified by Roy himself.

Traditionalist Indonesian Islam is characterised by tolerance for local custom, and this may explain the support provided for Roy by the former President, and head of NU, the late Abdurrahman Wahid. However, this is not the same as saying that Roy's teaching could be considered as representing, or integrating, a form of local custom. In fact, quite the contrary is the case. It is 'local' in a literal sense, and sits in a long history of heterodoxy in Javanese Islam. It is also consistent with a contemporary (twentieth century) debate concerning the partial adoption of local language in congregational worship, where Indonesian replaced Arabic for the Friday sermon. Roy's teaching reveals, however, no indication of 'traditional', non-Islamic, religious or spiritual belief or practices. That is, Roy's piety is not necessarily in question, nor is his acknowledgment of the core requirement of the Islamic faith in relation to prayer.[79] Perhaps, more accurately, it cannot be concluded from the evidence that Roy saw himself as promoting a syncretic deviation from Islam. The teaching itself appears to fall within a mainstream interpretation of *bid'ah*, being a sincere but unorthodox attempt to improve religious performance.

The absence of more detailed facts in relation to specific events and incidents does not allow a judgment as to what extent Roy was deliberately provocative or arrogant, as proposed by MUI. Certainly his language offended conservative community elements, and his attempts at doctrinal interpretation (in his publications) reinforced the sense of offence. It is also reasonable to conclude that the

---

example, Bush (2008: 178) who records that the years covered by the case study (2002–2005) correspond to a period in which the number of such local laws reached a peak.
79 Core requirements of the faith were canvassed in the trial, as will be seen in Chapter 6.

distribution of leaflets on the second anniversary of 9/11 may have been a deliberate provocation. Roy's apparent assertiveness in promoting his views speaks of his personal drive and commitment, but falls short of a comprehensive social or political agenda. Despite this and his lack of affiliations with major organisations, his legal problems attracted the support of high profile Indonesian Islamic liberals (evidenced by the roles of Abdurrahman Wahid and Ulil Abshar Abdalla). This arguably elevated his case to the status of a proxy for a broader conflict in contemporary Indonesia between proponents of conservative and liberal approaches to Islam.

Sequence of events

One key observation from the sequence of events is the apparent absence of any obvious correlation in time between the leaflets and *fatawa*.

The first *fatwa* was not issued until nearly two years after the production of the first leaflet, and a further year passed before the second *fatwa* was issued. The reasons for the relatively large gaps between the appearance of the leaflets and the *fatawa* could be explained in different ways, and evidence has not been identified in the research to resolve this question. Roy claimed not to have been aware of the first *fatwa* until advised by a third party, approximately ten months later. This may indicate that despite being geographically close, there was limited or no communication either between the parties or in the community more generally, which may explain the timeline. Nonetheless the timespans involved are of interest. This is because they suggest that there was no urgency to respond in a formal way to Roy's teaching, despite the claim that the teaching offended against mainstream Islamic doctrine. That is, despite its significance, the existence of a doctrinal dispute alone may not have been sufficient to trigger a response from MUI. It might also be concluded that for much of the time social conflict was in fact limited. Roy himself sought to bring the authorities' attention to the emerging conflict in correspondence, but the situation evolved over at least two years. It seems, therefore, that reference to other events or influences is required to explain how the matter came to a head in 2005.

The state's enforcement action also forms part of what appears, from the documentary record, to be an increasing tempo of the events in and around Lawang in April/May 2005. The two elements of this state action are the closure of the *pesantren*, which followed the meeting convened by the *Bupati*, and Roy's arrest not long after the submission of a complaint by members of MUI Malang. Taking the police action first, there is little to explain the timing of these steps, nor to explain why Roy's arrest was considered necessary when the evidence indicates that a security presence at the *pesantren* prevented a demonstration on 6 May. The complaint and the charge laid under the Criminal Code, relate solely to the offence of 'disgracing' a religion, and refer to documents that had been in existence for some time (the second leaflet, and the first *fatwa*). On this basis – theoretically – the complaint, charge and arrest could have proceeded at a much earlier point.

On the information available, Roy was increasingly concerned about safety and security through early 2005. This may be an indicator that there were undocumented occurrences or communications that were drivers of the increasing pace of events. There is certainly evidence to suggest that Roy's media appearances may have added intensity to events in the lead up to his arrest by publicising, nationally, what had previously been a local issue. Prior to the carriage of Roy's interviews in national electronic media in early May 2005, it appears the greatest public exposure his teaching had received was in the *Sunan Ampel* seminar in Surabaya. There is also evidence to suggest that an unidentified group or groups from outside Roy's immediate location were becoming more vocal in their concerns about the impact of his teaching. (It is possible that these developments are connected, but there is no evidence supporting this conclusion except their proximity in time.) The security presence at the school suggests that the authorities considered protest or violence to be a realistic possibility, but there is little documentary evidence to explain the level or significance of this threat. There is certainly no indication though that conditions were so serious as to be leading to severe or widespread communal violence of the sort experienced in Poso. However, clearly, the concerns of the group from Pasuruan appear to have driven them to protest at – and possibly threaten – the *pesantren*.

Role of state authorities

Following from the above observations, it might be concluded that the authorities judged the existence of a threat to public order to be sufficiently serious to act in the way they did on 6 and 7 May 2005. The offence with which Roy was charged falls under the public order provisions of the Criminal Code, and the existence of protest action may have in part triggered their response. However, a distinction can be drawn between the laying of a charge and Roy's pre-trial detention (the charge and the elements of the offence will be discussed in detail in the following chapter).

Roy's teaching and conduct had caused a reaction among sections of the population, but there is no information to suggest that Roy or his followers were themselves a threat to others. Indeed, the evidence indicates that it was Roy and his followers who had been subjected to violence and intimidation. The timing of Roy's arrest, at the end of a day of protest, indicates that the police felt that the matter was urgent. Equally, the overnight questioning might indicate a desire to act both quickly and without attracting publicity or attention, or simply merely to intimidate and disorientate Roy. In the absence of further explanation, the police action in seeking the detention of Roy appears arbitrary, and almost counterintuitive given that the only obvious threat to public order was from other quarters.

Even less certainty surrounds the action of the *Bupati* in issuing the order closing the *pesantren*. No authority is given in the decision for this step, and the only specific legislative support is found in a provision giving a general indication that public order is a matter of interest to the District head. Roy's almost immediate arrest and detention essentially deprived the decision of any real significance. Indeed, the police action effectively renders the *Bupati*'s act symbolic. Given the ambiguity surrounding the District head's powers, it could be that the police action was in fact necessary to achieve the cessation of activities at the *pesantren*. This outcome certainly appears to be at the heart of the decision, but the question remains how this decision was arrived at. On the day of the decision the *Bupati* met with counterparts in the *Muspida*, in consultation with MUI and others. One issue is that the membership and history of *Muspida* potentially renders its civilian leadership nominal (although there is no evidence to indicate that the outcome was driven by the military or intelligence agencies in this case). Another issue in relation to the membership of the leadership group is the opportunity it might provide for collusion. While there is no clear evidence of this, it is quite apparent that the meetings provided an opportunity for the courts in particular to be prejudiced by information about local events and the perspectives of other state bodies, violating the principle of the separation of powers (*trias politika* in Indonesian). The issue of consultation with religious organisations will be dealt with in more detail below.

In short, it is difficult to avoid the conclusion that the *Bupati* overreached his authority and acted without sound legal foundation in issuing the decision. Whether or not the *Bupati* or any other relevant party might have thought his action lacked validity is not clear, however. Should it have been the case that the lack of clear legal authority was evident to the parties, then it could be concluded that the acts of the *Bupati* were a show of leadership designed to provide political endorsement for state action against Roy. There is a possibility this role may have been played for electoral reasons, given the upcoming voting for regional head. There is also a possibility that the *Bupati*'s leadership role reflected the need to provide civilian government legitimacy to a decision driven by a religious organisation, and carried into effect by various legal sector agencies.

Motivation for the fatawa

If the *fatawa* were directed at doctrinal matters, but not necessarily triggered by the existence of the disputed teaching, what then may have prompted them? Both *fatwa* refer to a number of considerations in their recitals and, given their format and intent, were not issued in response to an individual request for a religious ruling. Therefore, it is difficult to determine with accuracy any specific triggers for their production. However, the first *fatwa* references a letter from MUI Lawang dated 11 September 2003, which was also the date of the incident at the Singosari mosque (this is the only role played by the local level branch of MUI that can be identified). According to the letterhead of MUI Malang, the district-level branch is located in the town of Singosari, and not the district capital Malang. It is unclear whether the letter from the lower-level branch of MUI was a request for a ruling, or a formal complaint about Roy's teaching or the distribution of leaflets on 11 September 2003. Nonetheless, it is reasonable to conclude that the first *fatwa* was issued as a result of the events in Singosari, and this appears to be confirmed by the evidence at trial.

In the case of the second *fatwa*, the recitals refer to Roy's December 2004 letter to MUI Malang seeking guidance on procedures for worship, a copy of which was passed to MUI at the provincial level. It might be concluded that the second *fatwa* was a response to the need for more detailed doctrinal guidance regarding Roy's teaching. There is otherwise no other readily apparent reason for the issuing of this *fatwa* in February 2005.

There is relatively limited information revealing the extent to which the community was 'disturbed' by Roy's teaching. The evidence indicates that for much of the time there may not have been any specific or acute problem, but there are several critical incidents of protests by other Indonesian Muslims – specifically, the disturbance at Singosari, and the protests mounted by the group from Pasuruan. No definitive information is available to confirm their identity or the manner in which they organised themselves, or any affiliation to established organisations. Prior to 2005, only the incident at the mosque in Singosari stands out as an event of some consequence. This cannot be taken, however, to demonstrate that the broader community or particular sections of the community may not indeed have been upset or concerned by Roy's leaflets, or the existence of his *pesantren*. There is, however, a clear sense that events escalated in 2005.

Roy's references to the situation as being 'conflict prone' suggests that there was potential for actual conflict to break out, and it might be presumed that this was based on attitudes or opinions expressed by members of the local community. The fact that the *pesantren* came under physical threat from groups in 2005, and was under the protection of the authorities around the time of his arrest, bears out these concerns. There is no explanation offered by the parties for why disturbances broke out in 2005, and their scale, frequency and impact on the public remain unclear. The protests were, however, associated in witness statements with the additional publicity given to Roy's teachings through the public event at *Sunan Ampel* in Surabaya in April, and through the television coverage in May.

Endorsement of the teaching

Not long after the incident at the mosque in Singosari Roy commenced the process of seeking approval – the 'legalisation' of his publications. This process was to take nearly eighteen months and to involve a wide range of parties, up to and including the President (if only as a recipient of correspondence). It is not clear from the documentary evidence where the suggestion arose that official endorsement of the publications was either needed or recommended. Nor is it clear why Roy wrote in the first instance to the provincial government, but it appears that the government representatives did not feel competent to deal with the matter, quickly engaging the Department of Religion. The Department's research body did not provide a formal response on the leaflets until February

2005. Immediately prior to this response, Roy was also advised by the Department that the *pesantren*'s mission statement revealed errors in Islamic law – referencing the first *fatwa*, and implicitly alleging that Roy was propagating deviant teachings contrary to law, and suggesting he cease his activities. A short time later the Department received advice from MUI East Java that Roy's teachings were in error, together with a request to distribute the second *fatwa*. (This follows an earlier request from the Department for MUI's opinion on the mission statement.)

As indicated, there is no information pointing to the reason Roy initially sought formal endorsement of his leaflets, although a working assumption might be that engaging in this process was a sensible response following the events at the mosque in Singosari. In which case, and given that he appears not to have sought approval immediately after publishing the leaflets, it might be reasonable to accept that this was a purely pragmatic gesture on Roy's part. The Department and MUI, on the other hand, were confident not only in declaring Roy's teaching invalid, but also in declaring that he was not entitled to express his interpretation of doctrine, nor actively promote it. Ultimately the Departmental response that it does not authorise public documents rendered the request for legalisation a fruitless and meaningless exercise. What the process does reveal is that the Department aligned itself with MUI, or rather adopted MUI's judgment upon the material, effectively outsourcing the assessment of matters of doctrine to the non-government sector.

Role of MUI

The series of exchanges between MUI and the Department are of interest, as they seem to demonstrate not only cooperation between MUI and the Department on matters of doctrinal interpretation, but also at the level of policy-setting and implementation. This cooperation appears to be accepted as given on both sides, and there is a congruence of approach, particularly in relation to the adoption or promotion of security policy. The provincial office of the Department specifically approached MUI for its view. For its part, MUI also assumed it was appropriate – or at least opportune – to request that the Department assist with distributing the second *fatwa* through the departmental office network.

In relation to matters of government policy and implementation there are a number of indications that MUI either assumed a status or prerogative in the field of administration or, at the least, actively lobbied state agencies. The first *fatwa* is copied to a list of key legal and administrative officials, consistent with those later engaged in the decision-making process of the *Muspida*. It also includes in its operative section a direct call to the civil administration to take action to uphold Islamic law. The second *fatwa* cross-references the key legal instrument, Law 1/PNPS/1965, and the Department of Religion was aware that the East Java branch was considering Roy's case, suggesting communication between the two.

Just as it is not easily determined which party – MUI or the Department – was driving the relationship, equally it is not easily determined precisely how the *fatawa* became central to the administrative and legal process. Did the police, for example, have a copy of the first *fatwa* at the time the complaint was lodged in 2005 because it had been distributed to them earlier? Was it provided by the complainant or was it requested? The result, in any event, was that by cross referencing the *fatwa* in the police charge, a formal link was made between state law and Islamic law. This arguably gives MUI and its doctrinal interpretation a pre-eminent position, and it is reasonable to assume that MUI was at least a cooperative partner in this process. With the emerging pattern of links between MUI and conservative Islamic groups – supported and reinforced by the evidence arising from the case study – the outcome is effectively the promotion of sectarian points of view through state mechanisms.

Conclusion

It appears that the enforcement action against Roy following the convening of the *Muspida* was a coordinated government response to a growing protest movement. Closure of the *pesantren* had the effect of de-legitimising Roy's activities, and the arrest and detention had the effect of physically silencing him by removing him from the public domain. These actions appear to have been taken as a result of decisions reached in consultation with MUI, and the evidence supports the view that the action was taken at the instigation of MUI, with MUI having the appearance of driving the agenda overall. While its profile derives from its status as *fatawa*-giver, there is a strong sense that it has – de facto – a place in the legal/administrative hierarchy, a position that allowed it to act in more than just an advisory capacity.

The case study needs also to be seen in the context of national, and international, developments. An important part of the national context is the evolving role of MUI which, at the time of these events, was taking a firm stand against 'liberalism', acting either in concert with, or in sympathy with, conservative Islamic groups in Indonesia. The case study provides supporting evidence for MUI's conservative posture. There is no unambiguous evidence that MUI took advantage of Roy's case to orchestrate a crisis requiring state intervention. This was, however, in effect the allegation raised by the defence team. Scholarship supports the view that MUI develops and maintains links with conservative Islamic groups and a key representative of a sub-national branch of MUI in this case – Bashori – certainly maintained such links. A key question raised by the case study, then, is whether it provides evidence that MUI actively exploited the events and the legal/administrative framework to pursue sectarian ends.

This notion, together with the close relationship established by the case study between MUI and government administration, and law and policy implementation in the field of religious affairs, raises important questions about the realisation of the constitutional protection for freedom of religion. In short, the MUI-state relationship suggests a tendency toward preferencing among doctrinal interpretations. Taking into account the historical evidence of variation in approaches to Islam, and the continuing existence of major divisions in Indonesian Islam, the tendency is clearly selective. It also reflects an unwillingness, or incapacity, among representatives of the state to evolve beyond pre-democratic approaches to government, relying on an outmoded ideology of state security, and the legal and administrative frameworks that implemented it. As Rawls places particular emphasis on the role of the judiciary as an exemplar of public reason, the next chapter will deal with the way in which ordinary trial courts also contribute to negotiating the boundaries between religious authority and state authority, and to public reason.

6 Case Study Part 2 – Innovation on trial

In the previous chapter it was shown how Yusman Roy developed and disseminated a variant interpretation of Islamic ritual prayer. The focus was on the reaction of the local community and particularly of representatives of sub-national branches of MUI. It was also seen how rulings in the form of *fatawa* were produced in response to Roy's activities, and events evolved over a number of years before culminating in his arrest. This chapter presents the second part of the case study, focusing on the legal process including the criminal trial, taking up the narrative from the point of Roy's arrest in May 2005. Roy's case moved swiftly through the Indonesian court system, concluding with his conviction on 30 August 2005. A first level appeal was rejected in September of that year, and a Supreme Court challenge was rejected the following January.

In this chapter I describe the legal process in detail by reviewing the prosecution and defence cases, and the evidence presented at trial, including the evidence given by expert witnesses for both the prosecution and the defence. This evidence in particular is valuable in that it addresses the matters of religious doctrine raised by the MUI *fatawa*. I noted in Chapter 2 that Rawls places special emphasis on the place of judges in the conduct of public reason. Chapter 3 demonstrated that the Constitutional Court (MK) has heard several cases involving issues of religion and religious freedom and, most relevantly for the purposes of the research, including judicial review of the Blasphemy Law. In this chapter it will be seen how a trial judge confronts the challenge of addressing a prosecution which centres on an issue of religious doctrine. The prosecution of Roy's Islamic innovation is in many ways the centrepiece of the book, as the case presents an Indonesian citizen confronted with the force of the state implementing criminal provisions that seek to protect religion. As noted in Chapter 3, there is no capacity in lower courts to consider the constitutionality of law, and equally the MK is not competent to hear appeals in individual cases. This enhances the value of a case study of a trial under the Blasphemy Law by illustrating in greater depth the issues arising from the enforcement of this law.

The indictment

As seen in the previous chapter, the police complaint charged Roy with breach of art 156a of the Criminal Code. This article provides as follows:

> Whosoever intentionally publicly expresses sentiments or commits an act:
>
> a   that fundamentally and by its nature is hostile, abuses or disgraces
> b   a religion practised in Indonesia
>   with the intention that persons should not practise any religion at all
>   that is based on Belief in Almighty God
>
> will be subject to a jail sentence of five years.

The Indictment (*surat dakwaan*)[1] also included a subsidiary charge of breaching art 157 of the Criminal Code. This article, discussed in Chapter 3, provides:

> Whosoever broadcasts, exhibits, or affixes writing or drawings in public, the contents of which contain statements of hostility, hatred or contempt between or towards groups in Indonesian society, with the intention that their contents be known or better known by the public, is liable to a jail sentence no longer than two and one half years or a fine.

In support of the primary charge, the indictment alleged that the following acts were committed:

- Commencing in 2002 Roy instructed his students in conducting prayer and that an *Imam* is obliged (*wajib*) to read Qur'anic verses using Arabic with translation 'into *bahasa Indonesia* or Javanese or the local language'.[2]
- Roy produced and required (*memerintahkan*) his students to distribute the materials to the local community.
- Roy produced a VCD containing a discussion by him and including the following statements:

  - 'No person can enter heaven if they only speak Arabic, there is no restriction on *sholat* accompanied by translation'.
  - 'If anyone says that *sholat* is not valid when accompanied by translation, that thinking is extremely stupid, they do not realise they are misleading themselves and mislead many others'.
  - 'I curse every *imam sholat* who deliberately doesn't translate using a language understood by their congregation, this results in their congregation being misled, I curse them'.
  - 'I urge all to begin broadcasting this from the towns to the furthest corners of Indonesia to begin using *sholat* accompanied by translation'.

---

1 Indictment, Attorney-General's Office Kepanjen.
2 *bahasa kaumnya* – literally 'tribal' or 'clan' language.

- Three hundred copies of the VCD were made and handed over to his students and by his students distributed to the 'Muslim community' in the area.
- That these acts made the 'Muslim community' both in and around the *pesantren* and those far from the *pesantren* disturbed because they considered (*menganggap*) the teaching given by the accused 'deviates from norms (*kaidah*) and constituted a deviant act', consistent with the *hadith* 'that means more or less [*sic*] "you should pray as you know that I pray"'.
- MUI Malang District and MUI East Java Province released *fatawa* that declared Roy's teaching a 'deviant innovation and that *sholat* conducted by him was invalid (*tidak sah*)'.

In relation to the subsidiary offence, the indictment refers once again to the distribution of the leaflets and VCD (including also the summaries of the Qur'anic references in the leaflets, and Roy's statements in the recording).

The defence presented a series of objections to the indictment, founded principally on human rights grounds. The defence argued that Roy's conduct was not criminal in nature, but, rather, consistent with his right to religious freedom protected in articles 28E and 29 (2) of the Constitution. It was also argued that Law 39/1999 on Human Rights (arts 22, 74 and 77) obliged the government and all members of the community, including MUI, to respect and protect human rights. Moreover, it was argued that the District Court was not competent to hear the case and the police investigation was invalid because it was the responsibility of the Human Rights Commission to investigate occurrences of human rights violations. The defence objection, in short, was that the prosecution had the effect of criminalising Roy's conduct. It was also claimed that the prosecution failed to provide evidence that Roy had instructed his *santri* to distribute the leaflets and VCDs, and that no specific details (times and dates) were provided for the acts alleged to have been performed by Roy.

The closing submission by the prosecution was read before the Court on 18 August 2005. Following usual Indonesian court procedure, the written submission consisted of a restatement of the indictment, and summaries of the evidence (evidence in the case will be discussed in the following section). No submission was made to the Court on the subsidiary charge under art 157 of the Criminal Code. As will be discussed below, the Court ultimately found for the prosecution on this second charge, which makes the absence of any submission appear to be a critical omission in the trial.

The substance of the prosecution submission was a review of the elements of the offence set out in art 156a. It stated that the facts demonstrated the distribution was in order to ensure that members of the public read the leaflets, and that Roy was aware that as a result there would be views 'pro and kontra' his teaching, and that the material was distributed in public places. The prosecution then provided definitions of the key words in the offence: hostility, contempt and disgracing. The statement explained that the word 'disgracing' is based on 'dirt' (*noda*), 'pockmarked' (*bercak*), something that 'soils' (*mencemari*), or 'makes dirty' (*mengotori*) and thus 'disgracing' (*penodaan*) is to soil, to dirty the cleanliness (*kesucian*) or destroy the prestige (*merusak keagungan*) of something. The closing argument then detailed over approximately six pages the evidence provided at trial concerning the core elements of Roy's teaching and the issues raised by witnesses as to its validity.

Evidence

Evidence was given at the trial by all individuals who were interviewed by the police following Roy's arrest on 6 May 2005. The police collected a total of eight statements between the evenings of 6 and 7 May, and a further – ninth – statement was taken from Roy himself in the early hours of 7 May. While information relevant to the case study is contained in the police statements, the references to evidence in this chapter draw on the judgment.[3] The judgment includes summaries of the evidence provided and, while these are not verbatim, they draw from notes taken by court staff and the judges during the trial, and are therefore assumed to be representative of the material before the Court. I include where it is available material from other sources, such as submissions made by the parties, to supplement the material found in the judgment.

Prosecution witnesses

Four of these witnesses were affiliated with MUI (at the sub-national level) and two were members of the Department of Religion (one of these also had an association with MUI). One witness was a former assistant at Roy's *pesantren*, and the remaining two were local community representatives, from the RT/ RW.[4] Expert evidence was also provided, including by one of the staff members of the Department of Religion, and this evidence will be dealt with in a subsequent section.

Evidence was given by the individuals who initially lodged the complaint with police. These witnesses were the complainant (*pelapor* – literally 'reporter', the one making the police report) Machmud Zubaidi, the head of MUI Malang, and the two individuals identified as witnesses (*saksi*) in the police report – Muhammad Achwan, the head of MUI Tajinan (one of the sub-districts making up the District of Malang), and Luthfi Bashori, the head of the MUI Malang *Fatwah* Committee. Zubaidi was first directly exposed to Roy and his teachings at the seminar conducted on 30 April 2005 at the State Islamic University, *Sunan Ampel*, Surabaya, where Roy appeared as a speaker and the VCD was

3 Kepanjen District Court Decision. All references in the section following are from the judgment.
4 Material from these individuals was referred to in the previous chapter; the RT/RW is the neighbourhood or citizen's association, see also previous chapter.

played. He had previously read the leaflets and received a copy of the VCD in his role as head of MUI Malang. Zubaidi explained that the 2003 *fatwa* was issued because of a report from and discussions with MUI Lawang, and as a result of the leaflets and VCD being distributed. Zubaidi stated that the community was disturbed by Roy's actions, and that this had been conveyed to him by members of the community as well as to other *ulama* at MUI. He himself was disturbed by the teaching because 'if the teaching continued then pity (*kasihan*) the community [which would] become increasingly disturbed and would stray from the right path (*tersesat*)'.

Zubaidi also gave evidence as to the grounds upon which the teaching was considered deviant. He explained that it was inconsistent with the *hadith* 'pray as you know that I pray' and the opinions of the schools of Islamic jurisprudence (*madzhab-madzhab*) 'because *sholat* is the virtue of piety meaning devout members of the *umat* must conform to the conduct of the Prophet' and there can be no human element in the readings, which are in the language of revelation.[5] As to the significance of the *fatwa* Zubaidi told the Court: 'the intention of the *fatwa* was guidance so that the accused would return to the teaching of the Prophet concerning the method of performing *sholat*'. Further he gave evidence that 'MUI cannot press (*memaksakan*) its opinion but can only issue a *fatwa* . . . if a *fatwa* is not followed this is a risk which is the personal responsibility of those that do not follow it'.

The evidence of Zubaidi is of interest due to his position as head of MUI Malang and as complainant to the police. However, Luthfi Bashori of the MUI Malang *Fatwa* Committee also played an important role, not only because he was head of the *fatwa* issuing body, but – as discussed in Chapter 5 – he was a point of contact for other religious leaders in the region, and he published his views on the Roy case. In his evidence Bashori confirmed that he received complaints by telephone about Roy's conduct. He

> received many telephone calls from several towns asking about the said teachings on *sholat* the point being that they were disturbed and what is more there were those who asked: 'Why can't Malang stop this teaching, if it can't be done they will come to Malang'.

Bashori stated that it was his dislike of such 'anarchist' behaviour and to prevent 'unwanted' events that he reported the case to the police.

Bashori gave evidence that the issue of dual language prayer was discussed by the local MUI *ulama*. Not a single one confirmed the teaching, and so MUI issued its *fatwa*. In his opinion, Bashori felt that the teaching disgraced religion, as it was something that devalued (*melecehkan*) *sholat*; he added that a

---

5 A view conforming broadly to the description of Islamic doctrine in Chapter 1.

translation from Arabic was not in accordance with Islamic teaching, and in his opinion the acts of the accused sullied (*mengotori*) Islam.

Other prosecution witnesses attested more directly to the key events. A former student at the *pesantren* gave evidence that he personally assisted with distribution of the leaflets together with other students. He stated that during his time at the *pesantren* (it is not specified how long he remained there) he had not observed any trouble or heard any complaints from neighbours or from anywhere else. A further key witness, Habib Alaydrus, was the head of MUI Lawang and gave evidence that he had received copies of the leaflets, and to his knowledge members of the community became disturbed particularly when the witness explained the teaching to them, following which they burnt the leaflets. He also observed that the community became even more disturbed following the television broadcast about Roy's teaching.[6] In his role as head of the local branch of MUI he stated that he received 'reactions' about the teaching from *kyai* most of whom were responsible for *pesantren* in Jakarta, Surabaya, Malang, Pasuruan, Semarang and Bangli. He himself, as a *kyai* and member of the *umat* Islam, 'was very offended with the attitude of the accused which was observed in the VCD and moreover at the *pondok*, where the word "God" was displayed inside a picture of a horseshoe'.[7]

Defence witnesses

The defence team presented eight witnesses at trial including four former students from Roy's *pesantren*. The remaining four defence witnesses were expert witnesses, two in the field of law and human rights and two in religion. Although holding semi-official responsibilities, the local community representatives could be considered the only independent witnesses interviewed by the police, in that they appear not to have had an affiliation with either MUI or with the *pesantren*.

Evidence was provided by four former students, although little of substance arises from this material. All four stated clearly in their evidence that they only used translations in the course of family prayer sessions, although two claimed to have, in fact, led prayers at the *pesantren* (whether or not this included Friday group prayers is not clear). Three of these individuals were involved in the distribution of pamphlets, two were assaulted during the visit to the mosque at Singosari, and one also appeared as a speaker on the VCD. Three of the students observed that Roy did not curse local *ulama* in order to threaten them, but

---

6 National television stations carried stories about Roy in the days leading up to his arrest; see Chapter 5.
7 The letterhead carries the logo of the *pesantren*, which is in the shape of a horseshoe with the name written around the outside edge, and Arabic script displayed inside the horseshoe.

rather as an appeal or reminder to them, one proposing that it is God that is cursing (rather than Roy himself). One witness stated, for example, 'that an *imam sholat* who doesn't use translation will be cursed is not meant as a threat but a reminder and the one giving the reminder was the accused'.

Roy's own evidence is presented last in the judgment of the District Court. He explained that an *Imam* was obliged to use translation of the readings during *sholat* 'because it was the right of followers to understand the readings'. Roy acknowledged that the leaflets admitted into evidence were those distributed by his students and that he himself had authored them. He informed the Court that the statement 'extremely stupid' used in the VCD was a form of 'shock therapy' for his own students and that he accepted that offence had been caused by his cursing of those who did not adopt his teaching, but that he 'sought the truth not enemies'. Roy stated that his teaching on dual-language prayer was his own interpretation and that he found it very beneficial, although he did not intend to disgrace religion or to spread hostility.

Expert evidence

The judgment refers to five individuals as being 'expert' witnesses (*saksi ahli*). Two experts provided testimony for the prosecution on the religious issues raised by Roy's teachings: Achwan Mukkarom, the head of the Malang office of the Department of Religion; and Abdusshomad Buchori, a representative of the East Java (provincial level) MUI.[8] The religious experts called by the defence team were Imam Ghozali Said and Ulil Abshar Abdalla. The judgment does not record the specific source of their expertise but, as discussed in the previous chapter, Ulil Abshar Abdalla is a leading figure in JIL. Two other experts – Solehuddin and Abdul Latief Fariqun – were called by the defence and provided evidence, respectively, on the history of the provisions under which Roy was charged, and on human rights and the Indonesian constitution.

In his evidence Mukkarom explained that there could be no other language but the language of revelation in *sholat*. He stated that the method of *sholat* had been determined by God through the angel Gabriel to the Prophet, and that according to *fiqh* the accused's teaching was deviant. Mukkarom also stated, though, that the use of translation as promoted by Roy was not a problem if he performed this as an individual – the problem was proposing that others do so (*mengajak orang-orang lain*). In his view, the teaching disgraced Islam because *sholat* was a pillar of religion and, although changes had been made to

---

8 The defence team objected to both experts, given their affiliation with, respectively, the government and MUI. The Defence Statement claims in particular that Buchori's evidence lacked independence as MUI was itself responsible for criminalising Roy's activities.

sholat in Turkey during the time of Ataturk, there was no difference of opinion about the matter in Indonesia.[9]

The representative of East Java MUI, Buchori, also reflected on past variations in Islamic practice. He stated that the Qur'anic references relied upon by Roy to support his teaching had also been used at the time of Abu Hanifah,[10] but were no longer used and were not relevant – moreover 'this was only the opinion of Israelis or Jews that curse Muhammad'. According to Buchori's evidence, Abu Hanifah provided a dispensation for an individual who was experiencing difficulty in Qur'anic study, but there had been no support in the four *madzhab* for *sholat* with translation. Buchori described disgracing religion as meaning an 'individual' interpretation of the Qur'an, and accordingly invited Roy to return to the true teaching because his teaching was a new approach, considered deviant (*model baru dianggap sesat*). He then went further and described Roy's teachings as 'sinful' (*fasik*): the acts of a person of faith who breaches the Qur'an. Nonetheless Buchori then also gave evidence that there was no regulation that prohibited the use of translation during prayer, rather it arose as a matter of interpretation.[11]

For the defence, Said observed that Islamic teaching was based on the Qur'an and *hadith* but that a deeper understanding of these sources was not easy and could only be attained in steps. He stated that opinions among Muslims differed on prayer, and that those opinions that do not deny God or the work of Mohammed were not deviant. Whilst Roy's teaching was incorrect (*apabila ajaran tersebut salah*) it was not to be categorised as deviant, because it still acknowledged God and Mohammed. On the question of the *hadith* referred to frequently in the case – 'pray as you know that I pray' – Said explained that this arose due to the range of methods of prayer in use at the time of the Prophet and that the *hadith* in question required Muslims to emulate the Prophet.

In his evidence Said addressed the question of the relevance of the many Qur'anic references relied upon by Roy. Said stated that these do not support the argument that *Imam* were obliged to use translation during prayer, however he again emphasised the distinction applied above between deviant and incorrect

---

9 This had only come about in Turkey due to the power of the ruler, the witness argued. Ataturk encouraged the use of Turkish during worship causing 'controversy which has lasted to this day' (Mango 1999: 497). Ataturk was considered progressive by Indonesian secularists but ignorant of Islam by more conservative Muslims (Federspiel 2009: 111). Abd-Allah (2007: 6–8) relates a very early historical example of an innovation in prayer introduced by the second caliph 'Umar, reinforcing that differences over proper procedure are of long standing.

10 The founder of the Hanafi school, considered to be the most liberal of all Sunni schools of Islam, and understood to have believed that individual Muslims should be given the benefit of the doubt in matters of personal faith (Jackson 2006).

11 '*pengaturan secara tegas larangan sholat menggunakan terjemahan tidak ada tetapi melalui penafsiran-penafsiran*'.

teachings, stating that Roy's interpretation was merely incorrect. This situation called for dialogue and advice as well as 'development' (*pembinaan*) rather than a declaration of deviancy. If dialogue and development did not result in a change in the teaching, Said felt it was up to the public to evaluate (*maka masyarakat yang akan menilai*).

Abdalla gave evidence that it was very inappropriate for Roy's case to become a criminal matter. He noted that there was an inheritance of classical literature spanning many centuries that revealed a very wide range of differences on matters of law, politics, society, *aqidah* and philosophy. In his opinion, a matter such as Roy's – a difference of opinion in the field of *fiqh* – had never been criminalised. He stated that whilst Roy's views were not in accordance with the opinions of the majority of Sunni *ulama*, it was not a strange opinion and could still be accommodated within *fiqh*. He observed that in Hanafi *fiqh*, the *umat* knew of Abu Hanifah's permission for *sholat* in Persian, and while accounts of this suggest he had withdrawn this opinion, there is, in fact, no indication in the Hanafi teaching that this was so.[12]

In Abdalla's view, there were no differences of opinion in Islam concerning the requirement to conduct prayer, but there were differences of opinion about the Prophet's *sholat* and interpretations also differed among *ulama* about this. Given the extraordinary differences about the Prophet's *sholat*, Roy's teachings should not be considered strange for being a new approach. As to the issue of what matters are appropriately categorised as 'deviant', Abdalla's evidence was that only differences of *aqidah* could be so categorised and that if the ethics of dialogue in matters of *fiqh* were valued, Roy's opinion could be considered as 'less superior' (*pendapat yang tidak unggul*).

Abdalla was the only expert to address the question of the status of the MUI *fatawa*. He expressed the traditional view that in Islamic law a *fatwa* – whether personal or institutional – was non-binding and merely a legal opinion. MUI *fatawa* in his opinion were of the same status as an individual *fatwa*, that a *fatwa* does not have the force of compulsion (*tidak dapat dipaksakan*), and that in Islamic law the person requesting the opinion is not obliged to follow it. In his opinion, the strength of a *fatwa* lies in the quality of its theoretical grounding (*dalilnya*) and that the categorisation of 'deviant' – he repeated – was only used in matters of *aqidah*. Whilst he did not agree that other *ulama* could be obliged to use translation, in Abdalla's opinion, differences on matters of *fiqh* should not be brought to a legal forum but resolved through dialogue.

The first legal expert called by the defence – Solehuddin – argued that the Blasphemy Law was introduced to protect the interests of the state and society

---

12 See Hosen (2012) for a detailed treatment of the Hanafi jurisprudence, and his discussion about the 'old' debate about recitation in languages other than Arabic.

in relation to matters of religion.[13] He stated that the Law required the issuing of a joint decree (*surat keputusan bersama* or SKB)[14] prior to proceeding to the use of art 156a, and described 'contempt for religion' to mean the elements of an act or statement breaching fundamental teachings of a religion. Solehuddin also expressed the view that contempt could be addressed by groups within Islam toward other Islamic groups, between different classes, among ethnic groups and between different races. Latief stated that, as a member of the United Nations, Indonesia had concrete obligations to honour and protect the rights of its citizens and that a conflict between laws should be resolved in favour of the superior (higher level) law (although it is not clear from the judgment which of the laws relevant to the case he was referring to here).[15]

Defence case

The defence case was summarised in two closing arguments, one presented by Roy's legal representatives and another by Roy himself. The approach of both statements was to focus primarily on the religious issues in the case, although the legal team did raise a challenge in relation to legal procedure and discusses the elements of the charges. Overall, the defence amounted largely to an attempt to convince the Court of the correctness of Roy's interpretation of Islamic doctrine, even when arguments were made in relation to the elements of the crimes.

Legal team

One key question of law raised by the defence in this case was, in essence, an argument of statutory interpretation, namely the proper relationship between art 156a of the Criminal Code and Law 1/PNPS/1965. The defence argument emphasised that the Presidential Decree established a warning procedure, and that in Roy's case no formal warning was provided, and referred to the evidence given by Solehuddin. The defence proposed that the Court take into consideration the fact that the Decree – which was elevated to the level of legislation in 1969 – remained in force, despite the insertion of art 156a into the Criminal Code. The argument put here was that the spirit (*jiwa*) of the Blasphemy Law

---

13 See Chapter 3 for further background on the offence and the Presidential Decree by which it was initially established.
14 The instrument issued under the administrative procedures established in Law 1/PNPS/1965 warning that particular conduct should cease; see discussion of *Bakorpakem* Chapter 3.
15 The witness may have been suggesting a conflict between Law 1/PNPS/1965 and constitutional protections, or with Indonesia's human rights legislation; see Chapter 3 for a discussion about the constitutional challenge to the Law, which post-dated the Roy case by several years.

was different to that in the Criminal Code and reflected the times in which it was developed, the objective being the protection of social needs in religious life; the existence of the preliminary warning process indicated that the legislators did not intend to immediately criminalise acts.

In relation to the elements of the crime the defence provided a lengthy summary of the evidence of Abdalla. The first issue raised was the precedent claimed for the use of languages other than Arabic in Hanafi jurisprudence. The defence reiterated this point, and argued specifically that Abu Hanifah permitted the use of Persian for the reading of the *fatihah*, or confession of the faith during prayer. Moreover, this was not an example of dual-language prayer, but one of permitting prayer entirely in a language other than Arabic.

The most extensive argument presented in the defence statement concerned the application by MUI of the term '*sesat*' in the *fatawa*. The defence returned to the argument provided in expert evidence that it was only appropriate to apply the term in the context of *aqidah* or the core question of Islamic faith, not in matters of *fiqh*. The statement noted that throughout Islam's history differences of opinion have been debated, and not resulted in legal process. It quoted the evidence of Abdalla, in which he described the contemporary trend of MUI *fatawa* being accepted as binding:

> My opinion about MUI is that there is an inappropriate trend, one that is not good, this is the tendency at the moment. *Fatwa* that are issued by an organisation are taken to be binding. It is a great shame that *fatwa* issued, whether at the central, regional or district level are used as a binding legal decision, because there are several groups in society that try to force their wishes on other groups. This tendency has never occurred in the history of Islam.[16]

The defence statement expanded on this with a further observation about the contemporary role of MUI:

> We cannot prohibit people from spreading their teaching, rather what we must do is accept differences. Because of MUI's attitude of immediately declaring that a group is deviant, an ugly prejudice has arisen between groups in society.

To illustrate the significance of MUI's role in declaring particular behaviour to be deviant, the statement referred to the co-existence of the two large national Islamic organisations, NU and Muhammadiyah. Under the subheading 'The

16 This particular observation by the defence team does not appear in the summary of evidence in the Court's decision. Nonetheless the judgment does reflect the broader point that MUI *fatawa* should not be considered binding.

MUI fatawa are capable of exacerbating differences in thought between NU and Muhammadiyah that had already abated and aims to divide the Islamic community with violent means', the defence statement observed: 'in the history of the development of Islam in Indonesia in general and especially on Java the Islamic community has known extremely strong differences of opinion between NU and Muhammadiyah'. Acute differences involving matters of Islamic principles had died out leading to a period of dialogue between the two large Islamic organisations, however the defence drew the Court's attention to its concern about a contemporary trend of intolerance, reflecting earlier episodes in which the two mass organisation had declared the other to be deviant.[17]

The statement also highlighted the opinion provided in evidence by Said. He stated in evidence that both the translation of the Qur'an and of the Friday sermon had been debated in modern Indonesia. In 1917, the work of Professor Mahmud Yunus in translating the Qur'an was considered deviant – although his efforts were not 'criminalised'. This later led to the development of an official translation of the Qur'an produced by the Department of Religion. Further, the early prohibition on the use of languages other than Arabic during the Friday sermon (*Khotbah Jumat*) evolved during the twentieth century, and the sermon was now able to be delivered in Indonesian. The statement also reflected the view advanced by Roy himself:

> To the extent that the content of *sholat* is a communication with God, this has to be understood (*dimengerti*). Who is bold enough (*siapa yang berani*) to declare that this is not Islam and is criminal. Differences in the conduct of *sholat* using dual languages is not a difference of *aqidah* . . . and if wrong, this should only be declared wrong in a *fatwa*, not deviant.

The defence statement also provided a brief commentary on the facts surrounding the disturbance in the community including a significant allegation about the conduct of MUI. It argued that the local community was not disturbed by anything done by Roy himself, but rather that they were scared by the arrival of a group from outside (*dari luar kampung* – from outside the village) coming in the name of the Islamic community (*Ummat Islam*). The statement identified this group as the *Forum Umat Islam*, a group declaring itself to represent the entire Indonesian Islamic community, whose pressure and threats (*tekanan dan ancaman*) caused concern in the neighbourhood of Roy's *pesantren*. Moreover, the defence alleged that this group was organised by the Malang branch of MUI (*serta diorganisir oleh MUI Kabupaten Malang*), although the source of this specific allegation is not clear. The community's concern was so great that nightly watches were instituted to guard the village from an attack by outsiders.

---

17 The submission accords with the scholarship on this point, discussed in Chapter 4.

Roy's statement

The day following the presentation of the defence statement by Roy's legal representatives, he himself delivered a statement to the Court. This long statement, amounting to thirty-four pages of text, included eighty-seven Qur'anic references and included as appendices the two leaflets by which Roy disseminated his teaching. The question of language and linguistic competence was a central theme in the statement. Roy stated, for example:

> My religion is Islam, not Arabian (*tidak beragama Arab*). As Islam actually isn't identical to Arabia. And Arabia also is not identical with the Islamic religion. . . . I am one of the vast majority of Indonesians who don't fully understand Arabic and there are many Indonesians that don't understand Arabic perfectly and they also want to perform *sholat* safely and without being intimidated by the threat of arbitrary criminal sanction.[18]

Roy stated that matters internal to religion could only be resolved by reference to the Qur'an and a matter of pure religion should not be subject to the Criminal Code, a human creation. He also appealed to the government to end its discrimination against this group of Indonesians and not to crush their human right to freedom of belief, proposing that the Court, as fellow Muslims, should emphasise Islamic brotherhood (*ukhuwah Islam*) over division.

In relation to the role of MUI, Roy observed that out of respect for MUI he had made three approaches to them in writing with no response. Roy further stated that MUI gave the impression that its religious rulings were the most accurate and that 'MUI was the one and only authority (*penguasa*) on *ijtihad* in Indonesia'. He went on:

> And if there is an opinion on Islam from a member of society that is opposed to that of MUI accordingly it is our fate to be faced with criminal prosecution. So far as we understand the matter of *ibadah* especially concerning *sholat* that it is a matter of a personal communication between an

---

18 Roy is not alone in his appreciation of the practical difficulties that arise from the need to be familiar with Arabic. The Persis leader, Ahmad Hassan, was of the opinion that while Arabic was necessary for the study of religious sources, a person who taught only Arabic 'would not succeed' (Federspiel 2009: 74). This question has been under consideration for many centuries in Indonesia and scholars have, for example, used religious texts in Arabic transliterated into local languages since at least the 1600s (Umam 2013: 254). Umam (2013) discusses the work of one nineteenth-century Javanese teacher, Muhammad Salih Darat, who prepared his own instructional texts and expressed very similar views to those of Roy. Salih's writings included the observation that 'Islam became widespread despite the fact that many people did not understand Arabic; if understanding of Arabic is a precondition for being complete in Islam, then the majority would never become fully Muslim' (Umam 2013: 260).

individual and their God and is not subject to impeachment by anyone according to their law of God.

Roy linked the personal nature of devotion to the fate of the nation: in his view the 'failure' of *sholat* (*gagalnya sholat*) had a serious impact on the moral development of the nation. He explained this as being due to the fact that religious devotion could not make an impression on an individual's mind when they failed to comprehend its content. The failure of the moral development of the nation would lead to an increase in corruptors and terrorism, 'along with numerous other forms of wickedness'. This, he proposed, was the result of the efforts of those with a 'fanatical interest in Arabic'. With such significant implications for the nation, Roy questioned why MUI continued to support a form of *sholat* that relied only upon Arabic.

Court decision

The trial of the charges against Roy commenced one month after his arrest, in early June 2005. The judgment, delivered approximately two months later, on 30 August, repeated at length the contents of the indictment and the closing statement of the prosecution. It also included much briefer summaries of the closing statements by the defence and Roy, and more extensive summaries of the evidence given by witnesses in the trial (drawn on in the preceding discussion of the evidence). The Court made a number of key findings expressed in a formulaic manner in a series of paragraphs each commencing with 'Considering, . . .' ('*Menimbang*, . . .') and followed by a statement summarising a particular element of the case.[19]

The Court found: evidence from witnesses including the accused showed that from 2003 Roy instructed his students[20] in a method of leading *sholat* with translation into *bahasa Indonesia*; that this teaching was the product of Roy's own thinking; and Roy then developed the idea that *Imam* must translate the readings used in *sholat*. It found further that Roy produced leaflets and made his students distribute them in, among other places, Singosari, Tulungagung, Lawang and the Arjosari bus terminal in Malang.

The Court held that with the existence (*dengan adanya*) of the leaflets and VCD, various opinions arose about the accused's teaching: 'on the one hand

---

19 Butt (2006: 117–119) describes this formula as standard in Indonesian courts (proposing that it reflects French judicial style), although he focuses his attention on the decisions of the Constitutional Court.

20 Here the Court uses the term *murid* (student), which in Indonesian is usually associated with those attending a state or other secular place of education, rather than *santri*, the term for students at a *pesantren*. This may indicate the Court did not identify the *pesantren* as a legitimate place of Islamic study, or that it wanted to avoid the use of religious terminology.

there were those who said the accused's deeds disgraced (*menodai*) religion and there were also those who considered that the accused's actions did not disgrace religion'. Referring to the trial evidence, the Court noted that opposing views were submitted by the experts called by the prosecution and defence and concluded:

> from the summary of the various conflicting opinions previously stated, the Court concludes that a single view cannot be derived from the experts concerning whether the deeds of the accused are a form of disgrace toward religion or not, instead being a difference of opinion that can be accommodated within *fiqh* that requires dialogue in order to find legal sources that can act as a guide concerning the accused's deeds.

The Court duly acquitted Roy of the first charge.

As to the elements of the second charge, the Court determined that 'the meaning of broadcasting, showing (*mempertontonkan*) writing or pictures [*sic*] here is the existence of an act of the deliberate displaying (*menunjukkan*) or distribution (*menyebarkan*) of writing with the objective of that writing or picture being known by another'. The Court held that Roy's students distributed the leaflets, that the VCD was produced in order to make his teachings known, and that the leaflets were distributed on more than one occasion and in different locations. Accordingly, Roy's acts were held to fulfil the first element of the subsidiary charge.

The Court went on to state that the elements of the second offence required that the contents (of the material made publicly known) express feelings of hostility, hatred or contempt. It held that the proceedings revealed that *kyai* and members of the community who read the leaflets or watched the VCD 'were offended because within the said leaflets or VCD could be found words from the accused that should people not adopt his teachings then they were cursed and there were also found the words "extremely stupid" (*goblok pol*)'. Further, the Court noted the witnesses called by the prosecution: 'stated the words of the accused made them offended and annoyed (*tersinggung dan panas hati*) and this constitutes a form of contempt toward people that do not adopt the accused's teaching'. Furthermore, the witnesses stated that the community reacted to the leaflets, 'so that there arose hostility among the *ummat Islam* and moreover when the accused's students distributed the said leaflets some were struck [assaulted] by the community, which demonstrated their dislike of the leaflets . . .'. The Court (*Majelis*) therefore found this element proven.

The third element of the offence the Court described as being 'toward groups of Indonesian citizens'. It then defined this concept:

> In this situation, the meaning of the word 'group' must be interpreted widely, that is not restricted to ethnic group or traditional community, or

group of citizens as intended by art 131 *Indische Staatsregelling*[21] but rather according to developments with the times (*perkembangan zaman*) and developments in religious life, it must be interpreted as 'a religious community' (*kumpulan umat beragama*), so that this element carries a meaning that feelings of hostility, hatred or contempt [can be] directed towards fellow members of a religious community or toward other members/ religious communities.[22]

From the facts revealed in the proceedings the existence of the leaflets and VCD the Court held that:

> there occurred a reaction from religious leaders (*tokoh-tokoh agama*) that constitute an Islamic religious community that stated their feelings of offence and objection to the words of the accused that declared [them] cursed should they not adopt his teaching and extremely stupid, this religious community described by the expert witness Ulil Abshar Abdalla as followers of Sunni *ulama*.[23]

The Court then concluded that a religious community, being one which opposed the accused's teaching, constituted a 'group of Indonesian citizens', and therefore found this element fulfilled and the charge proven.

Appeals

Both the defence and prosecution lodged appeals against the decision at first instance with the High Court of Surabaya, which handed down a decision on 22 November, 2005.[24] The High Court's decision consists primarily of a recitation of the indictment and a brief summary of the decision of the lower court. There is no evaluation of any arguments raised before either court by either party, and no evaluation of any kind of the charges, the evidence or the reasoning of the lower court. The decision simply states that the appeal court affirms the verdict of the Kepanjen District Court.

The Roy case subsequently came before the Supreme Court of Indonesia in January 2006. A summary of the decision of the Supreme Court of 27 January

---

21 A Colonial-era regulation which, Katjasungkana (2008: 485) explains, entrenched racial segregation and discrimination by defining three racial groups, and assigning to each a separate civil code, the groups being Europeans, 'Foreign Orientals' and 'natives'.
22 This interpretation appears to be consistent with jurisprudence of the Indonesian Supreme Court which held in a 1962 case involving art 156 that the teachers and administrators of a *pesantren* could constitute a 'group' despite being all Muslims (Soerodibroto 2009: 99).
23 Abdalla's evidence on this point was that dual-language prayer was not in accordance with the opinion of the majority of Sunni *ulama*.
24 Surabaya High Court Decision 361/PID/2005/PT.SBY

2006 indicates that both parties lodged appeals, although the Court refused to accept the defence case and dismissed the prosecution's appeal without providing any reasons for either decision.[25] As a result, the decision of the Kepanjen District Court is the only judicial record of any substance in the Roy case.

Blasphemy – a case note

A dispute about religious doctrine lies at the centre of the Roy case study and accordingly religious issues were embedded in all stages of the legal process. Both the prosecution and defence cases and the evidence of expert and other witnesses were heavily focused on the question of whether the teaching should be considered deviant. The Court, however, withdrew from the religious issues, despite their prominence, by not ruling on the contentious issue of 'blasphemy' and by not engaging with the question of whether *fatawa* have any role in Indonesian legal process. The Court's finding on the second charge appears initially to have avoided any direct engagement with matters of religious doctrine. The Court, however, arguably made an indirect ruling on a matter of faith and, moreover, the finding on this charge seemed to stretch the interpretation of the facts and law, possibly as a means of finding a way to deliver a conviction, and in response to public pressure (Hosen 2012: 12).

There is much to be said about matters raised in the trial that the Court fails to rule on. This reflects not only on the Court's attitude to the issue of faith, but also on the stances of the parties (MUI, legal agencies and the defence) to the whole legal process. All parts of the legal process including the trial were framed almost entirely around a debate founded in religious doctrine, and therefore an explanation needs to be found – given the Court's ambivalence to faith – as to why this was so. The Court also avoided any discussion at all about human rights, thereby removing the need to consider the extent to which the existing criminal law might conflict with Indonesia's comprehensive protection for freedom of religion.

Failure of primary charge

The Court's decision in relation to the charge of disgracing a religion is a critical part of the case study. This is due to the significance of the religious issues for the parties and for MUI as a key protagonist in the case, and the profile they assumed in the trial. The failure of the charge under art 156a might be

---

25 Indonesian Supreme Court Decision No. 75 K/Pid/2006. It appears that the defence appeal was lodged out of time, arguably due to a delay in transmitting the appeal documents, which the defence blamed on poor court administration (letter from LBH Surabaya Pos Malang to Chief Justice of the Supreme Court, 27 December 2005). The summary of the Supreme Court decision does not make any reference to the issue of the timeliness of lodging the appeal.

considered a reasonably serious blow to the prosecution. The penalty carried by this charge of five years imprisonment is double the penalty carried by the subsidiary offence.[26] The lack of information contained in the appeal court judgments makes it difficult to determine what motivated the appeals lodged by the prosecutor; however, it could be inferred that failure of the charge carrying the more severe penalty was likely a significant factor in the appeals.

The failure of the prosecution to succeed upon this charge raises questions as to its approach to the case, particularly as it was noted above that no closing submission was made at trial on the subsidiary charge. The emphasis placed on the primary charge may reflect the fact that this offence carried the heavier penalty. It may also be evidence, however, of the fact that the case was approached as a trial about religious doctrine.

The absence of any discussion in the judgment about the elements of the crime and the nature of the offence, in even a general sense, leaves significant issues unanswered. This decision should not be considered unique in this regard. Butt (2006: 102–103) comments on the training and competence of Indonesian career judges, noting the relatively brief six months of formal training and the general absence of a doctrine of judicial method (when compared to their civil law judicial counterparts in France for example). Indonesia's Judicial Commission has also sponsored analysis, which revealed issues in the 'competence, independence and impartiality' of judges in trial courts (Colbran 2009: 287).[27] Colbran (2009: 288) observes that these findings reflect 'poorly on the competence' of the judiciary and may 'reflect inadequate professional qualifications'. Accordingly, beyond the formulaic presentation of the judgment (based on a series of statements of 'considerations'), it is not unreasonable to conclude that judicial method in Indonesia is characterised by limited general legal competence and a lack of rigour in analysis.

The offence itself is expressed in ambiguous terms in the Criminal Code. The charge contains two subparagraphs:

a   sentiments or acts that are hostile, abusive or disgracing toward a religion
b   with the intention that person not practice religion based on Belief in Almighty God.

26 Indeed, unlike the subsidiary offence which is expressed as a term of imprisonment 'up to' two and a half years, the term of imprisonment for art 156a is expressed as being (precisely) five years.
27 The research was conducted in 2007–2008 and was based on the analysis of eighty-two decisions made in District and High Courts in nine locations across Indonesia, the majority being in criminal cases. Flaws observed included accepting inadequate, incorrect or incomplete indictments; contradictions between legal considerations raised in decisions and the verdict rendered; the absence of relevant legal considerations; and, little appreciation of human rights or wider principles of justice (Colbran 2009: 286–288).

There is no conjunction between the two subparagraphs such as 'and' or 'or', therefore it is not clear whether the law requires that sentiments or acts be both offensive in one of the ways specified *and* be of a nature to discourage religious adherence, or whether it is sufficient for either limb to be satisfied.

There was no indication at any point in the legal process that Roy was alleged to have discouraged religious adherence. To the contrary, his actions were directed toward improving the quality of prayer within the context of Islam. Expert evidence by the defence also argued that Roy was not challenging any of the fundamental precepts of Islamic faith, and therefore any such allegation would have been strenuously refuted. Should it have been the case that both elements of the offence were required to be proven, it is highly likely that the prosecution would have failed on the first charge.

The prosecution was based on evidence that Roy's teaching was not supported by Islamic scholarship. In its closing argument, indeed, the prosecution focused entirely upon the primary charge, and argued that the adoption of an unorthodox teaching was in itself an act that disgraced religion. This may suggest that the prosecution assumed that the two sub-parts of art 156 were expressed in the alternative. Even if this were the case, it seems unusual that a statement to that effect was not included in the closing argument, if not also in the indictment.

The Court may well have been prepared to entertain the possibility that Roy's teaching amounted to disgracing of Islam. This interpretation arises only by inference from the fact that the Court relied on a conflict in the expert evidence on the status of using translation as part of *sholat*. That is, had either a unanimous view emerged in evidence that the teaching conflicted with doctrine, or had the defence failed (for some reason) to call any expert evidence on this point, it would have been open to the Court to accept the position advanced by the prosecution through its expert witnesses.

There may also arguably be a contradiction between the Court's response to the two charges. The Court was prepared to find that Roy's language amounted to an expression of contempt (see further below) and did not specifically state that the words 'extremely stupid', or any other statements made by Roy, were 'hostile'. Nonetheless the first charge presented an opportunity to the Court to make a finding about Roy's attitude in general, or his words and actions; for example, that his words were abusive. This would arguably have been sufficient for a finding against Roy on subparagraph 'a' of art 156, avoiding any need to address the issue of whether or not he disgraced Islam.

The second charge

The actions prohibited in art 157 are broadcasting, exhibiting or affixing writings or images. On the plain meaning of the words of the article none of Roy's acts come within the scope of the acts prohibited. Roy is not alleged to have broadcast in the conventional sense of publishing his writing via electronic media, although the VCD was played in public and there was media coverage of Roy in the days leading up to his arrest. These were entirely indirect activities and not within Roy's control. The distribution of leaflets and the VCD might be considered a form of exhibiting of his writing or thoughts but, again, these actions do not seem to fall within the ordinary meaning of the word 'exhibit'.[28] There is also no evidence that any of his writings were affixed, or posted, in public places. It is thus arguable that the offence created by art 157 is intended to capture specific types of conduct, none of which Roy, in fact, engaged in. Despite the considerable scope for interpretation required to establish unambiguously that the relevant conduct was properly captured by the provision, the Court made no effort at all to discuss the nature of the acts identified in the Criminal Code.

Evidence for the Court's lack of concern for the text lies in its finding that broadcasting or showing meant 'displaying or distributing' with the objective of making the contents known. This conflation of all the components of this element of the offence moves away from the actual text of the article by redefining the concept of broadcasting and freely mixing terminology. The evidence relating to the key acts was, of course, unequivocal and not contested by the defence: Roy's teachings were disseminated and made publicly known and this was the very objective of producing the leaflets and VCDs. The Court's finding that the leaflets and VCD were distributed with the intention of making their contents know appears to have been considered sufficient to sustain the finding on this element of the second charge.

A further question that arose from the findings of fact by the Court was whether Roy's conduct could be defined as promoting hostility, contempt or hatred, having declared that a finding on any one of the concepts was sufficient. At its simplest, the Court's decision rested on the finding that Roy's statement 'extremely stupid' caused offence, and it described this statement as showing contempt. It was arguably open to the Court to find that this phrase was contemptuous of others – being those that might not accept the recommendation to use translation. However, in discussing this issue the Court also repeatedly referred to the feelings of hostility that arose in the community. It recalled that the community was offended and annoyed by the teaching, and by Roy's cursing of those who did not adopt it. This approach is consistent with a broader trend in modern blasphemy law, as Pringle (2006: 35) argues that the contemporary understanding includes two important features: understanding the conduct as 'fomenting of civil disorder', and involving 'an offence to the beliefs of believers'.

The evidence about reactions to the teachings is mixed, in the same way as the expert evidence regarding whether or not the teaching disgraced Islam.

---

28 The Indonesian word used in the Criminal Code is *mempertunjukkan* which can also mean to 'demonstrate', 'show' or 'perform' and so may indeed be more specifically intended to cover forms of artistic display.

Evidence was given that the community immediately surrounding the *pesantren* did not react in any overt, and certainly not in a physical, way to the teaching, which was underway for some years prior to the violent protests in 2005. The reactions referred to are, in fact, those reported to or communicated via MUI representatives and, ultimately, a threat from outside the immediate community that brought the events to a head on 6 May 2005. Were it not for the specific statement that Roy's words constituted a form of contempt, the finding on the second charge would have rested entirely on the reaction to his actions, rather than on the actions themselves.

The Court was also required to consider the question of whether Roy's actions were 'against' or 'among' 'groups' in Indonesian society. It determined that 'groups' could be interpreted to include a religious community, and also that the acts or sentiments referred to in art 157 could be directed toward members of other religious communities or towards fellow members of a religious community. The Court's approach therefore reflects the opinion put to it by the defence expert Solehuddin in his evidence that this element of the crime could be interpreted to include conflict among groups within Islam. The Court added further depth to the definition of group by adapting evidence given by Abdalla, holding that offence had been caused to religious leaders who constituted an Islamic community, and also to a community of followers of Sunni *ulama*.

The ruling is confused on this point, as it refers both to a community of leaders and a community constituted by followers. What is interesting, however, is the Court's decision to specify the particular nature of the community by reference to one of the major Islamic sects. No more was made of the point, and therefore it is difficult to determine why this step was taken. It may have been out of an excess of caution on the part of the Court, to ensure that it had placed an adequate level of definition around the concept of a group in society, and this would appear to be the point made by the evidence of Solehuddin. However, this is potentially at odds with its approach to the first offence. Having avoided making any finding on the evidence advanced by the parties as to whether Roy's teaching was supported by doctrine, on the second charge the Court nevertheless stepped into the field of doctrine (even if only at a relatively high level). The finding about the nature of the group offended is either or both a recognition that religious doctrine is necessary in contributing to the resolution of a charge of this nature, or an inherent categorisation of Roy's teaching as being outside mainstream Sunni teaching. Both these interpretations, the issue of the role of doctrine generally, and the contribution the trial made to an intra-Islamic debate, are discussed further below.

Absence of art 156

As discussed in Chapter 3, there is a further related offence in the Criminal Code under art 156. This provision makes it an offence to publicly express feelings of hatred, hostility or contempt against one or more groups in Indonesian society. The absence of this offence from the indictment and from the judgment of the District Court is notable for two reasons. First, it appears to capture quite adequately Roy's activities as found by the Court. The elements of this offence are expressed in general terms and do not carry the ambiguity carried by the acts found within art 157. Therefore, it was open to the prosecution and the Court to consider that Roy's statements made in the leaflets and the VCD amounted to the public expression of hostility or contempt. Equally, the Court's finding in relation to the nature of his acts being among or against a 'group' sits comfortably within the wording of art 156.

Second, the Court had further reason to refer to art 156, due to the fact that this provision itself clearly addresses the concept of 'group'. Following from its initial description of the offence, art 156 goes on to define 'group' for the purposes of both this 'and the following article'. That is, despite providing a relevant definition of 'group' for the purposes of Indonesian criminal law, the Court, when discussing this in relation to art 157, failed to cross reference the preceding article. 'Group' is defined as 'each part of the Indonesian people that is different from one or more other parts because of race, country of origin, religion, place of origin, heredity, nationality or status according to constitutional law'.

There is no clear requirement in the law that the person committing the offence be identified directly or indirectly with a *different* group within Indonesian society to that against which the acts are said to be directed. However, the colonial origins of the public order offences in the Criminal Code, discussed in Chapter 3, are reinforced by the final group category found in art 156. Personal status is no longer a feature of Indonesian law but was a distinct and important part of pre-Independence law. Under this framework, individuals were categorised according to particular forms of identity including those enumerated in art 156 (as was noted above). Therefore, it might be inferred that the intention behind art 156 is to prohibit members of one such group causing public disturbance through expressing hatred etc. for members of another group. This much would appear to be logical also from the notion of maintaining public order in a pluralist society such as Indonesia.

Accordingly, it is possible to conclude that the proper interpretation of art 156 – and so of art 157 – requires that the acts constituting the offence be directed toward members of a *different* group. As seen above, the Court defined the group to whom offence was caused as being Sunni *ulama*. In doing so the Court is either acknowledging Roy as leading a deviant sect within Islam, or alternatively expressing the opinion that Roy is not practising 'Islam' at all. To make any such finding inherently engages the Court in determining matters according to doctrine. Taken on its face, the application of art 156 establishes a higher threshold for categorising religions, and thus carries the more significant implication – were it deployed in this case – that Roy is, in fact, a member of a 'separate' religion.

It is possible that a calculation was made by both prosecution and the Court that the phrase 'against or among groups' in art 157 provided more latitude. If, as argued, a finding under art 156 appears necessarily to involve understanding

Roy's teachings as taking him outside Islam, then it is possible this may have caused this provision to be deliberately avoided. That is, art 157 may, in fact, have better suited the circumstances of the Roy case, due to the fact that his sentiments were expressed – arguably – in relation to fellow Muslims, and thus were disseminated 'among' a group, if this is understood as meaning 'within'. If this was, in fact, the case then the further definition provided by the Court of offence being caused to Sunni *ulama* was probably unnecessary. It was also argued above that this approach could be seen as a doctrinally based assessment of Roy's teachings, thus bringing the treatment of art 157 very close to that which would result from the application of art 156.

The human rights question

The District Court does not address the human rights issues raised in the defence statement. I considered Indonesia's human rights framework in Chapter 3, where I argued that religious freedom is well protected both in the Constitution and in legislation. It was also noted there that there is a division of responsibilities between different levels of the Indonesian judiciary, such that constitutional issues (the compatibility of legislation with the Constitution) cannot be handled by lower courts, nor the Supreme Court. It would, however, be appropriate for a court of general jurisdiction to consider potential conflict between different pieces of legislation – in this case the Criminal Code and human rights legislation.

The Human Rights Law holds that international conventions are incorporated into Indonesian law, but it is not clear whether a lower court would consider it appropriate to refer to international law, particularly since its own constitution is not within its scope. Assuming that the Court was competent to consider human rights, it is not clear that this would have been of assistance to the defence. If the Court had turned to the Human Rights Law, it may well have considered that the terms of art 22 of that law reinforced the prosecution argument. This provision expresses the right to religious freedom as both the right to choose a religion and belief and to worship 'according to the teachings of his religion and beliefs'. It is possible that this provision would be interpreted as requiring that the teachings in question be consistent with doctrine. Clearly, as this was precisely the issue arising in the case, human rights legislation may not have been of any assistance.

Role of *fatawa* in the case

One or both *fatawa* were referred to in all stages of the legal process up to and including the trial. Commencing with the police charge, subsequently in the indictment, and throughout the evidence provided by witnesses, including from the expert witnesses, the issuing of *fatawa* by MUI is a consistent and important feature of the legal process. Despite this, the Court makes no explicit reference in its decision to the *fatawa*, nor to the role played by MUI. Its silence on these matters leaves unresolved the issues raised about the relationship between the formal expression of Islamic doctrine in *fatawa* and the state legal process.

The *fatawa* were admitted into evidence and are referred to as such in both the closing statement of the prosecutor and in the judgment of the Court. Besides these references, the documents themselves are given no status or afforded any attention by the prosecution or the Court. In one sense, the *fatawa* are therefore reduced to playing a supporting role only. One reason may be that there is no formal nexus in Indonesian law linking Islamic rulings to the state legal system except in those cases where legislation has so stipulated (see Chapter 4). In the absence of such a link, the prosecution – and the Court itself – may not have been in a position to refer directly to the *fatawa*. This might reflect either discomfort in doing so, or that it simply did not occur to an Indonesian lawyer to do so. Another reason may be that the *fatawa* were always considered to be evidence of the concern felt by Islamic scholars and by members of the community toward Roy's teaching and activities. Once the legal process had progressed as far as the trial, evidence provided to the Court by the witnesses spoke to the charges and provided the information necessary for the Court to perform its function. So from a practical standpoint the virtual disappearance of the *fatawa* as the case passed through the legal process may reflect the different focus and methods arising at trial. Overall, the decision of the Court might be seen as maintaining the status quo position that there is no formal recognition provided in Indonesian law for the *fatwa* as an Islamic legal instrument.

Another reason may also lie in the Court's reaction to the conflict among expert witnesses on matters of Islamic doctrine. This conflict was the reason given by the Court for finding the charge of disgracing a religion not proven. Had the Court decided to address the question, it would have faced the challenge of consistent evidence from both prosecution and defence experts that individuals cannot be compelled to follow *fatawa*, as they are non-binding instruments designed to provide guidance which may be adopted, or not, at the discretion of the individual. It would have been difficult for the Court to 'enforce', adopt, or otherwise take notice of the *fatawa* when they are non-binding.

Role of religious doctrine in the trial

Chapter 5 described the increasing tempo to the events in the case study through 2005, and the trial forms the peak of this series of events. It can be assumed that there was a high level of interest locally in the legal process, if only by inference from the media attention given to the Roy case and the support provided by high profile individuals such as the former President Wahid. Video recordings of the trial[29] reveal that the public area at the rear of

---

29 The VCDs were located during fieldwork and are on file with the author. The recordings were made by the defence team.

the courtroom was filled with young Muslim men, who periodically responded vocally to evidence, particularly during the testimony of Roy himself. The charge under art 156a was developed and presented to the Court on the basis that Roy's teaching itself was in error. This question is fundamentally a matter of religious doctrine which, as noted above, consumed the parties to the trial and dominated the evidence. For this reason, as discussed above, the Court's withdrawal from the field of religious debate stands out because it brought an important and passionately defended doctrinal conflict to an abrupt halt.

What arises from reviewing the evidence is not only that there was agreement as to the status of *fatawa* but that the extent of the disagreement between the parties as to the status of Roy's teachings was not as significant as might have been expected. The prosecution's expert witnesses maintained that bilingual prayer was not acceptable, yet also admitted that no clearly identifiable doctrine prevented the practice. On this point, though, the representative of MUI East Java aligned Roy's justifications for his teaching with views of Israelis and Jews, which speaks of a highly defensive and prejudiced approach to Islam. Equally, the defence experts do not refrain from acknowledging that the teaching was an innovation, just not one of the forbidden kind. They also clearly identified weaknesses in Roy's scholarship, and considered his opinion to be flawed.

Despite this broad level of consensus there was a considerable amount of testimony that addressed matters of Islamic jurisprudence. This evidence included references to the schools of Islamic jurisprudence – *madzhab* – in particular the Hanafi school. Evidence was also given concerning the interpretation of *hadith* ('pray as you know that I pray'), together with a critique of Qur'anic references. In fact, the most extensive critique of Roy arguably came from the defence expert witness Said.

Even in the absence of such intense desire on the part of the parties to lay out competing views, the nature of the charges and the events that gave rise to them inherently required an assessment of religious doctrine. It would be very difficult for a court to determine whether a claim that a religion – any religion – had been 'disgraced' or was the subject of hostile or otherwise abusive criticism without some evidence being produced about what is considered appropriate according to that religion. Hearing evidence from religious experts might well be the most appropriate way to explore the issues. It is also probably a necessary approach in an offence of the kind expressed in art 157, which could be considered to cover a variety of acts of vilification including – as seen here – on religious grounds.

Reinterpreting the trial

There are compelling reasons to reinterpret the trial as more than a legal event. This conclusion is driven by the approach to choice of charges, the technical or legal weaknesses evident in the decision, and by the stance of the parties, who approached the trial as a debate over religious doctrine. There are unsatisfactory elements in the way in which the charges were interpreted by the Court and also in its key findings. There is also an asymmetry in the failure of the prosecution to address the Court on the second charge, despite this being the charge upon which the prosecution succeeded. There is also the failure of the Court to address or try to reconcile the charges with Indonesia's human rights framework.

The intense focus on religious issues was a natural consequence of the nature of the allegations, and of the first charge in particular, but there are also other dimensions to this approach that need to be highlighted. One issue is the need to reconcile the consensus position that *fatawa* are non-binding with the adoption of, or at least references to, the *fatawa* in the legal process. Another issue is the defence team's concerns about the role of MUI – expressed in its closing argument – about advancing its religious views in society, and indeed MUI's own vigorous promotion of the *fatawa*. There are also potential contradictions in the positions put by both sides in the trial. For example, the evidence given by MUI representatives about the status of *fatawa* might be said to contradict their approach which included distributing both rulings among government agencies. (Unless the converse is the case, and there is an appreciation that distribution of *fatawa* via government networks compensates for their status as unenforceable opinions.)

One way to understand the role of the *fatawa* is therefore to consider that MUI may well be aware of the limitations of *fatawa* from the standpoint of Islamic jurisprudence, and also aware that – as seems to have been the case from analysis of the trial – Indonesian law does not explicitly recognise the rulings as having any force. The legal process could therefore be understood as a mechanism for MUI to further promote its views about religious doctrine. It is important to acknowledge though that the criminal process involved three state agencies – the police, prosecutors and courts – all of which are independent. However, as was seen in the previous chapter, there was ample opportunity for all parties to understand MUI's position, and all of the independent legal agencies were party to coordination measures and were recipients of the *fatawa*.

The trial was also revealing in the frequent references to the *umat* – a specific reference to the community of Islamic believers – as opposed to the community surrounding the *pesantren*, or Indonesian society more generally. At no point were Roy and his followers declared to be outside Islam, but the continued description of those upset or offended as being 'the *umat*' potentially leads to the conclusion that Roy was considered not of that group. Ultimately, the Court's blurring of the elements of art 157 and the issue of group identity meant that this issue was not explored in any depth.

Roy's closing statement points to a broader agenda which, while personal to him, also has historic resonances given the context of the heterodoxy of Javanese Islam discussed in Chapter 4. He explicitly distanced himself from 'Arabic Islam', and promoted a patriotic desire to contribute to the moral development of the nation (an idea that formed a key part of the leaflet released on Independence Day 2003). This defence of his own, local, Islam is an expression of his desire to engage intellectually with his faith, a task made difficult in his view for those with limited Arabic language skills. But the theme was developed by him to embrace national development. Roy clearly expressed his fear that the Arabic element of worship limited the potential of the nation to fight terrorism and corruption. Roy appeared at all times to be sincere in his view that translation improves the capacity of the congregation to communicate with God, but his teaching also carries another, nationalist, dimension.

Finally, the defence team's closing statement became an opportunity for it to raise potentially explosive allegations of collusion between MUI and hardline Islamic groups. Evidence given at trial confirmed that MUI representatives were contacted by unknown groups from locations some distance from Lawang, notably Pasuruan, which was the origin of the group that descended on the *pesantren* on 6 May 2005. There is no indication in the evidence or any other material that supports this claim by the legal team, but the proposal that MUI in some way coordinated the aggression against Roy and his followers is consistent with the defence's view about MUI, which was that it was forceful in promoting its views on Islam. More than this, though, it reflects outright suspicion of MUI's motives and methods. Manipulation of events in the manner claimed would not necessarily negate the sincerity of MUI's position on a point of doctrine, but would be an indication of a desire to promote that view at any cost.

Conclusion

The legal process, including particularly the courtroom, was a forum for a confrontation between two opposing views about Indonesian Islam. Despite the lack of traction with the Court on matters of doctrine and jurisprudence, what occurred was nonetheless arguably a trial of Islamic values in contemporary Indonesia. Competing views of what amounts to 'blasphemy' or a deviant Islamic practice was on trial. The parties in this were orthodox, conservative, Islam (represented by MUI) and liberal Islam (represented literally and in person by witnesses including Ulil Abshar Abdalla and through the indirect support of Abdurrahman Wahid), with Roy providing an authentic pretext for these views to be publicly aired. Taken to its furthest extreme, the claims made by the defence team could be taken to suggest that MUI engineered the case both through lobbying of government and legal agencies, and collaboration with radical groups.

Taken from a more technical perspective, the trial presents a more complex and – at times – frustrating picture. Many issues were poorly explored or left unaddressed by the Court, and the ambiguity of the law and the ambivalence of the Court's response to the elements of the crime make it difficult to draw firm conclusions about this important component of the case study. Most importantly, the Court chose not to enter into a debate on Islamic doctrine but rather to shut it down. Its reasons for doing so remain unclear. The *fatawa* were also not explicitly recognised by the Court. Accordingly, I propose a reinterpretation of the trial to recast it as, in effect, a formal, public and state-sanctioned forum for the continuation by other means of the intra-Islamic debate about innovation that took place in the community. In this sense, Roy's trial can be seen as a proxy for the broader confrontation in Indonesia between orthodox Islam represented by MUI, and liberal Islam, represented not so much by Roy himself but by those who came to his defence.

7 Islam, public reason and the state

This book explores the liberal nature of contemporary Indonesian constitutionalism by considering how the legal and political order post-Soeharto reflects elements of a comprehensive political theory, and to what extent. The form of liberalism chosen for this study was John Rawls' political liberalism, which some scholars have sought to apply to Indonesia and to Islam. Rawls' thinking about the ideal form of a constitutional democracy takes particular account of the interplay of competing comprehensive world views and was inspired by the experience of Western nations with religious conflict during previous centuries. I chose a case study of a prosecution under Indonesia's 'blasphemy' Law to consider the relevance of a political theory designed to provide a framework for managing value pluralism, and the respect for religious freedom as a fundamental constitutional right.

As stated in Chapter 1, the question of whether Rawls is compatible with Islam involves further inquiry as to the nature and scope of Islam, as well as where or how normative Islam is constituted. In the case of Indonesia there has been longstanding conflict about piety, devotion and what constitutes valid or deviant conduct. This conflict reflects the existence of diverse non-state authorities on Islam. There has also been ongoing contestation over the role of Islam as a source for state law and policy. In current day Indonesia, the law seeks to both promote and protect religion, but these potentially complementary functions in fact promote contradictions in the constitutional order. That is, notwithstanding the right to religious freedom in the Constitution and other law, the blasphemy regime facilitates the promotion of orthodox interpretations of religion. Jurisprudence (scholarship and superior court rulings) also establishes that all law must be consistent with an overarching obligation that the Indonesian state be based on Belief in Almighty God.

In the area of non-state Islam, the influential non-government Muslim organisation MUI seeks to promote 'Islamic law' as widely as possible. MUI has an important stake in determining the doctrine that pertains in cases of blasphemy or deviant interpretations of Islam. It also plays a prominent role supporting law enforcement in cases of blasphemy relating to Islamic practices. The case study of a blasphemy prosecution shows how the law is implemented against an Indonesian Muslim, and Muslims seem to account for a large number of those prosecuted under the blasphemy regime. I adopted this case study to demonstrate that the concept of religious pluralism is not only an inter-faith question. In a Muslim majority nation it is possible for issues of religious freedom and pluralism to arise within the majority faith. That is, there is the clear potential for conflict between 'religious' values and 'liberal' values, including religious freedom, even when working in the context of a majority single faith within a multi-faith constitutional democracy. In this final chapter I will consider the application of Rawls to Indonesia, reviewing the findings of previous chapters and exploring the views of scholars who have considered the compatibility of Rawls with Indonesia and with Islam.

Case study of post-Soeharto Indonesia

Chapter 2 introduced Rawls' political liberalism, which is the political theory from which the concept of public reason derives. Public reason can be understood as a mechanism of public justification in a constitutional democracy. Rawls, with other liberal theorists, is concerned with developing a response to the 'fact of pluralism', which is the recognition that a diversity of world views is a permanent feature of life in a democracy. Rawls traces the roots of political liberalism to the Western political experience with religious toleration when, during the Reformation, competing claims for authority were grounded in rival theologies. He proposes, instead, that no comprehensive world view should prevail in contests within a constitutional system.

In that chapter it was seen that some opponents of this thinking draw inspiration from different philosophical sources, these other sources also being themselves Western in origin. The so-called 'communitarian' critique, broadly, promotes group identity in preference to individual rights and reflects, it was argued, the Romantic tradition. Another interpretation of liberalism (drawing on Hobbes) is the source of the criticism that an overlapping consensus is not possible in the face of fundamental differences in values, and that (only) *modus vivendi* is possible. *Modus vivendi* is described by Rawls as a consensus based only on group or self-interest. It was also seen that arguments have been raised that, even in the West – supposedly the context in which Rawls may be found most suitable – those of faith may find the constraints of public reason unacceptable. I tried to highlight in that chapter that it may not be possible to reconcile arguments inspired by different philosophical sources. It should also be recalled that Rawls developed his political liberalism specifically in order to give meaning to the fundamental rights of individual citizens in a constitutional democracy. Despite its origins in Western political philosophy, his thinking is – some argue – not seen, or only imperfectly realised, in the West. It was also shown that critics of Rawls appear to be in agreement with him that freedom of religion is a fundamental constitutional right. *Modus vivendi* cannot obtain in circumstances where the individual pursuit of interests may suffer systematic injury under a regime, and conscientious pursuit of religion or belief, even that involving 'false acts', must be free from coercion. Rawls places a particular importance on the role of judges as 'exemplars of public reason', identifying a key role played by decision making in superior courts and the contribution of Indonesian courts is considered below.

I then dealt with the nature of contemporary jurisprudence about the place of religion in Indonesian legal and constitutional thinking in Chapter 3. Here it was seen that the historical urge on the part of some Indonesian Muslims to secure a place for Islamic or syariah law in the Constitution has been persistent. A similar urge is seen in jurisprudence that argues that Islamic law can, and indeed should, be codified or reflected in national law. It was seen that the laws protecting faith are expressed in several provisions that span a wide range of conduct, and none address Islam specifically. Only one of the provisions of the Blasphemy Law is – on its face – designed to deal with what scholars have called 'religious offences' (addressing deviant expressions of faith, but not mentioning Islam specifically). The other criminal provisions are less specific and are better characterised as 'offences against religion'. These provisions are, by their language and location in the Criminal Code, clearly directed at contributing to the maintenance of 'public order', and some are inherited from the colonial era. A key provision (art 156a of the Criminal Code) is widely accepted as being in need of redrafting. Its structure is ambiguous and it contains a key concept that is capable of multiple interpretations (*penodaan* – disgracing religion). I think it is particularly interesting to note that this is very similar to a provision in Egyptian law that has been deployed against minority faiths in criminal prosecutions. Overall, it was argued this is a de facto blasphemy regime because none of the laws contain a word directly corresponding to 'blasphemy'. Blasphemous conduct may be captured by the law, depending upon the circumstances and support that might be found in religious doctrine. The MK has specifically invited religious parent organisations to act in support of state management of religion in the context of upholding the validity of the Blasphemy Law.

Chapter 4 described the development, policies and *fatawa* of MUI, which advocates for the adoption of Islamic values in state law. It was shown how this policy is expressed and that there is a substantial list of legislation in which aspects of Islam are integrated. I also explored at some length the nature and characteristics of MUI *fatawa*. Islamic religious rulings are traditionally seen as non-binding, but MUI (only one of several *fatawa* issuing bodies in Indonesia) has developed a bureaucratic form of *fatawa* that it deploys in its self-appointed role as *mufti*, or religious adviser to the state. Innovation, or deviant approaches to Islam, have been addressed in its *fatawa*. *Fatawa* have also dealt specifically with innovation in worship, including a ruling on the activities of Yusman Roy. This area of doctrine is significant for the issue of religious freedom. This is because rulings on interpretations and practices go directly to the notion of the right to enjoy or pursue faith, particularly when directed at particular individuals (and indirectly their followers) as in this case study. Moreover, it was seen that there is a close correlation between a series of concepts, including innovation, blasphemy, heresy and apostasy. MUI purports to determine, nationally, standards of religious practice, and this, in combination with a state legal system highly receptive to Islam, gives MUI the capacity to play a significant role in influencing the character of Islam in Indonesia. Its ability to do this is significantly enhanced when its rulings not only set standards according to doctrine, but ultimately form part of the exercise of state power in criminal law, as shown by the Roy prosecution.

I detailed the facts and circumstances of this case study in Chapter 5, where we saw the promotion of a non-mainstream interpretation of Islam in East Java. The background to the case study reveals the manner in which MUI branches operate at the local level. MUI was engaged at the national level only following Roy's arrest, while events unfolded in East Java over a longer period and *fatawa* were issued at the local and provincial level. I noted that for some years prior to his arrest Roy's teaching did not give rise to unrest or to state action but there was a distinct intensifying of activity in 2005. It was suggested that the events in East Java in 2005 mirrored to some extent a rise in public activity particularly by MUI nationally. Media broadcasts featuring Roy probably served to raise the profile of this dispute and contributed to the acceleration of activity. The chapter details the manner in which MUI engaged with a range of state agencies, demonstrating that MUI is a capable and influential actor in promoting Islam and, in effect, advisor to government on religious matters. This role includes participation in significant bodies such as the regional leadership forum, or *Muspida*, and thus precipitating, or at least contributing to, the decisive action taken by state agencies including closure of the *pesantren* and Roy's arrest. I argued that the dispute can be interpreted as a proxy for the national-level dispute between orthodox and more liberal interpretations of Islam in Indonesia.

The examination in Chapter 6 of the criminal trial of Yusman Roy provided a practical example of the Blasphemy Law in action. It is also important because, given the nature of the distribution of judicial power in Indonesia, the MK in its ordinary judicial review function does not deal with specific cases (although Roy's prosecution was referenced in the application before the Court in that appeal). Equally, lower courts are unable to deal with matters of constitutional rights and the consistency of legislation with the constitution. For this reason alone it is valuable to consider the manner in which a blasphemy case proceeded in the Indonesian courts. This allows better consideration of the issues with the interpretation of particular provisions which, as noted, were accepted in the MK as requiring amendment. It also illustrates how *fatawa* contribute to criminal process. Evidence was led at trial about doctrine, and the *fatawa* were themselves not necessarily a key determinant of the legal issues in the trial. The District Court, however, withdrew from ruling on matters of doctrine on the primary charge of disgracing religion due to the conflicting evidence from religious scholars. This was perhaps a pragmatic step. I argued, however, that the Court rendered a decision on the subsidiary charge which, in any event, centred on a question of faith. It did this by finding that Roy's teaching on dual-language prayer offended Sunni Muslims, which may potentially amount to a ruling akin to apostasy by implicitly declaring his teachings outside mainstream Indonesian

Islam. Finally, as a prosecution of an Indonesian Muslim, the Roy case demonstrates one example of the way in which the blasphemy regime is deployed against members of the majority faith.

Rawls, Islam and the state

The application of a political philosophy that seeks to confine the role of faith in public discourse and in the decision-making of public officials appears at first sight to be problematic in the Indonesian case. Indonesian law has been, and continues to be, heavily focused on respect for and protection of religion, which is particularly evident in the prosecution of blasphemy cases. Notwithstanding this, the constitution remains neutral as to faith, and religious freedom is clearly a core feature of the Indonesian human rights framework. The case study highlights important features of the working of Indonesian constitutional democracy through the interaction of law, state power and religious authority. This is a focus of some of the work of Bowen (2003; 2005), who appears to be the only scholar to assess directly the applicability of Rawls' public reason to the case of Indonesian Islam.[1] He bases his conclusions about the nature of public reasoning in Indonesia on a detailed study of the interplay of Islam and legal processes.

An-Na'im (2008) also considers the case of Indonesia; however his particular focus is on the application of the idea of public reason to Islam and the state across the Muslim world, exploring the question of secularism. An-Na'im considers the consequences for both the state and Islam of the desire to integrate syariah into state law, which, as has been seen, is a subject of debate in Indonesia. Bilgin (2011) accepts, largely without qualification, the relevance of Rawls to Muslim states, although both he and An-Na'im consider Rawls particularly pertinent to Western liberal democracies. Fadel (2008: 17) focuses on Muslim experience in liberal democracies but excludes from his analysis citizens in Muslim majority jurisdictions. I will explore below the relevance of the various qualifications adopted by these writers.

Bowen (2003) seeks to adapt the notion of public reason to an understanding of the interplay of values in the Indonesia legal system – specifically in the context of family law and inheritance disputes in Aceh. Bowen (2003: 11) sees a distinction between the Western liberal orientation of Rawls' public reasoning and the fact that, for Muslim people, public values are derived from religious text. Bowen concludes that Rawls' version of public reason is not what we observe in Indonesia. In his view, particularly with respect to Islamic law and *adat* (traditional law), public reasoning retains a foundation in comprehensive

---

1 In his examination of the question of secularism and the Indonesian state Elson (2010: 340) refers to Rawls' political liberalism as an example of a model of religious toleration but goes no further in his analysis. He does not apply Rawls explicitly.

doctrines, and the ensuing conception of justice is not a political conception in the sense intended by Rawls, but one that is 'public and also Islamic' (Bowen 2003: 11–12). He concludes that whatever the rule of law is taken to mean, it must incorporate Indonesian value pluralism (Bowen 2003: 257).

Bowen (2005: 152–153) extends this work in an effort to see whether lessons from Asia can be applied to an understanding of Western society. He identifies three normative frames of reference in Indonesia: a social group that exists as political community (referring to special autonomy for Aceh); social norms that provide legitimacy to self-governance of communities (reliance on *adat* or traditional law); and the existence of Islamic norms governing family disputes (marriage and inheritance law, including special legal processes provided for Muslims in family law) (Bowen 2005: 166–167). He seeks to answer the question 'whether the presence in a legal system of laws that are based on revelation is compatible with the idea of an overlapping political consensus' (Bowen 2005: 153). Bowen (2005: 169) responds that in Indonesia there is evidence of 'competing universalistic normative structures', which demonstrates that there is only a 'convergence' or 'reasoned *modus vivendi*', not agreement on a set of shared normative starting points.

An-Na'im (2008: 6) challenges what he describes as two 'dangerous illusions': that the state's coercive power should be used to enforce Islam and that Islam should be kept out of the public life of the community of believers. He argues (An-Na'im 2008: 7) that protecting the desire of individuals to live in accordance with their beliefs requires that the state should not enforce Islam and adds further (An-Na'im 2008: 279):

> The claim of some Muslims to have the religious right and obligation to enforce Sharia through state institutions must be forcefully blocked because it constitutes an immediate and total repudiation of the right of all citizens to believe in Islam or another religion or opinion.

The state should, rather, restrict itself to upholding constitutional and other safeguards to free and fair debate (An-Na'im 2008: 281). An-Na'im (2008: 7) contests the notion of an Islamic state for two reasons: first, because it is a 'postcolonial innovation', which includes a 'totalitarian' view of law and policy; and second, because of the difficulty of ascertaining what Islamic authority (the enforcement of syariah) means to Muslims at large.

An-Na'im (2008: 84) discusses the possibility of a religiously neutral state that nonetheless retains a connection between Islam and the development of public policy.[2] He observes, correctly, that Rawls 'accepts the possibility of

---

2 It is not possible or desirable, he argues, for any society to keep its religious beliefs and commitments out of political choices and decisions, as this risks 'forcing religious reasoning into the domain of fugitive politics' (An-Na'im 2008: 275).

invoking comprehensive doctrines in public reason for particular situations' and adopts the distinction Rawls makes between a 'more or less well ordered society' and a 'nearly well ordered society' (An-Na'im 2008: 99). In the former, political values are well developed and there is no need for reference to comprehensive doctrines in public reason; in the latter case, an explanation of how comprehensive values affirm the political values can help to legitimise the notion of public reason. An-Na'im (2008: 101) suggests that the former is more characteristic of the United States, and therefore the concept may not resonate with postcolonial Asian societies whose historical and social conditions leave them as currently 'less well ordered'. For him it is a mistake to seek to exclude religion from public reason (An-Na'im 2015: 279).

An-Na'im (2008: 97–101; 2015) proposes instead the adoption of a concept that he labels 'civic reason', acknowledging that there are 'obvious overlaps' between this idea and Rawls' public reason. This he describes more recently (An-Na'im 2015) as a 'friendly amendment' to Rawls. Civic reason 'entitles all citizens to publicly debate any matter that pertains to or reflects on public policy and governmental or state action' and its objective is to 'diminish the impact of claims of religious exclusivity on the ability to debate issue of public policy' (An-Na'im 2008: 93). Despite the fact that the two phrases express the same concept, An-Na'im maintains that there is a distinction between them. An-Na'im (2008: 100–101) argues that there are 'risks of transplanting' Rawls' ideas to Islamic societies at large because Rawls' model society assumes a developed and stable constitutional order, something An-Na'im believes is absent in many majority Muslim societies.

An-Na'im's (2008: 139) call to separate religion and the state does not relegate faith to the private domain; indeed, he argues that Islamic principles can be proposed for adoption as official policy or legislation:

> but such proposals must be supported by civic reason, which means that reasons can be debated among all citizens without reference to religious beliefs. But the practical operation of civic reason requires the safeguards of constitutionalism, human rights and citizenship.

At the same time, he states 'it is imperative that no particular view of Shari'a is coercively imposed in the name of Islam, because that would inhibit free debate and contestation' (An-Na'im 2008: 278). He (An-Na'im 2008: 275) explains:

> the internal transformation of religions is critical for the survival of religious traditions and the legitimacy of religious experience. Every orthodox precept the believers take for granted today began as a heresy from the perspective of some other orthodox doctrine and may well continue to be considered heretical by some believers.

Separation of church and state secures the 'legal and political space in which this transformation can happen' (An-Na'im 2008: 275–276). This 'secular' state enables freedom of belief and provides an opportunity for development in doctrine, without which there is 'no possibility of peace within or between religions': '[t]he secular state also secures effective possibilities for preventing an exclusivist and authoritarian religious group from threatening the essential interests of any segment of the population' (An-Na'im 2008: 276). An-Na'im (2015: 280–281) expands on this issue by invoking a clear distinction between 'nation' and 'state'; governments change, but state institutions live on despite changes in national politics and must, he appears to argue, be bound by constitutionalism and human rights standards.

On the specific question of freedom of religion, An-Na'im (2008: 117) acknowledges there is a conflict between syariah and human rights, but holds that it is possible and 'indeed necessary to reinterpret Islamic sources in order to affirm and protect the freedom of religion and belief'. He states that the relevant syariah principles concerning apostasy and related crimes 'have rarely been strictly and systematically applied in the past' but their existence 'constitutes a fundamental conflict with the premise of the universality of human rights, and is a source of serious violation of the freedom of religion and belief in practice' (An-Na'im 2008: 118). The inconsistencies between these syariah principles and 'religious freedom from an Islamic perspective', and the proper application of the religious neutrality of the state, eliminates 'any possibility of negative legal consequences for apostasy and related consequences' (but not the social consequences) (An-Na'im 2008: 118). To conclude, An-Na'im (2008: 122) states that 'because belief in Islam presupposes and requires the freedom of choice and can never be valid under coercion or intimidation', therefore there should be no negative legal consequences for apostasy and related concepts.

Fadel (2008) examines the compatibility of Rawls with Islamic thought, seeking grounds in Islam for a reasonable overlapping consensus. He attempts to provide a 'doctrinal roadmap' of Islamic resources which could 'be used to articulate a set of theological and moral commitments that would plausibly allow committed Muslims to endorse Rawlsian constitutional essentials for the right reasons' (Fadel 2008: 6). Fadel (2008: 6) looks to Islamic theology and ethics, rather than Islamic law, in overturning claims of irreconcilable differences between 'orthodox Islamic commitments and liberal constitutional democracy'. Developing the notion of pluralism within Islam he observes that there is a 'historical messiness' in Islam and reducing it to 'tidy doctrines' 'inevitably privileges some Muslim traditions (specifically, the written tradition of orthodoxy) and marginalises non-conforming Muslim views' (Fadel 2008: 6, 11).[3]

Fadel's (2008: 17) approach to Muslim states is similar to An-Na'im's in that he asserts that large numbers of Muslims live under authoritarian regimes, rendering meaningless any attempt to search for a commitment to democratic principles. He also assumes that the experience of religious conflict in the West

---

3 Cf. March (2009), who takes a contrary view.

is a 'but for' condition for the rise of liberal institutions (Fadel 2008). Interestingly, Fadel (2008: 18–19) also assumes that Muslim societies are largely homogenous in their relationships with their faith, and there is an 'absence of actual pluralism in most Muslim majority societies, especially Middle Eastern countries'.[4] Nonetheless, he concludes that, in a well-ordered society, there would not be support for a state to 'compel religious belief or punish heresy', that the primary obligation of a political order is to provide space for Muslims to live according to their faith (and seek salvation), and the political order must allow a 'modicum' of freedom of thought and pluralism (Fadel 2008: 35). Accordingly, Fadel (2008: 67) considers that Islamic substantive law and moral theology 'allowed for the introduction and acceptance of arguments within Islamic law that mimic Rawls' notion of public reason as defining the limits of legitimate political discourse'.

Bilgin (2011) too considers that Rawls is not automatically relevant in a Muslim context. He argues there are 'structural impediments' that prevent political liberalism being adopted for societies that 'fall short' of certain conditions (Bilgin 2011: 6). According to Bilgin (2011: 3), the requisite sociological conditions are an acceptance of tolerance born of the experience of prolonged religious conflict, and a democratic society that encompasses diverse world views. How can Rawls be applied in a society lacking the democratic culture political liberalism supposes (Bilgin 2011)? Despite this reservation, Bilgin (2011) argues emphatically that 'political liberalism offers ample conceptual and normative resources in the advancement of democracy in Muslim societies'.

Political liberalism itself is not embraced uncritically, as Bilgin (2011: 66) notes that 'without reasonable pluralism Rawls' idea fails'.[5] Even if politico-sociological conditions have not produced Rawlsian reasonable pluralism, Bilgin (2011: 64–66) argues that it may be possible to generate reasonable pluralism through developing political toleration of religion, and impartiality of the state toward religious views.[6] The consequences of reasonableness for religious doctrines are summarised by Bilgin (2011: 40) in the following way:

1) A politically reasonable religious doctrine accepts political liberalism as offering no drawbacks, and it may live by its tenets when it is ready to cooperate with others in order to reach fair terms of political conduct;

---

4 Mohr and Hosen (2011: 6–7) provide some statistics on the prevalence of democracy among Muslim states: ten countries declare themselves to be Islamic states; twelve predominantly Muslim countries declare Islam as the official state religion; eleven declare the state to be secular; and, a further eleven (including Indonesia) have no declaration as to whether they are secular or possess a state religion.

5 'Reasonableness' is one of the most discussed aspects of Rawls political liberalism but arguably deserves more explanation than it receives (Bilgin 2011: 21).

6 As noted in Chapter 1, Bilgin (2011) does not use national case studies, rather he explores the work of Locke on toleration and Adam Smith on state neutrality.

2) A politically unreasonable doctrine engages in cooperation but favours its own interests over the terms of cooperation, in which case the idea of public reason cannot be fully realised; and
3) A doctrine unwilling to cooperate at all will be opposed by a political liberal order.

He considers that the 'mainstream majorities' in most Muslim societies could fit within the first category, the third category is represented by 'marginal but vocal radical militant groups', and the second category 'cannot be trusted and thus cannot be offered fair terms', although such a group may transform over time, as has been seen with numerous Islamist parties (Bilgin 2011: 40–41).

Political liberalism, states Bilgin (2011: 55–56), does not 'espouse a privatized religion' but, following his analysis of the different postures among religious doctrines above, he observes that 'the robust representation of religion in political society poses a significant challenge to the political liberal prospect'. He does not agree with claims that Muslim countries are not electoral democracies because Islam is antithetical to democracy, since the same claim was made in decades past about Catholic nations, and is no longer the case (Bilgin 2011: 56).[7] Fundamentally, he asserts that political liberalism 'need not be confined to the societies of particular historical experiences' although for this to happen 'political reasonableness must prevail over the political calculus of citizens' (Bilgin 2011: 116–117). Moreover, 'political reasonableness naturally forbids the political imposition of religious beliefs and values and prohibits discrimination' (Bilgin 2011: 50).

Pluralism and liberalism in Indonesia

The expectations of a constitutional democracy reflecting Rawls' vision of public reason can be summarised as follows. Public reason is reasoning in the public space that addresses questions of public good represented by issues of fundamental political justice and constitutional essentials. It should result in political stability based on allegiance to political ideals and values. Public reason applies in particular to judges and especially to superior court judges. Public reason assigns special priority to basic rights, liberties and opportunities and affirms measures that assure all citizens adequate means to make effective use of these rights, liberties and opportunities. Judicial reasoning must fit the relevant body of constitutional principles, justified in terms of the public conception of justice. It cannot involve personal ideals and moral values nor

---

7 Using data published by Casanova, Bilgin (2011) records that in the 1970s only one quarter of Catholic majority nations were electoral democracies, but the proportions are now reversed and three quarters of Catholic majority nations have become electoral democracies.

the religious or philosophical views of others. Judicial reasoning must appeal to the most reasonable understanding of justice that all citizens might reasonably endorse.

Bowen's view about the nature of public reason in Indonesia is borne out by the case study. Indeed, the case study arguably demonstrates that the current interpretation of *Pancasila*, which demands an overarching commitment to religion, extends or perhaps further entrenches the place of faith in public decision making. Bowen's later (2005) invoking of the notion of *modus vivendi* marks a further, and perhaps more comprehensive, rejection of Rawls. An-Na'im includes Indonesia as a case study in his examination of Islam and the secular state, but does not express a conclusion in the clear terms used by Bowen. He proposes, however, that there has been constant negotiation and recalibration of 'the Islam-state-society equation in different phases of postcolonial Indonesian political history' (An-Na'im 2008: 251). In his view, this contest has contributed to 'damaging some aspects of constitutional democracy', and he finds the debate over Islam and the state in Indonesia beset by 'false dichotomies' and 'unnecessary dilemmas' (An-Na'im 2008: 249, 260). Much of this arises from the longstanding debate about the idea of secularism in the Indonesian context (An-Na'im 2008: 260–266). In short, An-Na'im (2008: 261) considers that Indonesia's traditions of tolerance and pluralism do, in fact, reflect the notion of the secular state as he describes it.

An-Na'im provides a far more detailed consideration of Rawls' thinking than Bowen. He correctly observes that the inclusion of explicit references to faith in public reasoning is captured by Rawls, reflecting simply a 'less well ordered' state. In addition, An-Na'im's work addresses the question of religious freedom. Accordingly, he is exploring Rawls more directly 'in context'; that is, he considers the sort of constitutional fundamental specifically envisaged by Rawls in explaining public reason. This is not a feature of Bowen's work. Furthermore, An-Na'im deals with the same broader political context that underlies Rawls' political liberalism, namely the existence of religious diversity within a single faith, and the motivation among some to access state power in the name of faith. As a result, An-Na'im's work is highly relevant in the context of the case study. Moreover, An-Na'im's analysis of the nature of Islam and Islamic reform, including concepts such as apostasy, is of particular relevance to the case study's subject of innovation in Islam and the Blasphemy Law.

An-Na'im's 'civic reason' is largely indistinguishable in its substance and the function it plays in civic discourse from 'public reason'. The key argument raised for creating a new term for the same concept is to address the likelihood that developing or transition states may not replicate the political stability of a more advanced constitutional democracy, such as the United States. This approach does not take account of the arguments seen in Chapter 2 that there are, in fact, no states – including the US – that replicate Rawls' ideal model. Rawls' model, as is acknowledged by An-Na'im, concedes that there may be a need for comprehensive doctrines to form part of public reasoning. (In his 'wide view' of public political culture, the 'proviso' allows comprehensive doctrine to be admitted subject to later being argued in terms that do not rely on a comprehensive doctrine.) Another reason for the 'friendly amendment' is An-Na'im's insistence that it is vital for religious views to be promoted in public debate. The case study arguably demonstrates how difficult it is to reconcile these two propositions. An-Na'im's more recent expression of the important distinction between state institutions and national governments reinforces the significance of the lessons from the Indonesian case study examined here. It is indeed a very careful balancing act required to shelter the state from religion (An-Na'im 2015: 275), because the motivation to permit space for the advancement of religious values in state law ultimately conflicts with the commitment to religious freedom.

An-Na'im's work serves as a guide to the consequences of a failure to more clearly promote religious freedom. In particular it reinforces the argument, seen in Chapter 2, that a degree of consensus about a predominant comprehensive worldview does not amount to public reason. Equally, public deliberation or reasoning does not amount to public (or civic) reason. An-Na'im's thinking about strictly controlling the access of religious doctrine to state authority is founded in large part upon his concerns about religious authoritarianism. Mainstream or elite views about faith can be translated into state law, which results in compulsion in religion, which, he argues, is contrary to Islam and the right to religious freedom. The case study of the blasphemy regime in Indonesia reveals just such a set of conditions.

Bowen may be correct in his view that public reason as envisaged by Rawls does not prevail in Indonesia, but the consequences of that condition are articulated in the work of An-Na'im. The consequences include that under a form of *modus vivendi* there is potential for constitutional rights to be overridden in pursuit of the aspiration to respect religious values. Indonesia as a functioning constitutional democracy has not been subject to political instability for some time, or a lack of constitutional maturity that An-Na'im suggests is the case in many Muslim majority states. It can, however, be considered 'unstable' in the sense intended by Rawls. That is, public reason is not fully realised as a consequence of the ongoing drive to actively recognise and indeed implement aspects of Islamic religious thought through state law.

The democratic threshold

Prior to considering some aspects of the Indonesian case in more detail, it is important to resolve the issues raised in the scholarship about the relevance of Rawls to Muslim majority states. The writers reviewed above all hold significant concerns about the capacity of most Muslim states to reach the threshold of mature democracy they see as implicit in Rawls. An-Na'im and Fadel consider most Muslim states to be insufficiently stable for a Rawlsian model, and Bilgin similarly sees 'structural limitations' as a barrier to the direct importation of Rawls. Bowen, too, holds reservations about the Western origins of Rawls' thinking.

It was seen in Chapter 1 that Indonesia's first Constitution had significant shortcomings and facilitated authoritarian rule. Indonesia was, nonetheless, a form of constitutional state for the latter part of the twentieth century, and principles of liberal democratic thought, including human rights, were prevalent in debates about constitutional reform during the 1950s. For that matter, as was observed in Chapter 3, religious freedom has always been a part of the Indonesian Constitution. Thus, while political transition took place relatively recently, in the early 2000s, Indonesia has now consolidated its place as a successful liberal democracy. Perhaps more importantly, it also has a long history of open and, at times, passionate debate about the liberal issues of tolerance, pluralism and the secular state. Accordingly, qualifications based on the origins of Rawls' model arguably do not apply in the case of Indonesia.

The Pancasila *state as religious state*

The blasphemy regime and related criminal provisions (offences against religion) are not inherently Islamic, but it has been shown how the law is used in Islamic doctrinal disputes and how Islamic law and argumentation forms part of the legal process in such cases. There is also a clear trend of Indonesian legislation being inspired by, or based on, aspects of Islamic law, which is consistent with jurisprudence arguing that it is appropriate for Islamic law to be a source for state law. The identification by the MK of a special place for faith, as a touchstone for the validity of law through its interpretation of *Pancasila*, reflects the strength of this line of thinking. The elevation of the first *sila* – which addresses *ketuhanan* or godliness – to this role is a key new development.

Indonesia's highest Court does not specifically invoke religion as part of its reasoning in the Blasphemy Case, as doctrine or a ruling on a specific issue is not relied on in its decision. This is partly a result of the case being about the constitutionality of the law rather than the determination of rights in a particular case. In this sense, the Court does not breach the limits described by Rawls for the reasoning of a superior court. In fact, the Court appears to be pursuing the task identified by Rawls – it is reasoning within the relevant constitutional principles and, arguably, attempting to express a conception of justice that the public might reasonably endorse. The commitment to godliness is not imported into the constitution or the process of reasoning from another source – it is constitutional text that demands interpretation.

In pursuing a 'middle path' through the issues in the Blasphemy Case, the Court seems to be attempting to tread a path that borders the legal/constitutional and the religious spheres. This mind-set can also be seen in the deliberations of the District Court in trying the Roy case. The trial Court declined to rule on the charge of disgracing religion, on the basis of conflicting evidence from religious scholars called by both the prosecution and defence teams. This, perhaps, reflects a view that a state court is not competent to rule on matters of faith, or that it is inappropriate for it to do so. The trial Court instead deals with the less contentious issue of public order, but, as was seen, this did not dispose of the religious issues. Rather, the trial Court rendered a de facto ruling on the status of Roy's teaching finding that it offended Sunni Muslims. The *fatawa*, which were important in the mounting of the charges and in the prosecution case, do not, however, appear to have received any formal recognition from the trial Court.

There appears to be an element in judicial thinking that while religion is to be acknowledged and respected, the interpretation of religion is out of bounds. The MK accordingly identifies a role for non-state Islam by inviting religious authorities to partner with the government in the area of determining what is and is not appropriate religious conduct or teaching. This statement indeed reflects the circumstances preceding the prosecution of Yusman Roy, which revealed the numerous points of contact between MUI and the state at the local level. It was also seen that the Department of Religion deferred to MUI on matters of doctrine, a further indication of the recognition by the state of a boundary between its competence and the competence of religious authorities.

In the case study, the state both validated the role of non-state religious authority, specifically MUI, and annexed it to the legal process. As An-Na'im (2008: 261) explains, however, the enforcement of religious law by the state 'only represents the view of the ruling elite and becomes the political will of the state rather than the religious law of Muslims'. In Indonesia, there appears to be an attempt to maintain a distinction between state power and religious authority in pursuing the so-called middle path. The outcome in this case is, however, not to prevent religion from entering into the resolution of disputes but, rather, state power is adapted for the purpose of enforcing a particular interpretation of religious doctrine, which contributes indirectly to promoting the authority of a distinct group within the majority faith, a matter I will return to below.

Despite the fact that the right to religious freedom is well entrenched in the legal and constitutional framework, it remains a very precarious right. The right has a dual status as both 'non-derogable' and yet open to lawful restriction in certain circumstances. As discussed in Chapter 3, the situation might be dealt with differently if there were a greater willingness to look further afield for assistance in developing a more nuanced reading of the law and Indonesia's human rights obligations. Courts are, however, required to give meaning to the provisions as they appear and the Constitution's human rights framework is compromised by the ability of the legislature to pass law concerning the respect for religious values, the rights of others, and public order. Even so, international human rights commentary encourages the strictest limit on the permissible restrictions on the right to religious freedom. In terms of public reason, applying such a restrictive scope to the meaning of the right to religious freedom reflects a failure to assign a special priority to a basic right and liberty, and to affirm the opportunity of all citizens to make effective use of the right.

Who (or what) is the umat?

I suggested in Chapter 3 that the MK's position on human rights in the Blasphemy Case showed a bias towards interpreting religious freedom as a form of group right. This was achieved through appearing to require consistency between both the internal and external religious forums and religious orthodoxy. I also proposed in Chapter 6 that the District Court in the Roy trial effectively excluded Roy from being among a group it identified as Sunni Muslims, on account of his allegedly deviant behaviour. Whether or not these judicial pronouncements are accurate reflections of domestic or even international human rights law, they could be said to assist in sustaining a particular concept of the *umat*. In Chapter 1 it was noted that a Muslim enters the community of the faithful when proclaiming the confession of the faith, and it has been seen that the events of the case study, as well as evidence in the prosecution, focused on this very issue. Those protesting against Roy were said to have come in the name of the *umat*, conforming with the requirement of *sholat* was described as being a requirement of members of the *umat*, and it was the distress among the *umat* caused by Roy's teachings that was his downfall.

The fuller implications of this approach are seen in the MK's consideration of the nature of the right to religious freedom. The Court acknowledges there is no limitation on the number of faiths that may be pursued in Indonesia but, at the same time, purports to oblige Indonesians to pursue their chosen faith only in a way consistent with 'correct' teaching and methodology. Ultimately, religious freedom in Indonesia therefore means the freedom to adopt a 'formal' religion. This reflects a commitment to a form of pluralism, and it was argued in Chapter 3 that the recognition of the right to religious freedom itself is a sign of this commitment. The case study, however, is of an intra-faith dispute. The promotion and protection of faith – under the overarching obligation of religiosity – protects all 'religions', but does not permit an individual to pursue faith in accordance with their own conscience or form of belief. As a result, Indonesian citizens are obliged to respect the religious beliefs of others by not contradicting or challenging the orthodox form of those religious beliefs. This was seen in the application of the public offence provisions of the Criminal Code where the onus is reversed and those who 'disturb' other citizens on grounds of religion are potentially criminally responsible for the deterioration in public order. It can also be seen in the text of art 22 of the Human Rights Law, which appears to require Indonesians to pursue their faith in accordance with religious teachings.

Returning to the critique of Rawls, it is clear that coercion in religion was considered unacceptable by all sides in the debate. Those who object to Rawls either on the grounds that *modus vivendi* as between different value systems is preferable (or merely a reality) or through a desire to see formal recognition of faith by the state, agree that restrictions on the freedom of religion are a fundamental injustice. *Modus vivendi* then, arguably, does not permit unreasonable intolerance within any given faith group. Equally, the scholars considered in the section above, writing primarily from a Muslim perspective, also highlight the critical issue of religious freedom and non-discrimination. It follows that any argument asserting the priority of conformity or membership of a group (however defined), when motivated by religious values, can only be in conflict with the concept of public reason. Or more broadly, following Bilgin, any lack of toleration or acceptance of pluralism is inconsistent with the nature and objectives of political liberalism.

This situation reflects the debates already identified as forming a fundamental part of Indonesia's constitutional journey. It is, in essence, a classic example of the stand-off between those motivated to pursue syariah and those motivated by liberal democratic values. The problem, as articulated clearly by An-Na'im, arises where state authority and state power are sought to be co-opted to impose a particular interpretation of Islam. In the case of Indonesia, this recalls the authoritarian strain of thought that was been prevalent in constitutionalism for much of the twentieth century. It has been argued that the Integralist (and authoritarian in effect) State owed a significant amount to the Romantic intellectual tradition, and this makes Larmore's observation about links between the Romantic tradition and the communitarian critique of liberalism particularly intriguing. The notion that there is something natural, or traditional, about the existence of religious groups that might be said to part of a *modus vivendi* fails to take account of a key consideration. It does not take account of the fact that (as Hooker observes) the *umat* is not static, nor of the fact that in a liberal democracy citizen's rights exist, at the very least, in parallel with other rights. Azra and Hudson (2008: 6) also argue that, while there is a 'richer understanding and practice of community' in Islam than is evident in the West, Indonesian Islam 'is entirely compatible with a strong form of individualism'.[8] Bowen's conclusion as to Indonesia displaying a reasoned *modus vivendi* among different normative systems may be an accurate assessment, but his analysis does not include matters of constitutional fundamentals. The case study suggests that, whatever the reality, there is a deficit under a blasphemy regime that comes at a significant cost to the status of individual citizens.

The rise of conservative Islam

MUI proclaims itself to be a '*rumah besar*' or a kind of 'broad Church' for Indonesian Islam. There have been clear examples of collaboration and coordination with Muslim organisations considered to be 'hardline' (*garis keras*) both at the national level and, as seen in Chapter 5, also the local level. There has to date been no room for collaboration with elements of Islam that may be considered 'liberal'. This is seen perhaps most prominently in MUI's national level *fatwa* against pluralism, liberalism and secularism in religion.[9] The

---

8 On the other hand, writing in the context of personal status systems, Sezgin (1999: 15) considers that 'as yet no society seems to have come up with an answer to the question of whose rights should prevail if the rights of the individuals and communities are in conflict; or to what extent a democratic regime should tolerate communal norms'.
9 Which had its counterpart in another Islamic organisation, Persis, and its policy on SIPILIS.

arguments raised on both sides in the trial of Yusman Roy could also be said to represent, broadly, the conflict in post-*Reformasi* Indonesia between liberal and conservative elements in Islam. MUI's efforts to claim a national leadership role are also seen in the role it played in a key national congress, held in the same year (2005) as the trial of Roy. That year, indeed, appeared to be a peak year for public activity by MUI and for efforts to tackle 'deviancy'.

Only one of several large, national Islamic organisations (and the only one without a mass membership), MUI claims a special role for itself as *mufti*, or adviser to the state on Islamic doctrine. One part of its self-proclaimed role includes the issuing of *fatawa*, and their promotion as guides to policy and legislation. It has been successful in numerous instances in this objective. Just as MUI at the local level was seen to be an adjunct to state agencies, so MUI at the national level has adopted a special role in the provision of guidance on Islamic issues. MUI was originally a creation of the state but has since evolved and sought to change its standing, becoming more clearly independent in its views. It would seem, in fact, that its relationship with government has largely reversed. No longer a creature of government, MUI takes the lead role in areas of law and policy, and the government responds.

It was noted in Chapter 4 that Indonesia has seen a divergence of views over many years on matters of Islam. Scholars have had greater difficulty more recently in identifying strands within Islam, and categories of Islam that were once a feature of Indonesian scholarship have become harder to define. There is, perhaps, ongoing polarisation between two extremes but this does not necessarily help to identify more accurately where MUI sits. Its embrace of more hardline elements within Indonesian Islam does not necessarily mean that it endorses radicalism or extremism. Certainly in relation to questions of innovation it seems to have adopted the position once held by Indonesian Modernists, such as Muhammadiyah, which views innovation from a conservative standpoint. A conservative approach to innovation tends toward the interpretation that all innovation is unacceptable. Variation in approach to ritual was considered at length in Chapter 4, and its close association with allegations of heresy and even apostasy was noted. There remain, however, different views on matters of doctrine and, importantly, on the significance of rulings provided in *fatawa*. Opinions were expressed on both subjects during Roy's trial and, indeed, the expert evidence was conflicting on the issue of dual-language prayer.

MUI has, nonetheless, mounted an effective campaign against liberal Islam, and measures such as its controversial *fatwa* have arguably contributed to rendering 'moderate' Islam in Indonesia largely inert. While different opinions may be seen, as they have been in the case study, what is critical is the influence carried by MUI. It appears to have gained prominence and authority, and this may reflect as much upon the attitude of the state as it does upon MUI or other national Islamic organisations. MUI is, ultimately, in an apparently unrivalled position to determine what amounts to a correct or incorrect interpretation of Islam, not only because of the authority it has assumed in relation to doctrine but also because of its capacity to influence the state. Its influence over the state does not reside simply in the national or policy level, as MUI is also capable of influencing individual cases, as was seen in the case study. The events in the Roy case suggest that MUI may have precipitated Roy's arrest and trial, and it played a decisive role in assisting government agencies to resolve the dispute. The *fatawa* also provided necessary content and weight to the criminal process, albeit they did not play a conclusive role in the Court's decision.

Rawls and Indonesian pluralism

There has been relatively little scholarly attention to the question of the influence of political theory in the Indonesian constitution. Scholars have identified that the constitution contains potentially conflicting doctrines. It has been noted correctly that the transformation of the constitution in the reform era, including the addition of a comprehensive human rights framework, marked a distinct move away from the Integralist State model. There has also been a substantial amount of scholarly attention to the influence of Islam, or the interaction between Islam and the state, and the accommodation in various ways of Islamic thought. There is no formal recognition of Islam at the constitutional level and freedom of religion is entrenched in a number of provisions in the constitution and law. This shows a recognition of the existence of religious pluralism, that is, the existence of different faith groups. The upholding of the validity of the Blasphemy Law, and the accompanying advancement of the commitment to godliness in the *Pancasila*, further extends the accommodation between state and faith. The injunction to maintain Indonesia as a state based in the Belief in Almighty God is, however, a very broad and poorly articulated concept.

The book highlights what I believe is a convergence between two complementary trends in Indonesia. One is the ever more important place of faith in Indonesian law and constitutional thought, as seen in the redefining of the *Pancasila* state as a religious state. At a more theoretical level, this movement and, specifically, the invocation of a partnership between the state and religious authorities by the MK, opens the possibility or the potential for a transfer of authority to non-state hands. The annexation to the state of religious authority to provide guidance on matters of religious values reveals a misapprehension about the nature of power in a constitutional democracy. At a more practical level, the manner in which the blasphemy regime is implemented invites ongoing engagement with religious authorities. Violations of public order laws may not always involve religious questions, and therefore might proceed without any issue of doctrine arising. However, when disputes about faith are at the heart of cases, as in the Roy prosecution, and when provisions from the Blasphemy Law are invoked, it is virtually impossible for the law to be interpreted and applied without reliance on religious advice. This is arguably a logical consequence of the nature of blasphemy laws. The motivation to apply the

Blasphemy Law, and the MK's upholding of the blasphemy regime, speak to the potency in Indonesia of the overarching sense of obligation to respect religion. To the extent that this reveals an absence of, or a weakness in, public reason in Indonesia is a commentary not on Indonesian social values, but on the nature of constitutional democracy in Indonesia.

The other element in this convergence is the continuing assertiveness of MUI as the national parent Islamic organisation, and its assumption of the role as the provider of guidance to the state on matters of Islamic doctrine. The particular characteristics of this trend are the eradication of both moderate doctrinal views and deviant variations from the public face of Islam in Indonesia, with MUI advancing a highly orthodox form of Islam. MUI demonstrates not only a clear doctrinal agenda, but a motivation to influence state law and policy, and to exploit opportunities to assert an authoritative view on doctrine. The existence of the Blasphemy Law, and the close collaboration between MUI and state agencies in particular, provide a crucial entry point for MUI into the criminal legal process. The law provides MUI the capacity to pursue and silence Islamic teachings considered to be deviant, thereby expanding in a new and important way the engagement between Islamic law and state law.

Blasphemy law sits at the intersection of state and religious authority, and the case study demonstrates that this legal regime illuminates the tensions inherent in the efforts to make a place for faith in Indonesia's constitutional order. These tensions are not new, as the modern Indonesian state has grappled with them since Independence. Efforts continue to be made to create an Indonesian state identity that is independent of two extremes: 'secular' or 'religious'. This is driven by a recognition that there is a form of pluralism 'hard-wired' into the constitution, but it is one that rests on a commitment to faith, and not a single religion. However, this middle path only further entrenches the place of faith in constitutional thought. More importantly it operates to cede authority from the democratic state: the state permits and encourages an independent source of authority to have influence in determining the extent to which Indonesian citizens can exercise their fundamental right to religious freedom.

Indonesia is neither an authoritarian state nor a fundamentalist theocracy – it is, in theory, a democracy that respects the rule of law. This is arguably, therefore, a political context to which Rawls' thinking can be applied, and concerns about the applicability of Rawls to Islamic states are not particularly relevant to Indonesia. His political liberalism deals with the nature of justice in a constitutional democracy with a particular concern for the respect of fundamental rights. For Rawls, citizens share equally in political power and, ultimately, under his framework the nature of justice and the legitimacy of law and state authority are determined by the state's management of diversity. In Indonesia, the experience of religious freedom and the quality of justice, broadly defined, is fundamentally compromised, as individual citizens can only experience faith in ways determined appropriate by the state, in partnership with non-state religious authorities.

The pluralist notions inherent in the constitution and the liberal principles they reflect have limited impact while their value is determined by authorities that are not formally part of the ordinary, publicly accountable institutions in a democracy. The state's drive to elevate respect for faith and a particular notion of national unity above individual justice represses diversity, and a liberal form of justice and the full benefits of democratic citizenship cannot be attained under these circumstances. Rawls' political liberalism has significant potential to contribute to thinking about Islam and democracy in Indonesia because Islam is not monolithic, and limits on the exercise of state power are just as relevant to members of the majority faith as they are to other faiths. The principle barrier to the application of Rawls' thinking in Indonesia is not theoretical incompatibility, but rather the ongoing influence of prevailing approaches to power and authority which continue to reflect entrenched, authoritarian mind-sets.

Postscript

The case study at the heart of the book is in some ways peculiar to the times, but the broader issues I have considered are perennial in the study of Islam and the state in Indonesia. This is because the relationship between religion and the state in a nation of the faithful is a natural preoccupation, and is constantly evolving. As has been shown, the more concrete links between Islam, law and the state are subject to public debate on a regular basis in Indonesia. The personality and focus of Indonesian Muslim organisations are also subject to change. The make-up of leadership groups (including that of MUI) alters on a periodic basis, usually with some input from their membership. There is constant discussion about matters of doctrine and its application to everyday situations and social trends. Indeed, over recent years there has been a series of high profile public debates about issues including deviant sects, anti-pornography policy and law, and LGBT rights. Arguably, conservative voices seek to control policy and shut down debate in every new area of social reform.

One important development is a draft revision of the Criminal Code, which includes a suite of provisions concerning religion. This has been submitted to the DPR for consideration but its final form, and the timeline for passage through the legislature, remain a matter of speculation. Debate may well take some time to be concluded, if it is at all. Importantly, the draft Code maintains the current official neutrality as regards particular faiths – Islam is still not afforded special recognition. The most obvious difference between it and the current Code is structural, with the draft providing a separate chapter (Chap VII) to address 'Crimes Against Religion and Religious Life'. This appears to signal an intention to elevate the status of offences protecting religion. Equally significant is the introduction of a new legal construct, namely 'defamation of religion' (*Penghinaan terhadap Agama*). This offence (art 341) forms the first of the eight articles in the new chapter. Defamation is an offence known in Indonesian law but the draft Code provides no definition, nor elements of the offence in the context of religion. The clarification to the draft likewise offers no guidance on its interpretation. Rather, it simply notes that the Constitutional principle of *Ketuhanan* reflects the critical place of religion in society and defamation shows a lack of respect and offends against this feeling of religiosity.

A further provision (art 342) extends the possible subjects of defamation beyond 'religions adhered to in Indonesia' to include also 'the greatness of God' (*kegaungan Tuhan*) and 'the word of God and His character' (*firman dan sifat-Nya*). This offence carries a more severe penalty than the basic offence of defamation of religion (five years, as opposed to two). Clearly, the potential scope for this set of offences is very wide indeed. The clarification describes this as an indirect form of defamation that can cause disturbance in the relevant religious group, and that it is intended to guard against inter-group conflict. As has been seen in practice, disturbance can arise when a group takes offence at a particular statement, teaching or variant practice. This kind of provision is likely to reinforce the criminalisation of deviant behaviour. Given the character of the offence and its breadth, it may well capture actions that comprise 'religious offences' (recall the distinction between offences against religion and religious offences discussed in Chapter 3); that is, conduct which is considered contrary to specific religious teachings. It therefore has the potential to encompass acts that are blasphemous in the traditional sense.

The concept of *penodaan agama* – staining or disgracing religion – remains in place in a provision (art 343) that prohibits 'ridiculing, staining, or humiliating religion, Apostles, Prophets, holy books, religious teachings, or religious worship'. As in the current Code, this addresses, as much as anything, acts that vilify a religion or practice. As we have seen, however, the unusual concept of *penodaan* is opaque, and open to potentially wide interpretation. The draft also retains a provision (art 344) prohibiting the broadcasting or display of writing, pictures or recordings that are defamatory or offensive (pursuant to arts 341 and 343).

Another notable development in the draft is the creation of a separate offence (art 345) of incitement – specifically, the prohibiting of incitement in any form that 'denies/negates (*meniadakan*) belief in a lawful religion' (*agama yang sah*). As I observed in my discussion of the current art 156a, there is some ambiguity in that provision as to whether the offence it creates requires this kind of action (attacking religious adherence itself) as well as other offensive behaviour, or whether they are, in fact, to be read in the alternative. Providing for this in a separate offence removes this ambiguity, and emphasises that the promotion of atheism is considered unacceptable in Indonesia. Not only is religious adherence thereby virtually mandatory, this provision only protects assaults upon lawful or valid religions. Criticism of, or even outright attacks upon, minority or deviant versions of established faiths is, accordingly, permitted.

In a more positive development, the draft includes the offence of blocking or disrupting places of worship and religious ceremonies (art 346), and ridiculing people or religious officials in the course of worship (art 347). Moreover, the disgracing or destruction of places of worship is also prohibited (art 348). The draft, in short, appears to reflect the strong trend which I have identified within Indonesian law and jurisprudence to seek both to protect religious adherence and to promote religious freedom. The approach taken also offers remedies to some of the shortcomings identified in the current suite of criminal offences relevant to religion, including in the Blasphemy Law. By expanding the range and clarifying the focus of offences dealing with religion, however, the draft may well create further difficulties for minority voices.

This book has focused, deliberately, on the legal and judicial domain. The courts are a forum to contribute to the delivery to citizens in a democracy of their right to equal treatment. Much of the literature about Rawls and the potential contribution of public reason in different political and social settings addresses public reason in social and political discourse. I have chosen to consider, rather, the obligations of the state and of state officials, and the very particular role of judges. This study of the Indonesian blasphemy regime and the treatment of those who pursue variant teachings within the majority faith also deals specifically with the kind of fundamental constitutional rights highlighted by Rawls as critical in a democracy. I have sought to show here that intra-faith religious debates can and do exist, and ensuring that state law and policy, and the administration of justice, respond fairly to divergent approaches to faith can be very challenging in practice. I do not seek to judge the correctness of any particular religious perspective, but rather to reinforce that there ought to be appropriate rules about the exercise of political authority in a pluralist nation that possesses a broadly liberal constitutional framework.

Bibliography

International instruments

General Comment Adopted by the Human Rights Committee Under Article 40, Paragraph 4, of the International Covenant on Civil and Political Rights, Addendum, General comment No 22 (48) (art. 18), CCPR/C/21/Rev.1/Add.4, 27 September 1993

International Covenant on Civil and Political Rights

Universal Declaration of Human Rights

Legislation and legislative instruments

Constitution of the Republic of Indonesia 1945

Code of Criminal Procedure

Criminal Code of Indonesia

Decision of the Attorney General 108/JA/5/1984 On the Establishment of the Coordinating Body for the Monitoring of Mystical Beliefs in Society

Decision of Malang Regent No 180/783/KEP/421.012/2005

Law No 1/PNPS/1965 Concerning the Prevention of Abuse and/or Disgracing of Religion

Law No 5 of 1969 Declaring Several Decisions and Regulations of the President to be Laws

Law No 1 of 1974 on Marriage

Law No 39 of 1999 on Human Rights

Law No 18 of 2001 on Special Autonomy for the Province of Nanggroe Aceh Darussalam

Law No 16 of 2004 on the Public Prosecutor (*Kejaksaan*)

Law No 32 of 2004 on Regional Government

Law No 40 of 2007 on Limited Liability Companies

Law No 19 of 2008 on Sovereign Syariah Securities

Law No 21 of 2008 on Syariah Banking

Law No 44 of 2008 on Anti-Pornography

Law No 33 of 2014 on *Halal* Product Assurance

Presidential Decree No 1 of 1965 Concerning Prevention of Abuse and/or Disgracing of Religion

Presidential Decree No 10 of 1986 Concerning the Regional Leadership Council

Qanun No 11 of 2002 on the Implementation of Islamic *Syariat* in the Fields of *Aqidah, Ibadah* and *Syi'ar* Islam

Cases

Constitutional Court Decision 12/PUU-V/2007 ('Polygamy Case')
Constitutional Court Decision 19/PUU-VI/2008 ('Religious Courts Case')
Constitutional Court Decision 140/PUU-VII/2009 ('Blasphemy Case')
Indonesian Supreme Court Decision No. 75 K/Pad/2006
Kepanjen District Court Decision 461/Pid.B/2005/PN.Kpj ('Roy Case')
Surabaya High Court Decision 361/PID/2005/PT.SBY

Books and journal articles

Abd-Allah, Umar F. 2007, 'Creativity, Innovation and Heresy in Islam' in Vincent J. Cornell & Omid Safi (eds.) *Voices of Islam*, Volume 5: *Voices of Change*, Westport, CT: Praeger Publishers.

Ackerman, Bruce 1994, 'Political Liberalisms', *The Journal of Philosophy*, vol. 91, no. 7, pp. 364–386.

Adams, Wahiduddin 2011, 'Fatwa MUI Dalam Perspektif Hukum dan Perundan-Undangan' [MUI *Fatwa* from the Perspective of Law and Legislation], paper presented at MUI seminar Jakarta, July.

Adji, Omar Seno 1984, *Hukum (Acara) Pidana Dalam Prospeksi* [Criminal Procedure in Action], Jakarta: Penerbit Erlangga.

Afrianty, Dina 2011, 'Indonesia's Islamic Educational Institutions and Radicalism Among Muslim Youth', *ARC Federation Fellowship Islam, Syariah and Governance Background Papers Series*, No. 8, Centre for Islamic Law and Society, Melbourne Law School, University of Melbourne.

Agrama, Hussein Ali 2012, *Questioning Secularism: Islam, Sovereignty and the Rule of Law in Modern Egypt*, Chicago: The University of Chicago Press.

Alavi, Karima 2007, 'Pillars of Religion and Faith', in Vincent J. Cornell (ed.), *Voices of Islam*, Volume 1: *Voices of Tradition*, Westport, CT: Praeger Publishers.

Alfitri 2008, 'Religious Liberty in Indonesia and the Rights of "Deviant" Sects', *Asian Journal of Comparative Law*, vol. 3, no. 1, pp. 1–27.

Amnesty International 2014, *Prosecuting Beliefs: Indonesia's Blasphemy Laws*, London: Amnesty International.

An-Na'im, Abdullahi Ahmed 2008, *Islam and the Secular State – Negotiating the Future of Shari'a*, Cambridge, MA: Harvard University Press.

——— 2011, 'Beyond *dhimmihood*: Citizenship and Human Rights', in Robert W. Hefner (ed.), *The New Cambridge History of Islam*, Volume 6, *Muslims and Modernity: Culture and Society since 1800*, Cambridge: Cambridge University Press.

——— 2015, 'Islamic Politics and the Neutral State: A Friendly Amendment to Rawls?', in Tom Bailey & Valentina Gentile (eds.), *Rawls and Religion*, New York: Columbia University Press.

Anwar, M. Syafi'i 2007, 'The Clash of Religio-Political Thought: The Contest between Radical-Conservative Islam and Progressive-Liberal Islam in Post-Soeharto Indonesia', in T.N. Srinivasan (ed.), *The Future of Secularism*, New Delhi: Oxford University Press.

Arblaster, Anthony 1984, *The Rise and Decline of Western Liberalism*, Oxford: Basil Blackwell.

Asad, Talal 2003, *Formations of the Secular: Christianity, Islam, Modernity*, Stanford: Stanford University Press.

Asshiddiqie, Jimly 2005, *Konstitusi dan Konstitutionalisme Indonesia* [The Indonesian Constitution and Constitutionalism], Jakarta: Indonesian Constitutional Court.

Azra, Azyumardi 2005, 'Islam in Southeast Asia: Tolerance and Radicalism', *CSCI Islamic Issues Briefing Paper Series 1*, Centre for the Study of Contemporary Islam, University of Melbourne.

Azra, Azyumardi, Afrianty, Dina & Hefner, Robert W. 2007, 'Pesantren and Madrasa: Muslim Schools and National Ideals in Indonesia', in Robert W. Hefner and Muhammad Qasim Zaman (eds.), *Schooling Islam: The Culture and Politics of Modern Muslim Education*, Princeton: Princeton University Press.

Azra, Azyumardi & Hudson, Wayne 2008, *Islam Beyond Conflict: Indonesian Islam and Western Political Theory*, Aldershot: Ashgate Publishing.

Bahlul, Raja 2003, 'Toward an Islamic Conception of Democracy: Islam and the Notion of Public Reason', *Critique: Middle Easter Studies*, vol. 12, no. 1, pp. 43–60.

Bashori, Luthfi 2006, *Musuh Besar Umat Islam* [The Great Enemy of the Islamic Community], Jakarta: LPPI.

Bell, Gary 2008, 'The Importance of Private Law Doctrine in Indonesia', in Tim Lindsey (ed.), *Indonesia: Law and Society*, Annandale: The Federation Press.

Berlin, Isaiah 1984, 'Two Concepts of Liberty', in Michael Sandel (ed.), *Liberalism and Its Critics*, Oxford: Basil Blackwell.

Bilgin, Fevzi 2011, *Political Liberalism in Muslim Societies*, London: Routledge.

Blitt, Robert 2010, 'Should New Bills of Rights Address Emerging International Human Rights Norms? The Challenge of "Defamation of Religion"', *Northwestern Journal of International Human Rights*, vol. 9, no. 1, pp. 1–26.

Bohmann, James 1995, 'Public Reason and Cultural Pluralism: Political Liberalism and the Problem of Moral Conflict', *Political Theory*, vol. 23, no. 2, pp. 253–279.

Bourchier, David 1999, 'Positivism and Romanticism in Indonesian Legal Thought', in Tim Lindsey (ed.), *Law and Society in Indonesia*, Annandale: The Federation Press.

Bourchier, David & Hadiz, Vedi 2003, *Indonesian Politics and Society: A Reader*, Hoboken, NJ: Routledge.

Bowen, John 1989, 'Salat in Indonesia: The Social Meaning of an Islamic Ritual', *Man*, New Series, vol. 24, no. 4, pp. 600–619.

—— 2003, *Islam, Law and Equality in Indonesia: An Anthropology of Public Reasoning*, Cambridge: Cambridge University Press.

—— 2005, 'Normative Pluralism in Indonesia: Regions, Religions, and Ethnicities', in Will Kymlicka and Boagang He (eds.), *Multiculturalism in Asia: Theoretical Perspectives*, Oxford: Oxford University Press.

Bruinessen, Martin van 2013, 'Introduction: Contemporary Developments in Indonesian Islam and the "Conservative Turn" of the Early Twenty-First Century', in Martin van Bruinessen (ed.) *Contemporary Developments in Indonesian Islam: Explaining the 'Conservative Turn'*, Singapore: ISEAS.

Bubalo, Anthony, Phillips, Sarah & Yasmeen, Saminah 2011, *Talib or Taliban? Indonesian Students in Pakistan and Yemen*, Sydney: The Lowy Institute for International Policy.

Burhani, Ahmad Najib 2005, 'The 45th Muhammadiyah Congress: Contest Between Literal-Conservative and Liberal Moderate Muslims in Indonesia', *Studia Islamika*, vol. 12, no. 1, pp. 185–189.

Bush, Robin 2008, 'Regional Sharia Regulations in Indonesia: Anomaly or Symptom' in Greg Fealy and Sally White (eds.), *Expressing Islam: Religious Life and Politics in Indonesia*, Singapore: ISEAS.

―――― 2009, *Nahdlatul Ulama and the Struggle for Power within Islam and Politics in Indonesia*, Singapore: ISEAS.

Butt, Simon 2006, *Judicial Review in Indonesia: Between Civil Law and Accountability? A Study of Constitutional Court Decisions 2003–2005*, unpublished PhD Thesis, University of Melbourne.

―――― 2010, 'Islam, the State and the Constitutional Court in Indonesia', *Pacific Rim Law & Policy Journal*, vol. 19, pp. 279–301.

―――― 2014, 'Asia-Pacific: Judicial Responses to the Death Penalty in Indonesia', *Legal Studies Research Paper No. 14/67*, Sydney Law School.

Butt, Simon & Lindsey, Tim 2012, *The Constitution of Indonesia: A Contextual Analysis*, Oxford and Portland, OR: Hart Publishing.

Campbell, Tom 2001, *Justice*, New York: St Martin's Press.

Cohen, Joshua 2003, 'For A Democratic Society', in Samuel Freeman (ed.), *The Cambridge Companion to Rawls*, Cambridge: Cambridge University Press.

Colbran, Nicola 2009, 'Courage Under Fire: The First Five Years of the Indonesian Judicial Commission', *Australian Journal of Asian Law*, vol. 11, no. 2, pp. 273–301.

―――― 2010, 'Realities and Challenges in Realising Freedom of Religion or Belief in Indonesia', *International Journal of Human Rights*, vol. 14, no. 5, pp. 678–704.

Cook, Michael 2004, *Commanding Right and Forbidding Wrong in Islamic Thought*, Cambridge: Cambridge University Press.

Cornell, Vincent J. 2007, 'Introduction' in Vincent J. Cornell (ed.), *Voices of Islam*, Volume 1: *Voices of Tradition*, Westport, CT: Praeger Publishers.

Cotterrell, Roger 1997, 'The Concept of Legal Culture', in David Nelken (ed.), *Comparing Legal Cultures*, Aldershot: Dartmouth.

―――― 2004, 'Law in Culture', *Ratio Juris*, vol. 17, no. 1, pp. 1–14.

Crouch, Melissa 2012, 'Law and Religion in Indonesia: The Constitutional Court and the Blasphemy Law', *Asian Journal of Comparative Law*, vol. 7, no. 1, pp. 1–46.

Cumming, Robert Denoon 1969, *Human Nature and History: A Study of the Development of Liberal Political Thought*, 2 Vols., Chicago: The University of Chicago Press.

Dalacoura, Katerina 2003, *Islam, Liberalism and Human Rights*, London: I.B. Tauris.

Department of Religion 2007, *Kompilasi Peraturan Perundang-Undangan Kerukunan Hidup Umat Beragama* [Compilation of Laws and Regulations on Harmony in the Life of the Religious Community], 9 ed., Research, Development and Training Institute, Department of Religion, Jakarta.

Dhofier, Zamakhsyari 1982, *Tradisi Pesantren: Studi Tentang Pandangan Hidup Kyai* [The Pesantren Tradition: A Study of the Life View of a Cleric], Jakarta: LP3ES.

Dombrowski, Daniel 2001, *Rawls and Religion: The Case for Political Liberalism*, Albany: State University of New York Press.

Drakeley, Steven 2014, 'Indonesia's Muslim Organisations and the Overthrow of Sukarno', *Studia Islamika*, vol. 21, no. 2, pp. 197–231.

Durham, W. Cole Jr. & Scharffs, Brett G. 2010, *Law and Religion in National, International and Comparative Perspectives*, New York: Aspen Publishers.

Effendy, Bahtiar 2003, *Islam and the State in Indonesia*, Singapore: ISEAS.

Elson, R.E. 2010, 'Nationalism, Islam, "Secularism" and the State in Contemporary Indonesia', *Australian Journal of International Affairs*, vol. 64, no. 3, pp. 328–343.

—— 2012, 'Absent at the Creation: Islamism's Belated, Troubled Engagement with Early Indonesian Nationalism', Geoff Wade and Li Tana (eds.), *Anthony Reid and the Study of the Southeast Asian Past*, Singapore: ISEAS.

Fadel, Mohammed 2007–2008, 'Public Reason as a Strategy for Principled Reconciliation: The Case of Islamic Law and International Human Rights Law', *Chicago Journal of International Law*, vol. 8, no. 1, pp. 1–20.

—— 2008, 'The True, the Good and the Reasonable: The Theological and Ethical Roots of Public Reason in Islamic Law', *Canadian Journal of Law and Jurisprudence*, vol. 21, no. 1, pp. 5–69.

Fathurrahman, Oman 2011, 'Sejarah Pengkafiran Dan Marginalisasi Paham Keagamaan Di Melayu Dan Jawa (Sebuah Telaah Sumber)' ['A History of Infidelity and Marginalisation of Religious Thought in Malaysia and Java (A Study Resource)'], *Analisis*, vol. XI, no. 2.

Fealy, Greg & Hooker, Virginia (eds.), 2006, *Voices of Islam in Southeast Asia: A Contemporary Sourcebook*, Singapore: ISEAS.

Federspiel, Howard 1970, 'The *Muhammadiyah*: A Study of an Orthodox Islamic Movement in Indonesia', *Indonesia*, vol. 10, pp. 57–79.

—— 2009, *Persatuan Islam: Islamic Reform in Twentieth Century Indonesia*, Jakarta: Equinox.

Feener, R. Michael 2014, 'Official Religions, State Secularisms, and the Structures of Religious Pluralism', in Juliana Finucane and R. Michael Feener (eds.), *Proselytizing and the Limits of Religious Pluralism in Contemporary Asia*, Singapore: Springer.

Fenwick, Stewart 2009, 'Administrative Law and Judicial Review in Indonesia: The Search for Accountability', in Tom Ginsburg and Albert H.Y. Chen (eds.), *Administrative Law and Governance in Asia: Comparative Perspectives*, Abingdon: Routledge.

—— 2011a, 'Between Innovation and Intolerance: An International Perspective on Religious Freedom in Indonesia', *Jurnal Fatwa*, vol. 1, pp. 91–106.

—— 2011b, 'Yusman Roy and the Language of Devotion: 'Innovation' in Indonesian Islam on Trial', *Studia Islamika*, vol. 18, no. 3, pp. 497–529.

Finnis, John 2007, 'On 'Public Reason'', *Notre Dame Legal Studies Paper* No. 06–37/ *Oxford Legal Studies Research Paper* No. 1.

—— 2011, *Collected Essays*, Volume V: *Religion and Public Reasons*, Oxford: Oxford University Press.

Fitzpatrick, Daniel 2008, 'Culture, Ideology and Human Rights: The Case of Indonesia's Code of Criminal Procedure', in Tim Lindsey (ed.), *Indonesia: Law and Society*, Annandale: The Federation Press.

Franck, Thomas M 1997, 'Is Personal Freedom a Western Value?', *The American Journal of International Law*, vol. 91, pp. 593–627.

Freedom House, Undated, *Policing Belief: the Impact of Blasphemy Laws on Human Rights*, www.freedomhouse.org/sites/default/files/PolicingBelief_Egypt.pdf.

Freeman, Samuel 1994, 'Political Liberalism and the Possibility of a Just Democratic Constitution', *Chicago-Kent Law Review*, vol. 69, pp. 619–668.

—— 2003, 'Congruence and the Good of Justice', in Samuel Freeman (ed.), *The Cambridge Companion to John Rawls*, Cambridge: Cambridge University Press.

—— 2007, *Rawls*, Abingdon: Routledge.

Geertz, Clifford 1976, *The Religion of Java*, Chicago: University of Chicago Press.

Gibb, H.A.R. & Kramers, J.H. 1974, *Shorter Encyclopaedia of Islam*, Leiden: Brill.

Gillespie, Piers 2007, 'Current Issues in Indonesian Islam: Analysing the 2005 Council of Indonesian *Ulama* Fatwa No 7 Opposing Pluralism, Liberalism and Secularism of Religion', *Journal of Islamic Studies*, vol. 18, no. 2, pp. 202–240.

Glenn, H. Patrick 2000, *Legal Traditions of the World*, Oxford: Oxford University Press.

Gray, John 2000a, 'Mill's Liberalism and Liberalism's Posterity', *The Journal of Ethics*, vol. 4, pp. 137–165.

—— 2000b, *Two Faces of Liberalism*, Oxford: Blackwell Publishers.

Habermas, Jurgen 2006, 'Religion in the Public Sphere', *European Journal of Philosophy*, vol. 14, no. 1, pp. 1–25.

—— 2010, 'The "Good Life" – A "Detestable Phrase": The Significance of the Young Rawls's Religious Ethics for His Political Theory', *European Journal of Philosophy*, vol. 18, no. 3, pp. 443–454.

Halliday, Terrence & Karpik, Lucien 1997, *Lawyers and the Rise of Western Political Liberalism: Europe and North America from the Eighteenth to Twentieth Centuries*, Oxford: Clarendon Press.

Hamzah, Andi 2010, *KUHP & KUHAP, edisi revisi 2008* [The Criminal Code and Code of Criminal Procedure, revised edition 2008], Jakarta: Renika Cipta.

Hasan, Noorhaidi 2008, '*Reformasi*, Religious Diversity, and Islamic Radicalism after Soeharto', *Journal of Indonesian Social Sciences and Humanities*, vol. 1, pp. 23–51.

Hashemi, Nader 2009, *Islam, Secularism, and Liberal Democracy: Toward a Democratic Theory for Muslim Societies*, Oxford: Oxford University Press.

Hassan, Riaz 2006, 'Expressions of Religiosity and Blasphemy in Modern Societies', in Elizabeth Coleman and Kevin White (eds.), *Negotiating the Sacred: Blasphemy and Sacrilege in a Multicultural Society*, Canberra: ANU E Press.

Hayek, F.A. 1982, *New Studies in Philosophy, Politics, Economics and the History of Ideas*, London: Routledge.

Hayfa, Tarek 2004, 'The Idea of Public Justification in Rawls's Law of Peoples', *Res Publica*, vol. 10, pp. 233–246.

—— 2008, *The Problem of Public Justification in Political Philosophy: Rorty, Rawls and Habermas*, Saarbrücken: VDM Verlag Dr Müller.

Hefner, Robert W. 1995, 'Modernity and the Challenge of Pluralism: Some Indonesian Lessons', *Studia Islamika*, vol. 2, no. 3, pp. 21–45.

—— 2011a, 'Indonesia: Shari'a Politics and Democratic Transition' in Robert W. Hefner (ed.), *Shari'a Politics: Islamic Law and Society in the Modern World*, Bloomington: Indiana University Press.

—— 2011b, 'Introduction: Shari'a Politics – Law and Society in the Modern Muslim World', in Robert W. Hefner (ed.), *Shari'a Politics: Islamic Law and Society in the Modern World*, Bloomington: Indiana University Press.

—— 2013, 'The Study of Religious Freedom in Indonesia', *The Review of Faith & International Affairs*, vol. 11, no. 2, pp. 18–27.

Hirji, Zulfikar 2010, 'Debating Islam from Within: Muslim Constructions of the Internal Other', in Zulfikar Hirji (ed.), *Diversity and Pluralism in Islam: Historical and Contemporary Discourses Amongst Muslims*, London: I.B. Tauris.

Hooker, M.B. 2002, 'Introduction: Islamic Law in South-east Asia', *Australian Journal of Asian Law*, vol. 4, pp. 212–231.

────── 2003, *Indonesian Islam: Social Change Through Contemporary Fatawa*, Crows Nest, NSW: Allen & Unwin.

────── 2013, 'Southeast Asian Islams', *Studia Islamika*, vol. 20, no. 2, pp. 183–242.

Hooker, M.B. & Lindsey, Tim 2002, 'Public Faces of *Syariah* in Contemporary Indonesia: Towards a National *Madhab*?', *Australian Journal of Asian Law*, vol. 4, pp. 259–294.

Hosen, Nadirsyah 2004, 'Behind the Scenes: *Fatwas* of the *Majelis Ulama Indonesia* (1975–1998)', *Journal of Islamic Studies*, vol. 15, no. 2, pp. 147–179.

────── 2005, 'Religion and the Indonesian Constitution: A Recent Debate', *Journal of Southeast Asian Studies*, vol. 36, no. 3, pp. 419–440.

────── 2007, *Shari'a Constitutional Reform in Indonesia*, Singapore: ISEAS.

────── 2012, 'Pluralism, Fatwa and Courts in Indonesia: The Case of Yusman Roy', *Journal of Indonesian Islam*, vol. 6, no. 1, pp. 1–16.

Hughes, Thomas Patrick c.1885, *A Dictionary of Islam*, undated reprint of Premier Book House, Lahore from the original publication, London.

Human Rights Watch 2013, *In Religion's Name: Abuses against Religious Minorities in Indonesia*, Human Rights Watch, USA.

Ichwan, Moch. Nur 2005, '*Ulama*, State and Politics: *Majelis Ulama Indonesia* After Soeharto', *Islamic Law and Society*, vol. 12, no. 1, pp. 45–72.

────── 2006, 'Official Reform of State Islam: State Islam and the Ministry of Religious Affairs in Contemporary Indonesia (1966–2004)', PhD Thesis, University of Tilburg.

────── 2013, 'Towards a Puritanical Moderate Islam: The *Majelis Ulama Indonesia* and the Politics of Religious Orthodoxy', in Martin van Bruinessen (ed.), *Contemporary Developments in Indonesian Islam: Explaining the 'Conservative Turn'*, Singapore: ISEAS.

Indrayana, Denny 2008, *Indonesian Constitutional Reform 1999–2002: An Evaluation of Constitution-Making in Transition*, Jakarta: Kompas Book Publishing.

Inoue, Tatsuo 1999, 'Liberal Democracy and Asian Orientalism', in Joanne Bauer and Daniel Bell (eds.), *The East Asian Challenge for Human Rights*, Cambridge: Cambridge University Press.

International Crisis Group (ICG) 2002, 'Indonesia: The Search for Peace in Maluku', Asia Report No 31, Jakarta/Brussels.

────── 2006, 'Islamic Law and Criminal Justice in Aceh', Asia Report No 117, Jakarta/Brussels.

────── 2008, 'Indonesia: Implications of the Ahmadiyah Decree', Asia Briefing No 78, Jakarta/Brussels.

Ivison, Duncan 2002, *Postcolonial Liberalism*, Cambridge: Cambridge University Press.

Jackson, Roy 2006, *Fifty Key Figures in Islam*, London: Routledge.

Ka'bah, Rifyal 1999, *Hukum Islam di Indonesia: Perspektif Muhammadiyah dan NU* [Islamic Law in Indonesia: the Muhammadiyah and NU Perspective], Jakarta: *Universitas Yarsi*.

Kahin, Audrey 2012, 'Natsir & Sukarno: Their Clash Over Nationalism, Religion and Democracy, 1928–1958' in Hui Yew-Foong (ed.), *Encountering Islam: The Politics of Religious Identities in Southeast Asia*, Singapore: ISEAS.

Kahn, Paul W 1999, *The Cultural Study of Law: Reconstructing Legal Scholarship*, Chicago: The University of Chicago Press.

Kamenka, Eugene & Tay, Alice 1980, 'Social traditions, legal traditions' in Eugene Kamenka and Alice Tay (eds.), *Law and Social Control*, London: Edward Arnold.

Kaptein, N.J.G. 2004, 'The Voice of the *Ulama*: *Fatwas* and Religious Authority in Indonesia', *ISEAS Working Paper: Visiting Researchers Series* No 2, Singapore: ISEAS.

Katjasungkana, Nursyahbani 2008, 'Gender and law Reform in Indonesia: Overcoming Entrenched Barriers', in Tim Lindsey (ed.), *Indonesia: Law and Society*, Annandale: The Federation Press.

Kingsbury, Damien 2003, *Power Politics and the Indonesian Military*, London: RoutledgeCurzon.

Kymlicka, Will 1992, 'Two Models of Pluralism and Toleration', *Analyse & Kritik*, vol. 13, pp. 33–56.

Laffan, Michael Francis 2003, *Islamic Nationhood and Colonial Indonesia: The* umma *below the winds*, London: RoutledgeCurzon.

Larmore, Charles 1990, 'Political Liberalism', *Political Theory*, vol. 18, no. 3, pp. 339–360.

—— 2003, 'Public reason', in Samuel Freeman (ed.), *The Cambridge Companion to Rawls*, Cambridge: Cambridge University Press.

Lembaga Bantuan Hukum Surabaya [Surabaya Legal Aid Association] 2005, *Ketika kebebasan berkeyakinan kembali diadili: buku putih* [When Freedom of Belief is Criminalised: A white paper], Jakarta: LBH Surabaya and Yayasan Tifa.

Lembaga Pembinaan Hukum Nasional [National Law Reform Body] 1974, *Pengaruh Agama Terhadap Hukum Pidana* [The Impact of Religion on Criminal Law], Jakarta: LPHN.

Lewis, Bernard 1953, 'Some Observations on the Significance of Heresy in the History of Islam', *Studia Islamica*, no, 1, pp. 43–63.

Liddle, R. William & Mujani, Saiful 2002, 'The Islamic Challenge to Democratic Consolidation in Indonesia', paper presented at the International Conference on The Challenge of Democracy in the Muslim World, Jakarta 19–20 March.

Lindsey, Tim 1999, 'From Rule of Law to Law of the Rulers – to Reformation', in Tim Lindsey (ed.) *Indonesia: Law and Society*, Annandale: The Federation Press.

—— 2002, 'Indonesian Constitutional Reform: Muddling Towards Democracy', *Singapore Journal of International and Comparative Law*, vol. 6, pp. 244–301.

—— 2004, 'Indonesia: Devaluing Asian Values, Rewriting Rule of law', in Randall Peerenboom (ed.), *Asian Discourses of Rule of Law: Theories and Implementation of Rule of Law in Twelve Asian countries, France and the US*, London: RoutledgeCurzon.

—— 2008, 'Constitutional Reform in Indonesia: Muddling Towards Democracy', in Tim Lindsey (ed.), *Indonesia: Law and Society*, Annandale: The Federation Press.

—— 2009, 'Human Rights and Islam in South East Asia: The Case of Indonesia', in Hatem Elliesie (ed.), *Islam und Menshenrechte* [Islam and Human Rights], Frankfurt: Peter Lang Verlag.

—— 2012a, *Islam, Law and the State in South East Asia*, Volume 1: *Indonesia*, I. B. Taurus, London.

—— 2012b, 'Monopolising Islam? The Indonesian Ulama Council and State Regulation of the 'Islamic Economy'', *Bulletin of Indonesian Economic Studies*, vol. 48, no. 2, pp. 253–274.

Linnan, David 2007, 'Like a Fish Needs a Bicycle: Public Law Theory, Civil Society and Governance Reform in Indonesia', in Tim Lindsey (ed.) *Law Reform in Developing and Transitional States*, London: Routledge.

Loobuyck, Patrick & Rummens, Stefan 2011, 'Religious Arguments in the Public Sphere: Comparing Habermas with Rawls', in N. Brunsveld (ed.), *Religion in the Public Sphere*, Utrecht: Ars Disputandi.

Loughlin, Martin 2003, *The Idea of Public Law*, Oxford: Oxford University Press.

Lubis, Todong Mulya 1999, 'The *Rechstaat* and Human Rights' in Tim Lindsey (ed.), *Indonesia: Law and Society*, Annandale: The Federation Press.

Madjid, Nurcholish 1994, 'Islamic Roots of Modern Pluralism: Indonesian Experience', *Studia Islamika*, vol. 1, no. 1, pp. 55–78.

Maffettone, Sebastiano 2015, 'Foreword', in Tom Bailey & Valentina Gentile, *Rawls and Religion*, New York: Columbia University Press.

Mahmood, Saba 2005, *Politics of Piety: The Islamic Revivial and the Feminist Subject*, Princeton: Princeton University Press.

Majelis Ulama Indonesia [MUI] c.1995, *20 tahun Majelis Ulama Indonesia* [20 years of MUI], MUI, Jakarta.

———— 2005, *Kronologi Mengapa Yusman Roy Ditahan* [Chronology of Why Yusman Roy Was Detained], Law and *Fatwa* Committee, MUI Kabupaten Malang.

———— c.2007, *Mengawal aqidah Umat: Fatwa MUI Tentang Aliran-Aliran Sesat di Indonesia* [Guarding The Faith of the Islamic Community: MUI *Fatawa* on Deviant Sects in Indonesia], MUI, Jakarta.

———— 2010a, *Himpunan Fatwa Majelis Ulama Indonesia* [Collection of the *Fatwa* of MUI], MUI *Sekretariat*, Jakarta.

———— 2010b, *Himpunan Keputusan Musyawarah Nasional VIII Majelis Ulama Indonesia* [Collected Decisions of the Eighth National Conference of MUI], MUI, Jakarta.

———— 2010c, *Profile of MUI: Retrospective of the Indonesian Council of* Ulama – 35 *Years of Remarkable Progress*, MUI, Jakarta.

Mango, Andrew 1999, *Ataturk*, London: John Murray.

March, Andrew 2009, *Islam and Liberal Citizenship: The Search for an Overlapping Consensus*, Oxford: Oxford University Press.

Margiyono, Muktiono & Rumadi, Irianto S 2011, *No Middle Road: A Public Examination of the Decision of the Constitutional Court Concerning Review of Law No. 1/1965*, Indonesian Legal Resource Center, Jakarta.

Marshall, Anna-Maria 2006, 'Communities and Cultures: Enriching Legal Consciousness and Legal Culture', *Law and Social Inquiry*, vol. 31, no. 1, pp. 229–249.

Marshall, Paul & Shea, Nina 2011, *Silenced: How Apostasy and Blasphemy Codes Are Choking Freedom*, New York: Oxford University Press.

Masud, Muhammad 1993, 'The Definition of *Bid'a* in the South Asian *Fatawa* Literature', *Annales Islamologique*, vol. 27, pp. 55–75.

Masud, Muhammad Khalid, Messick, Brinkley & Powers, David 1996, 'Muftis, *Fatawas*, and Islamic Legal Interpretation', in Muhammad Khalid Masud, Brinkley Messick and David Powers (eds.), *Islamic Legal Interpretation*, Cambridge, MA: Harvard University Press.

McLaughlin, Nicole 2010, 'Spectrum of Defamation of Religion Laws and the Possibility of a Universal International Standard', *Loyola Los Angeles International and Comparative Law Review*, vol. 32, no. 3, pp. 395–426.

Menchik, Jeremy 2014, 'Productive Intolerance: Godly Nationalism in Indonesia', *Comparative Studies in Society and History*, vol. 56, no. 3, pp. 591–621.

Mir, Mustansir 2007, 'The Qur'an, the Word of God', in Vincent J. Cornell *Voices of Islam*, Volume 1: *Voices of Tradition*, Westport, CT: Praeger Publishers.

Mirza, Qudsia 2003, 'Sacred and Secular Blasphemies', *Griffith Law Review*, vol. 12 no. 2, pp. 336–361.

Mohamad, Goenawan 2007, 'Secularism, 'Revivalism', Mimicry' in T.N. Srinivasan (ed.), *The Future of Secularism*, New Delhi: Oxford University Press.

Mohr, Richard & Hosen, Nadirsyah 2011, 'Introduction: *Da Capo*: Law and Religion from the Top Down' in Nadirsyah Hosen & Richard Mohr (eds.) *Law and Religion in Public Life: The Contemporary Debate*, London: Routledge, pp. 1–12.

Mudzhar, Mohamad Atho 1993, *Fatwa-fatwa Majelis Ulama Indonesia: Sebuah Studi tentang Pemikiran Hukum Islam di Indonesia, 1975–1988* [Fatwas of the Ulama Council of Indonesia: A Study of Islamic legal thought in Indonesia] Jakarta: INIS.

——— 1996, 'The Council of Indonesian 'Ulama' on Muslims' Attendance at Christmas Celebrations', in Muhammad Khalid Masud, Brinkley Messick and David Powers (eds.) *Islamic Legal Interpretation*, Cambridge, MA: Harvard University Press.

——— 2011, '*Fatwa MUI Sebagai Obyek Kajian Hukum Islam dan Sumber Sejarah Sosial*' [MUI *Fatwa* as an Object of Islamic Legal Studies and a Source of Social History], paper presented at MUI conference Jakarta, July.

Muhaimin, Abdul Ghaffur 1995, *Ibadat and Adat Among Javanese Muslims*, Islam in Southeast Asia Series. Canberra: ANU E Press.

Nagel, Thomas 1999, 'Justice, Justice, Shalt Thou Pursue', *The New Republic*, Oct 25, pp. 36–41.

——— 2003, 'Rawls and Liberalism', in Samuel Freeman (ed.), *The Cambridge Companion to Rawls*, Cambridge: Cambridge University Press.

Nasution, Adnan Buyung 1992, *The Aspiration for Constitutional Government in Indonesia: A Socio-Legal Study of the Indonesian Konstituante 1956–1959*, Pustaka Sinar Harapan, Jakarta.

Niewenhuijze, C.A.O. Van, 1958, 'The Indonesian State and 'Deconfessionalized' Muslim Concepts' in *Aspects of Islam in Post Colonial Indonesia: Five Essays*, The Hague: W. van Hoeve.

Noer, Deliar 2010, *Administration of Islam in Indonesia*, Jakarta: Equinox Publishing.

Nussbaum, Martha 2001, 'Political Objectivity', *New Literary History*, vol. 32, pp. 883–906.

——— 2015, 'Introduction', in Thom Brooks & Martha C. Nussbaum (eds.), *Rawls' Political Liberalism*, New York: Columbia University Press.

Olle, John 2006, 'The Campaign against "Heresy" – State and Society in Negotiation in Indonesia', paper presented at 16th Biennial Conference of the Asian Studies Association of Australia, Wollongong, June.

——— 2009, 'The Majelis Ulama Indonesia versus "Heresy": The Resurgence of Authoritarian Islam', in Gerry van Klinken and Joshua Barker (eds.), *State of Authority: The State in Society in Indonesia*, Ithaca, NY: Cornell Southeast Asia Program.

O'Neill, Onara 1997, 'Political Liberalism and Public Reason: A Critical Notice of John Rawls, *Political Liberalism*, *The Philosophical Review*, vol. 106, no. 3, pp. 411–428.

——— 2015, 'Changing Constructions', in Thom Brooks & Martha C. Nussbaum (eds.), *Rawls' Political Liberalism*, New York: Columbia University Press.

Otto, Jan Michel 2010, 'Sharia and National Law in Indonesia', in Jan Michel Otto (ed.), *Sharia Incorporated: A Comparative Overview of the Legal Systems of Twelve Muslim Countries in Past and Present*, Leiden: Leiden University Press.

Oxford Dictionary of Islam, 2003, online at www.oxfordreference.com

Pink, Johanna 2003, 'A Post-Quranic Religion Between Apostasy and Public Order: Egyptian Muftis and Courts on the Legal Status of the Baha'i Faith', *Islamic Law and Society*, vol. 10, no. 3, pp. 409–434.

Platzdasch, Bernhard 2011, 'Religious Freedom in Indonesia: The Case of Ahmadiyah', *Institute of Southeast Asian Studies Working Paper: Politics and Security Series No. 2*, Singapore: ISEAS.

Pringle, Helen 2006, 'Are We Capable of Offending God? Taking Blasphemy Seriously', in E.B. Coleman and K. White (eds.), *Negotiating the Sacred: Blasphemy and Sacrilege in a Multicultural Society*, Canberra: ANU Press, pp. 31–41.

―――― 2011, 'Regulating Offence to the Godly: Blasphemy and the Future of Religious Vilification Laws', *UNSW Law Journal*, vol. 42, no. 1, pp. 316–332.

Rasyid, Dr. K.H.M. Hamdan 2003, *Fiqih Indonesia: Himpunan Fatwa-fatwa Aktual* [Indonesian *Fiqih*: A Collection of Actual *Fatawa*], Jakarta: Al Mawardi Prima.

Rawls, John 1971, *A Theory of Justice*, Cambridge, MA: Belknap.

―――― 1993, *Political Liberalism*, New York: Columbia University Press.

―――― 1999, 'The Idea of an Overlapping Consensus', in Samuel Freeman (ed.), *John Rawls: Collected Papers*, Cambridge, MA: Harvard University Press.

―――― 2001, *Justice as Fairness: A Restatement*, Cambridge, MA: Belknap/Harvard.

―――― 2002, *The Law of Peoples with 'The Idea of Public Reason Revisited'*, Cambridge, MA: Harvard University Press.

Ricklefs, M.C. 2001, *A History of Modern Indonesia Since c. 1200*, Basingstoke: Palgrave.

―――― 2007, *Polarizing Javanese Society: Islamic and Other Visions, 1830–1930*, Singapore: NUS Press.

―――― 2008, 'Religion, Politics and Social Dynamics in Java: Historical and Contemporary Rhymes', in Greg Fealy and Sally White (eds.), *Expressing Islam: Religious Life and Politics in Indonesia*, Singapore: ISEAS.

―――― 2012, 'Religious Elites and the State in Indonesia and Elsewhere: Why Take-Overs are So Difficult and Usually Don't Work', in Hui Yew-Foong (ed.), *Encountering Islam: The Politics of Religious Identities in Southeast Asia*, Singapore: ISEAS.

Ritter, Matthew A. 1999, 'Universal Rights Talk/Plurality of Voices: A Philosophical-Theological Hearing', in Mark Janis and Carolyn Evans (eds.), *Religion and International Law*, Leiden: Martinus Nijhoff Publishers.

Ruthven, Malise 1997, *Islam: A Very Short Introduction*, New York: Oxford University Press.

Saeed, Abdullah 2005, 'Introduction: the Qur'an, Interpretation and the Indonesian Context', in Abdullah Saeed (ed.), *Approaches to the Qur'an in Contemporary Indonesia*, London: Oxford University Press.

―――― 2006, *Islamic Thought*, London and New York: Routledge.

Saeed, Abdullah & Saeed, Hassan 2004, *Freedom of Religions, Apostasy and Islam*, Aldershot: Ashgate.

Salim, Arskal 2007, 'Muslim Politics in Indonesia's Democratisation', in Ross McLeod and Andrew MacIntyre (eds.), *Indonesia: Democracy and the Promise of Good Governance*, Singapore: ISEAS.

——— 2008, *Challenging the Secular State: The Islamization of Law in Modern Indonesia*, Honolulu: University of Hawaii Press.

Salvatore, Armando & Eickelman, Dale F 2004, 'Preface: Public Islam and the Common Good', in Armando Salvatore and Dale F. Eickelman (eds.), *Public Islam and the Common Good*, Leiden – Boston: Brill.

Sandel, Michael (ed.) 1984, *Liberalism and Its Critics*, Oxford: Basil Blackwell.

——— 1994, 'Political Liberalism', *Harvard Law Review*, vol. 107, pp. 1765–1794.

Scanlon, T.M. 2003 'Rawls on Justification', in Samuel Freeman (ed.), *The Cambridge Companion to Rawls*, Cambridge: Cambridge University Press.

Schaefer, David Lewis 2007, *Illiberal Justice: John Rawls vs the American Political Tradition*, Columbia: University of Missouri Press.

Scharffs, Brett 2011, 'Four Views of the Citadel: The Consequential Distinction between Secularity and Secularism', *Religion and Human Rights*, vol. 6, pp. 109–126.

Sen, Amartya 2007, *Identity and Violence: The Illusion of Destiny*, New York: W.W. Norton.

Sezgin, Yuksel 1999, 'A Comparative Study of Personal Status Systems in Israel, Egypt and India', *Working Paper*, The International Council on Human Rights Policy.

Sihombing, Ulil Parulian, Pultoni, Aminah, Siti, Roziqin, & Muhammad Khoirul 2012, *Injustice in Belief: Monitoring the Results of Cases on Blasphemy of Religion and Religious Hate Speech in Indonesia*, Indonesian Legal Resource Center, Jakarta.

Soerodibroto, R. Soenarto 2009, *KUHP dan KUHAP Dilengkapi Yurisprudensi Mahkamah Agung Dan Hoge Raad*, 5 ed [The Criminal Code and Code of Criminal Procedure Complete With Jurisprudence of the Supreme Court of Indonesia and the Netherlands, Fifth Edition], Jakarta: Rajawali Press.

Solahudin, Dindin 2008, *The Workshop for Morality: The Islamic Creativity of Pesantren Daarut Tauhid in Bandung, Java*, Canberra: ANU E Press.

Spinner-Halev, Jeff 2008, 'Liberalism and Religion: Against Congruence', *Theoretical Inquiries in Law*, vol. 9, no. 2, pp. 553–572.

Steiner, Henry & Alston, Philip 1996, *International Human Rights in Context: Law Politics and Morals – Text and Materials*, Oxford: Clarendon Press.

Stevens Alan M. and Schmidgall-Tellings A. Ed. (eds.) 2004, *A Comprehensive Indonesian-English Dictionary*, Columbus: Ohio University Press.

Sukma, Rizal 2003, *Islam in Indonesian Foreign Policy*, London: RouteldgeCurzon.

Tamanaha, Brian Z. 2004, *On the Rule of Law: History, Politics, Theory*, Cambridge: Cambridge University Press.

Tasioulas, John 2002, 'From Utopia to Kazanistan: John Rawls and the Law of Peoples', *Oxford Journal of Legal Studies*, vol. 22, no. 2, pp. 367–396.

Taylor, Charles 1995, 'Cross Purposes: the Liberal-Communitarian Debate', in *Philosophical Arguments*, Cambridge, MA: Harvard University Press.

Taylor, John 1967, 'An Approach to the Emergence of Heterodoxy in Medieval Islam', *Religious Studies*, vol. 2, no. 2, pp. 197–210.

Umam, Saiful 2013, 'God's Mercy is Not Limited to Arabic Speakers: Reading Intellectual Biography of Muhammad Salih Darat and His Pegon Islamic Texts', *Studia Islamika*, vol. 20, no. 2, pp. 243–274.

Voegelin, Eric 1974, 'Liberalism and Its History', *The Review of Politics*, vol. 36, no. 4, pp. 504–520.

Walker, Millidge & Tinker, Irene 1975, 'Development and Changing Bureaucratic Styles in Indonesia: The Case of the *Pamong Praja*', *Pacific Affairs*, vol. 48, pp. 60–73.

Weiss, Bernard 1996, 'Ibn Taymiyya on Leadership in the Ritual Prayer', in Muhammad Khalid Masud, Brinkley Messick and David Powers (eds.) *Islamic Legal Interpretation*, Cambridge, MA: Harvard University Press.

—— 2006, *The Spirit of Islamic Law*, Athens: University of Georgia Press.

Zamhari, Arif 2010, *Rituals of Islamic Spirituality: A Study of Majlis Dhikr Groups in East Java*, Canberra: ANU E Press.

Index

For Product Safety Concerns and Information please contact our EU
representative GPSR@taylorandfrancis.com
Taylor & Francis Verlag GmbH, Kaufingerstraße 24, 80331 München, Germany

* 9 7 8 1 1 3 8 3 6 2 8 5 7 *